ECONOMIC HISTORY

OPEN-FIELD FARMING IN MEDIEVAL EUROPE

AGRICULTURE

OPEN-FIELD FARMING IN MEDIEVAL EUROPE

A study of village by-laws

WARREN O. AULT

LONDON AND NEW YORK

First published in 1972

Published in 2006 by
Routledge
2 Park Square, Milton Park, Abingdon, Oxfordshire OX14 4RN
711 Third Avenue, New York, NY 10017

First issued in paperback 2014

Routledge is an imprint of the Taylor and Francis Group, an informa business

© 1972 Warren O. Ault

All rights reserved. No part of this book may be reprinted or reproduced or utilized in any form or by any electronic, mechanical, or other means, now known or hereafter invented, including photocopying and recording, or in any information storage or retrieval system, without permission in writing from the publishers.

The publishers have made every effort to contact authors and copyright holders of the works reprinted in the *Economic History* series. This has not been possible in every case, however, and we would welcome correspondence from those individuals or organisations we have been unable to trace.

These reprints are taken from original copies of each book. In many cases the condition of these originals is not perfect. The publisher has gone to great lengths to ensure the quality of these reprints, but wishes to point out that certain characteristics of the original copies will, of necessity, be apparent in reprints thereof.

British Library Cataloguing in Publication Data
A CIP catalogue record for this book
is available from the British Library

Open-field Farming in Medieval Europe
ISBN 0-415-37789-7 (volume)
ISBN 0-415-37652-1 (subset)
ISBN 0-415-28619-0 (set)

ISBN13: 978-1-138-86172-5 (pbk)
ISBN13: 978-0-415-37789-8 (hbk)

Routledge Library Editions: Economic History

Historical Problems:
Studies and Documents

Edited by
PROFESSOR G. R. ELTON
University of Cambridge

16

OPEN-FIELD FARMING IN MEDIEVAL
ENGLAND
A Study of Village By-Laws

OPEN-FIELD FARMING IN MEDIEVAL ENGLAND
A Study of Village By-Laws

W. O. Ault
Emeritus Huntington Professor of History
Boston University

LONDON · GEORGE ALLEN AND UNWIN LTD
BARNES AND NOBLE BOOKS – NEW YORK
(a division of Harper & Row Publishers, Inc.)

First published in 1972

This book is copyright under the Berne Convention. All rights are reserved. Apart from any fair dealing for the purpose of private study, research, criticism or review, as permitted under the Copyright Act, 1956, no part of this publication may be reproduced, stored in a retrieval system, or transmitted, in any form or by any means, electronic, electrical, chemical, mechanical, optical, photocopying, recording or otherwise, without the prior permission of the copyright owner. Enquiries should be addressed to the publisher.

© George Allen & Unwin Ltd 1972

British ISBN 0 04 942104 2 hardback
            0 04 942105 0 paper

Published in the USA 1972 by
HARPER & ROW PUBLISHERS, INC.
BARNES AND NOBLE IMPORT DIVISION

ISBN 06 4902501

GENERAL INTRODUCTION

The reader and the teacher of history might be forgiven for thinking that there are now too many series of historical documents in existence, all claiming to offer light on particular problems and all able to fulfil their claims. At any rate, the general editor of yet another series feels obliged to explain why he is helping one more collection of such volumes into existence.

One purpose of this series is to put at the disposal of the student original materials illustrating historical problems, but this is no longer anything out of the way. A little less usual is the decision to admit every sort of historical question: there are no barriers of time or place or theme. However, what really distinguishes this enterprise is the fact that it combines generous collections of documents with introductory essays long enough to explore the theme widely and deeply. In the doctrine of educationalists, it is the original documents that should be given to the student; in the experience of teachers, documents thrown naked before the untrained mind turn from pearls to paste. The study of history cannot be confined either to the learning up of results without a consideration of the foundations, or to a review of those foundations without the assistance of the expert mind. The task of teaching involves explanation and instruction, and these volumes recognize this possibly unfashionable fact. Beyond that, they enable the writers to say new and important things about their subject matter: to write history of an exploratory kind, which is the only important historical writing there is.

As a result, each volume will be a historical monograph worth the attention which all such monographs deserve, and each volume will stand on its own. While the format of the series is uniform, the contents will vary according to need. Some problems require the reconsideration which makes the known enlighteningly new; others need the attention of original research; yet others will have to enter controversy because the prevailing notions on many historical questions are demonstrably wrong. The authors of this series are free to treat their subject in whatever manner it seems to them to require. They will present some of their evidence for inspection and help the learner to see how history is written, but they will themselves also write history.

G.R.E.

PREFACE

This book is an outgrowth of a book of by-laws which the American Philosophical Society published for me in 1965 under the title, *Open-Field Husbandry and the Village Community, a Study of Agrarian By-laws in Medieval England*. That was intended for specialists. In the present volume I have had in mind readers with a wider range of interests. The by-laws have been translated and the 'Introduction' to the earlier work has been re-ordered, re-written and reduced by half. I am grateful to the American Philosophical Society for permission to make use of its publication in the production of this book.

I thank Professor G. R. Elton for valuable advice both general and specific. An indispensable collaborator at every stage was my wife.

W.O.A.

CONTENTS

GENERAL INTRODUCTION	*page* 7
PREFACE	9
INTRODUCTION	15
DOCUMENTS	79
Glossary	80
1. By-laws	81
2. Court Rolls	145
Index	175

INTRODUCTION

Introduction

In an open-field village the ploughlands lay in two or more extensive tracts. Each great field was divided into ploughstrips which were grouped in furlongs. The strips, many or few, of each landholder lay scattered through the tracts, intermingled with those of his neighbours. The origin of this arrangement has been explained in different ways but it is clear that if some villagers had ploughlands more outlying than the rest they would be at a disadvantage in making their way from the village crofts, to and fro, at the slow pace of oxen. Each year one of the great fields of a village lay fallow, that is, it was not under crop for an entire year. In this way the soil could maintain its level of fertility without manure, little of which was available. It was important in an age of subsistence farming with little carry-over that a landholder have no more of his ploughstrips in the fallow field than in those under crop.

Open-field villages in England go back to Domesday Book and beyond. Typical of them was the nucleated village where 'the eye sees only one village street, one set of fields'.[1] A tiny settlement of this type with only a few families we may call a hamlet, and there were isolated farmsteads also, with but one household. These three units of settlement—village, hamlet, and farmstead—were present in every region of England. In the highlands the hamlet and farmstead predominated, but compact villages were to be found wherever geographical conditions were favourable. In the midlands villages were the rule, but hamlets and farmsteads were not unknown, as, for example, in forest clearings. By the Norman Conquest the rural framework of England was largely complete. It was 'a world of neighbours' with all men within easy walking distance of each other.[2]

Most villages had a thin belt of woodland and waste and this afforded rough pasturage for the flocks and herds. But the best pasture was the stubble. Every landholder had a right to turn his beasts into the stubble of any field after harvest until seed-time which, in the case of a field lying fallow, would be a year. It is obvious that if the right of pasture was to be enjoyed by all and shared equitably there would have to be communal control, field-wide if not village-wide. The right of common

[1] W. W. Beresford and J. K. S. St Joseph, *Medieval England, an Aerial Survey* (1938), 62.
[2] R. Lennard, *Rural England, 1086–1135* (1959), 20-21.

pasture has rightly been called 'the determining idea' of the open-field system.³

The origin of the open-field system is shrouded in the mists of time. Some scholars are able to discern elements of it in what Tacitus wrote about the Germanic tribes *c.* AD 98: 'Lands proportionate to the number of cultivators are taken for tillage in turn by the whole body of them and then they divide among themselves according to rank; partition is rendered easy by the wide expanse of open ground. They change their ploughlands every year and yet there is land in abundance.' ⁴ Did the Anglo-Saxon invaders bring this method of land tenure and tillage, further developed, with them five centuries later? Scholars who believe this point to the passage in the Laws of Ine, 608–694: 'If ceorls (husbandmen) have a common meadow or other land divided into shares to fence and some have fenced their portion and some have not and [if cattle] eat up their common crops or grass, those who are responsible for the gap are to go and pay to the others who have fenced their part, compensation for the damage that has been done there. They are to demand with regard to those cattle such reparation as is proper.' ⁵ It is possible to assume that there is a reference here to a tract of arable divided into ploughstrips which need to be defended from trespassing beasts on one or more sides by a fence. Charters of the tenth century show that such tracts were in existence then and Dorothy Whitelock concluded: 'The normal practice was the open-field system in which each man held his strips in the common fields and one-half or one-third of the arable was left fallow each year. Along with the holding in the arable went rights in common meadows and pasture and in all the amenities of the estate.' ⁶

The right of pasture in and over a field when not under crop, then, is basic in the open-field system of agriculture. But Dr Joan Thirsk suggests that this may have been a later development in medieval England.

'It [the stubble] afforded useful feed for animals but was not indispensable if pasture and waste were plentiful. The fields needed manure to keep them in good health and it was obviously more economical to graze stock on the fields than to cart manure from elsewhere. But the need for manure might not be urgent until the fields were fairly intensively cropped. Under a rotation of crops and long years of grass men could have managed without. Thus, until population grew and land had

---

³ H. L. Gray, *English Open Fields* (1955), 47. Note the fact that it had no interior fences. It might well be protected from trespassing animals (and men) by ditches and hedges on one or more sides. In one sense of the word, therefore, it was not open.

⁴ J. G. C. Anderson's translation (1961), 132–4.

⁵ *English Historical Documents I* (1955), 368–369.

⁶ *Ibid.*, 70.

to be used economically we can envisage the possibility that the stubble in the arable fields was not used.'[7]

But the casual droppings of grazing cattle are unevenly distributed and their value much reduced through exposure.[8] Indeed, what cattle leave behind scarcely equals what they take away. For best results the whole of the crop residue, together with the infesting weeds and grasses, should be ploughed under early in the year of fallow, so that maximum nitrate fixation can take place, through which the soil, by 'resting', recovers its fertility.[9] Medieval man pastured the stubble not to keep the soil in good heart—his sharply observant eye told him that this did not follow [10]—but to keep his flocks and herds in good condition. This was especially important for the beasts of the plough, always given high priority. Good grazing was to be found on the headlands, balks, cartways and odd bits of land left unploughed, and the grasses and edible weeds of strips yet unploughed could be lopped off. (Cattle do not care much for straw.) Common pasture of stubble and fallow was a feature of open-field husbandry from the start, I think, and with it went communal control.

The practice of the New England pioneers supports this view. There too the arable lay in great fields and beyond the fields were woodland and waste—the 'cattle range'. A town might have several thousand acres of such land; Salem, Massachusetts, had four thousand acres. There might be several hundred cattle in the town herd. One or more herdsmen were contracted for and a town 'mark' was used for identification, for there was much inter-commoning. Even with such an abundance of pasture, however, every landholder had the right of pasture over the stubble of a great field in which his arable lay. So valuable was grazing the stubble that stints were established from the start, that is, each landholder was allowed to have so many horses and so many head of cattle, depending upon the size of his holding in the field. This right of 'commonage', as it was called, survived long after all other forms of communal control had vanished.

---

[7] *Past and Present*, No. 29 (Dec. 1964), 15.

[8] Half the nitrogen and more than half the potassium is in the urine which, in the open, is leached away by rainfall. In a feeding shed or barn the urine is absorbed by a bedding of straw or other organic matter, which then becomes, in effect, manure. Moreover, half the nitrogen in the dung volatilizes within forty-eight hours if left exposed to the air. Professor L. S. Thompson, Iowa State University, *Soils and Soil Fertility*, 2nd ed. (1957), ch. 10.

[9] 'Decomposition causes immobilization of the available nitrogen of the air by microorganisms of the soil.' *Ibid.*, 236.

[10] To increase the fertility of ploughland significantly barnyard manure should be spread on the soil evenly just before seed time at the rate of four tons to the acre and ploughed under without delay. L. L. Van Slyke, *Fertilizers and Crop Production* (1932), ch. 6.

EARLY BY-LAWS

The problem of the origin of the open-field will never be solved; documents are few and their meaning is uncertain. But we can find out a good deal about what the open-field system was like in the thirteenth century when documents at the local level become reasonably adequate. They are, however, almost exclusively manorial, so much so that formerly scholars made the manor the sole object of their study, unable or disinclined to penetrate to the vill that lay beneath, though it was both older and longer-lived.

Manorial documents are of several kinds. The Extent set forth in fullest detail what the lord of the manor was entitled to receive from his tenants in rent and services. It was based on the sworn testimony of a small group of tenants, generally unfree, the more worthy and knowledgeable sort, one supposes. Listed first was the parish church, its glebe lands and its tithes and their value; then the arable, meadows and woodland held by the lord in demesne; then the free tenants and their holdings, rents and labour service, usually light. Then a list (much longer) of customary tenants whose holdings, rents and services followed a set pattern; and lastly the cottagers with their crofts and, possibly, an acre or two of arable. A manorial Extent supplies us with the names of every tenant, with information about his economic and legal status.

Another class of manorial document is the reeve's account. Each year, after harvest, the manorial reeve set forth all receipts of rents and services for the year, the produce of demesne lands and livestock and the proceeds of the manor court. His disbursements were listed in complete detail. Placed in charge of his lord's economic interests, the reeve was concerned to show how he had met his obligations in the course of the year. The earliest extant accounts are those for the manors of the bishop of Winchester for the year 1208–1209. In the second half of the thirteenth century manorial accounts are plentiful.

The most valuable class of documents for the historian of rural life are the records of the proceedings of manor courts. Here, too, the interest of the lord was paramount; indeed as a final item at the end of the record of a session the scribe noted the sum total of proceeds accruing to the lord. Unfortunately manor court rolls are of still later date than Extents and accounts. The earliest roll known to Maitland was dated 1246.[11] In a search through more than thirty archives I have

---

[11] F. W. Maitland, *Select Pleas in Manorial and other Seigneurial Courts* (1888), xlii.

found none earlier, though there are a few prototypes which antedate Maitland's find.[12] Early rolls are rare not because so few have survived, however, but because the practice of recording the proceedings of manor courts had not yet become general.[13]

It is in the records of manor courts that village by-laws have been found, and they are to be seen in the earliest rolls. They are not easy to find; one may look through a series of rolls beginning with the first Edward and continuing with few gaps through the second Richard without finding any. In another series by-laws may be recorded with some regularity, together with the names of wardens elected to enforce them and a list of offenders, but this is rare. More often the names of the wardens are given and nothing more.

Sometimes, especially in an early roll where no by-laws are quoted, record was made of a fine for breaking one. For example, at Newington, Oxon., in 1270, 'John Garleche harboured Isabella contrary to the statute of autumn. Therefore he is fined 2d.'[14] It is probable that the statute referred to was the familiar by-law of harvest which provided that every able-bodied worker in the village must work as a reaper as long as there was anyone who wanted to hire him, and not glean. In breach of this village ordinance John had accepted Isabella as a gleaner. At Newton Longville, Bucks., in 1283, thirteen persons were presented by the wardens of autumn and fined 6d. each, but no record was made of which by-law or by-laws they had broken.[15] In the following year in the same manor it was ordered in court that the statutes of autumn of previous years be observed and enforced, but no note was made of what the statutes were.[16] In 1290, however, a list of thirteen by-laws was recorded,[17] and if we compare them with those of 1332 [18] we can see that there was little change in the intervening years. These by-laws deal with the basic problems of harvest and pasture in an open-field village. They are probably of considerable antiquity, as old in their essentials as open-field husbandry itself. There are comparable ordinances in other thirteenth-century manors, and the by-laws of later centuries are not dissimilar.

We may be certain, I think, that whenever an open-field husbandry was practical there were customary rules for its control whether or not reference was ever made to them in the roll of a manor court; and this must have been true in villages of divided lordship with no one manor court.

[12] W. O. Ault, 'The Earliest Rolls of Manor Courts', *Studia Gratiana* (1972).
[13] *Ibid.*
[14] Doc. 1.
[15] Doc. 196.
[16] Doc. 197.
[17] Doc. 8.
[18] Doc. 199.

PLOUGHING

Ploughing was the principal occupation on a medieval farm, calling for more labour on the part of man and beast year round than any other. The medieval plough was a wheeled instrument with mouldboard and coulter, drawn by four, six, or even eight oxen, depending on the kind of soil and its condition at ploughing time. In the autumn some land must be ploughed for winter seed; in the spring other land must be readied for the Lenten sowing. And fallow ground must be ploughed twice if possible. The first ploughing was to turn under the crop residue and weeds and grasses. This should be done before the onset of summer to allow time for the decomposition of the organic material. The second ploughing, less deep, aerated the soil and prepared it for seeding. It may be that more oxen were needed for spring than for autumn ploughing. Lack of fodder was perennial and after a winter on short rations the medieval ox, a scrawny beast, came to full strength slowly. Few peasants can have owned both a plough and the oxen to draw it. In Domesday Book 'only about half as many ploughs are listed as peasants'.[19] It was the need for cooperation in ploughing, perhaps, that induced the early early settlers to have their acres lie side by side, intermingled, in the open field. That is what happened in early New England where there were three times as many settlers as ploughs.[20]

Co-aration is not mentioned in any village by-law, however, early or late. 'We have a notion that this was done,' says Bennett, 'but little definite evidence exists to support this view.' [21] That tenants did combine in ploughing for their lord is clear. In a charter dated 1294 a villein tenant acknowledged his obligation to 'plough once in the winter sowing and again in the Lent sowing with as many oxen as he shall have yoked in a plough'. The custumal of Battle Abbey records in 1311 that every freeman who has a whole plough shall plough a whole acre at each boon work, 'and he who has less than a whole plough shall plough according to what animals he has yoked in the plough'.[22] In the village of Chalgrave, Beds., in 1313, the ploughing service of a tenant was thus defined: if he joins a beast of the plough to the plough team of another he will receive credit for his obligation of a boon ploughing. He must not, however, change his ox from one plough team to another without the lord's consent.[23] At Cockerham, Lancs., in 1326, 'Whoever has a

[19] E. Barger, *English Historical Review*, Vol. 54 (1958), 395–396.
[20] The New England settlers were 'compulsive' ploughers. After half a century they learned that corn, that is, maize, can be grown with entire success in a patch of cleared forest, Indian fashion, with the aid of a hoe.
[21] H. S. Bennett, *Life on the English Manor* (1937), 45.
[22] *Battle Abbey Custumals*, 148.
[23] *Bedfordshire Historical Record Society*, Vol. 28 (1950), 65–66.

holding of four acres of land shall bring one ox to plough with the lord's team twice a year and he shall give his lord 12d. for the ox if he does not have it.'[24]

Neighbour combined with neighbour, too, in ploughing their own acres. The Hundred Rolls tell us of a villager of Bolton, Lincs., who complained that he was 'unable to find ... a single neighbour who dared to yoke an ox to a plough with him because of the bailiff's forbiddance and power'.[25] In a manor court roll of Wakefield, Yorks., in 1286, 'It is found by an inquisition of neighbours that Richard de Tuthill was a companion of Roger de Bosco to plough jointly and at the time of ploughing cast him off so that his land had to lie untilled.'[26] Damages were assessed at 10s. and Roger was fined 12d. At Holderness, Yorks., in 1300 Richard Wilmot complained in the manor court of his neighbour Herbert Bowman, saying that with Herbert's consent and 'by an ordinance of the bondsmen' Herbert and his ox were 'associated' with him. Subsequently despite Richard's protest Herbert unyoked his ox and led it away. The jury said that the association of Herbert with Richard was a proper one and 'in the best place'. Herbert was fined 12d. and Richard's damages were assessed at 6d.[27]

No such ordinance has been found nor, ordinarily, would a village-wide provision be needed. Neighbours would combine informally. At Moundsmere, Hants., in 1327, one landholder accused another of having broken their agreement to plough together. The latter denied this, claiming that his accuser had withdrawn himself and refused to plough with him.[28] And at Thame, Oxon., in 1365, 'John de Roch complains of Robert Eliot of Eltoft ... John comes and says that on a certain day and year he made a pact with the said Robert that they should be partners for ploughing the land of the said John and Robert with equal animals going to the plough, which partnership is called marrows, for a year only.' Robert broke the pact.[29] 'Marrows' means 'to lend horses and men for labour to a neighbour and to receive a similar loan when needed'.[30] Arrangements such as these are common to this day among farmers whose capital is small. They never put them in writing and rarely do they need to go to law.

Strips of ploughland varied in length and in width. It has been sug-

---

[24] *Transactions of the Lancashire and Cheshire Antiquarian Society*, Vol. 69 (1954), 45.

[25] I, 351. Cited by G. C. Homans, *English Villagers of the Thirteenth Century* (1941), 78–79.

[26] *Wakefield Court Rolls*, III, 161.

[27] *Northamptonshire Record Society*, Burleigh MSS., 57-18. Herbert's ox was unyoked on a Monday, June 6th, and the court met on Friday, July 23rd.

[28] Winchester College MSS., 14411, cited in *Open-Field Husbandry*, 31.

[29] Thoresby Society, Vol. 15, 168. Cited by Bennett, *op. cit.*, 45.

[30] *Ibid.*

gested that the length of a selion was determined by the distance which a team of oxen could pull a plough without having to stop for a 'breather'. Alternatively, it is argued that furrows must be long enough to compensate for the inconvenience of having to turn the plough and team about. Another factor of length, no doubt, was the lie of the land; in the same village strips as short as 90 feet have been observed, and as long as 225 yards. Selions varied in width also. On light soil they could be considerably wider than in heavy clay where drainage furrows must be left at frequent intervals.

The area of a selion or strip was what could readily be ploughed in a day. The statute acre is 4,840 square yards, ideally a plot 22 yards wide and 220 yards long. It is clear that the 'medieval acre' was considerably smaller. It has been established by careful study that a day's work for a medieval plough and team was from one-third to two-thirds of a statute acre. Using a fourteen-inch steel walking-plough, drawn by two stout horses, my daily stint as a ploughboy was three statute acres.

No traveller through the English countryside can fail to notice the medieval acre strips which survive in pasture land as ridge and furrow. These are not perfectly straight. They have a slight sigmoid shape, the so-called 'plough twist'. 'When the ploughshare is lifted out of the ground at the end of the furrow there is a tendency for it to cut slightly wider and on setting it in on the other side the opposite tendency occurs and a slightly narrower furrow is cut. The result is a slight bend to the left at the end of each butt.'[31] But another theory is that the plough team pulled out to the left on the headland and thus 'the ploughman was able to keep the mouldboard pressed against the furrow slice'. The result was a selion shaped like a reversed 'S'.[32] The ridged shape of the strip, in cross-section, is a consequence of the method of ploughing: first a furrow was ploughed through the centre and then the others were cast inward toward it back and forth until the boundaries of the strip were reached on either side. Generations of this kind of ploughing in heavy soils would result in a ridge that might become too high at the centre for farming convenience. There was an easy remedy, and it is probable that in such a case the strip was ploughed the other way from time to time, that is, beginning at the sides and ploughing inward towards the centre. These two procedures are called respectively 'gathering' and 'casting'.[33]

Ploughstrips might be separated from each other by a balk of turf. These were sometimes wide enough to be of some value as mow-land or pasture. As population increased, many of the balks were ploughed up

---

[31] W. J. Slack, 'The Open-Field System of Agriculture and its Traces in Shropshire', *Caradoc and Severn Valley Field Club Transactions* (1927), 149.

[32] S. R. Eyre, 'The Curving Plough Strip and its Historical Significance', *Agricultural History Review*, Vol. III (1955), 87.

[33] Slack, *op. cit.*, 148.

and selions were separated by double furrows. These were easy to discern in a field of grain; in the broad furrow there was little depth of earth. Stalks were short and the spears of grain small.

Here and there in any great field there were bits of land of irregular shape and varied size, called 'gores', that had been left out because they could not be fitted into a furlong. There were, also, patches of unploughable land. Thus the pattern of each field was unique. At the end of each furlong a headland or 'fore-acre' was left unploughed. These were from fifteen to twenty-five feet wide and it was on them that the team and plough were turned; to turn a long plough and its team of four or six oxen hitched in pairs required considerable space. The headlands were used as rights of way for carts or as drove-ways for beasts, or they could themselves be ploughed to finish off a field.

Stealing a furrow could not possibly go undetected, but no by-laws dealing with this problem have been found. Trespass in ploughing is dealt with, but not until late medieval times. At West Drayton, Somerset, 'it is ordered at this court by the consent of all the tenants there that no one henceforth when he ploughs his land shall damage or trample the land of another sown with grain but shall turn his plough on his own land as before', on pain of 12d.[34] At Winterbourne, Stoke, Wilts., 'Our custome is that every tenant who turneth with the plough upon the next adjoining land that is sown shall make good the same again.'[35] And at Basingstoke, Hants., 'It is ordered that if anyone henceforth shall turn upon anyone's wheat with their plough or their horses they shall pay each time 3s. 4d.'[36] It would seem that by-laws such as these were called for because the tenants were no longer ploughing their selions at the same time of the year or even in the same year.

SOWING

No by-laws have been found that fixed a time for sowing, at least not till the sixteenth century. This is not surprising. Every farmer knew when he must sow if he would reap. Winter sowing must be done well before frost if seeds are to sprout and proper growth take place. In the spring the soil must be warm enough and the average temperature at a dependable level. Seed-time, then, may last a month, and sowings two weeks apart often ripen the same day. Medieval men might be well advised to sow Lenten seed 'when the oak leaves are as big as mouse ears', but there was no need of a by-law to that effect. Of course, coming to sow so late that you trample the ground of your neighbour whose seed had already sprouted was unneighbourly, and he might take you to

[34] Middlesex Record Office, Acc. 446-M6-570.
[35] *Wiltshire Archaeological and Natural History Magazine*, Vol. 34, 2. 1574.
[36] *History of Basingstoke*, 1586, 350.

court if you failed to make amends.[37] The first by-law that fixed a time, but not a day, for sowing is dated 1503: 'No one shall sow rye after the Feast of All Saints.' [38]

Where to sow was another matter. Sowing your acres, even one of them, in the fallow field was a cardinal sin, for it deprived your neighbours of their right of pasture. In the earliest court rolls there were instances of men punished for this.[39] The first by-law is dated 1352 and it comes from the village of Sedgefield, County Durham: 'This is an agreement by the neighbours of Sedgefield at the command and insistence of the steward and by the consent of the neighbours, that one-third of the fields of Sedgefield shall lie fallow every third year and if anyone shall sow any part of the said third contrary to the ordinance the products of the same shall be forfeited to the lord and in addition he shall pay half a mark.'[40] This ordinance may have been made necessary by a change from a two to a three field course of cultivation in this village. The sharp insistence of the steward and the heavy penalty suggest that it had been difficult to keep all the tenants in line. In a neighbouring village about the same date we find this: 'It is ordered by common consent that each of them shall have his lands under crop when everyone else does and let them lie fallow when the others do according to ancient custom.'[41] And at Bishop's Hampton, Warwickshire, in 1460 we find this record: 'By an agreement of all the tenants made in court in the presence of the steward it is ordered by the steward with the assent of all the tenants that they shall let one field lie fallow in turn every year and that all other fields be sown on pain of forfeiting their tenure.' [42]

When a field is under crop, in some villages, all selions must be sown, even to the 'outermost border and last land'. This was the subject of a by-law in the Oxfordshire village of Launton in 1587.[43] At Whitchurch, Hants., a similar by-law reads, 'Every tenant having any land in the fields shall annually keep in cultivation and sow all his outermost selions of any furlong commonly cultivated and not allow them to be idle and in fallow to the damage of his neighbours under pain of every one of them in default 10s.' [44] How would the neighbours be damaged if the tenant of the outermost selion of a furlong allowed it to lie fallow while the other selions of the furlong were under cultivation? Well, perhaps it was because it would grow up to weeds with wind-blown

[37] E.g., in Barkby, Leics., Merton College Muniments, c. 6590.
[38] Ampthill, Beds. Bedfordshire Record Society, L, 26–49.
[39] See below (under 'Pasture'), 72–76.
[40] P.R.O., Durham Cursitor Records, XII, 68 d.
[41] Durham Halmotes, 127. 1373–4.
[42] P.R.O. Eccl., 189–8.
[43] Westminster Abbey Court Rolls, 15565.
[44] Br. Mus. Add. Ch. 44604. 1668. A similar by-law is in the rolls of the manor of Scotter, Lincs., in 1598. Archaeologia, Vol. 46, 383.

INTRODUCTION 25

seeds. Or was it that the neighbours were thinking, too, about their right to pasture the stubble? The by-laws are all of late date. The owners of untilled plots may well have been absentees.

HAYING

In medieval times meadows were the gift of nature, not the work of man. The supply of hay, therefore, was strictly limited, and hay was the best, indeed about the only good fodder for animals penned up in winter. To quote Professor Homans, 'The greatest difference between medieval agriculture and modern is this humble but vital matter of hay.'[45] Meadows were to be found, for the most part, on the banks of a stream, but a roadside or headland might be worth mowing in a good season. Acre for acre meadow land was worth two or three times as much as arable.

How precious hay was in the sight of the lord of the manor is seen in the thirteenth-century records of the village of Newington, Oxon. Every virgater 'ought to mow the lord's meadow once a year until it is mown. He ought to tedder and rake the grass and take it to the lord's grange. For this service he shall have a wheaten loaf sufficient for two days and cheese worth a ha'penny and the mowers shall have among themselves one of the better sheep from the lord's fold, whichever they wish. One cheese and one basin of salt when all the hay has been carried.'[46] Provisions of this sort are familiar to readers of manorial Extents and they show, I think, that landlords were willing to pay a substantial bonus to see that their meadows were mown promptly and well. But even this did not always secure faithful service in Newington, as the following record from the manor court of 1300 reveals: 'The whole court is indicted for that they did not come in a body to mow the lord's meadow as they were summoned to do by the bailiff. But some tenants stayed home and took from each tenant not coming [to the mowing] 4d. by the assent of the tenants for the use of the tenants and not for the use of the lord and they are ordered therefore to make amends to the lord and on this they seek respite until the coming of the warden in order that they may consult about this with the warden. And they have a respite that upon the coming of the warden they will do in the premises whatever he shall deem best. Afterwards the whole court comes and puts itself at the mercy of the lord and his bailiffs except John Aleyn, Samuel Lornham, John Gane, John West, Hugh David, and John Goneyre. Fine 10s.' John West and Hugh David were the 'wardens of the mowers'. They were fined 12d. each 'because they did not do their

---

[45] *Op. cit.*, 41.
[46] *Rotuli Hundredorum*, II, 761.

office in due form in not rebuking the unjust mowers'. The other three named were fined 6d. or 12d. each 'for wrongful mowing the lord's meadows'.[47] It should be remarked that the deliberate revolt of a group of peasants against this particular labour service was not uncommon.[48]

The priority of the lord in hay time is illustrated by the following item from the Customs of Cockerham, Lancs.: 'No tenant shall hire servants whether men or women for the period of hay making until the lord has chosen whom he will on or near the Feast of St Peter in Chains.'[49]

In many villages the tenants too had meadows. In some cases they held them in common, that is, each year at hay time the co-parceners divided the meadow into plots or swathes in some equitable fashion. In the manor court of Holywell, Hunts., in 1327, a jury reported that 'William Bondley broke a by-law and entered the common meadow to the common damage'.[50] We may guess that William's offence was his failure to wait for the lotting of the meadow. In one of the halmotes of the Priory of Durham we find this record: 'It was ordered by common consent that each tenant shall come to make hay in the common meadow when summoned under pain of losing his portion.'[51] In other words, if you claim to have a share of the meadow you must come to the mowing when summoned as the others do. At Launton, Oxon., in 1440, 'it is ordered by the lord and his tenants that any tenant who has a parcel of meadow in East Brokemede shall not mow there now or ever until his neighbours are agreed under pain of 3s. 4d.'[52] That is, all must be in agreement about the dividing of the meadow before anyone can begin mowing. A by-law of Great Horwood, in 1483, makes much the same point.[53] At Kibworth, Leics., in 1486, 'It is agreed that each tenant shall be ready to divide the meadows indifferently before the Feast of Corpus Christi [May 25th] under pain of 40d.'[54] This court was held on April 27th. In the same manor, in 1538, 'It is ordered that all the inhabitants there shall be prepared to measure the meadow and set merestones there on a day agreed among them this side the Feast of Corpus Christi next [55] under pain of 12d.'[56]

[47] P.R.O., Court Rolls, Eccl. 26–41.
[48] R. H. Hilton, 'Peasant Movements in England before 1381', *Economic History Review*, 2d Series, Vol. 2 (1949).
[49] August 1st. *Transactions of the Lancashire and Cheshire Antiquarian Society*, Vol. 64 (1954), 46.
[50] P.R.O., Court Rolls, 3. c. 2, 179–22, *m*. 1.
[51] *Durham Halmotes*, 23. 1358. (1889.)
[52] Westminster Abbey Muniments, 15502 *d*.
[53] Doc. 167.
[54] Merton College Muniments, 6434.
[55] The Thursday after the eighth Sunday after Easter.
[56] *Ibid.*, 6442 *d*. Cited in *Open-Field Husbandry*, 34.

INTRODUCTION 27

Sixteenth-century by-laws are, as usual, more detailed. At Akeley, Bucks., in 1554, 'Hit is ordeyned and agreed att this courte that no man schall mowe in one of the meades until the whole meade be laydout ... Item that thre men be appoynted to the outer meade.'[57] In a tithe suit at Wigston, Leics., a peasant deposed as follows: 'In somer when the use to mowe there grass the parishioners being together doe amongste theym selves a grey and saye lett us begin and mowe longe medowe suche a day and sow that day they doe mowe longe medowe and hatters slade togeather as one medowe.'[58] Here is the way a meadow was lotted in the town of Billerica, Massachusetts, in 1658. 'The Lotts were drawne by the severall inhabitants whose names are here underwritten to the number of twenty and thre Lotts, besides the medows for the minister; which Lotts of meddow for the minister were joyntly agreed upon to be Layd out in the firste place accordinge to the beste discretione of a comittee appoynted for thyt worke.'[59]

Where the air is dry and the sun hot hay can be cut one day and stacked the next. In the damp climate of England, however, the mown grass will have to be turned at least once to dry it through and through. A thirteenth-century manual urged that 'the hay be tedded, dried and raked before it rains'.[60] Rained on, hay will have to be tedded again. At Elmley Castle there was a rule that 'the whole meadow shall be mown in one day'.[61] This could be important. In a number of villages midsummer day (June 24th) was set as the time for mowing, or the day before or the day after, depending upon the weather.

HARVEST

Hay time was followed after an interval of a few weeks by harvest. The time for beginning would depend upon the summer; there might be as much as three weeks' difference between a cold rainy summer and one that had been dry and fine. In Sussex wheat ripened a week to ten days earlier than in Yorkshire.[62] In medieval England the weeks of harvest were an anxious time of year; man subsisted so largely on the produce of his fields in those days and the weather, even in harvest time, was not reliable. The moisture content of grain must be within bounds or it will spoil; drying ovens were unimaginable.

The principle of procedure in harvest was haste without waste. That

---

[57] New College Court Rolls I, 3.
[58] Cited by W. G. Hoskins, *The Midland Peasant* (1957), 165.
[59] Records of Billerica, 7.
[60] *Fleta* Vol. 2, ch. 82. *Selden Society Publications* (1955).
[61] Worcester Record Office, 899: 95/4/60.
[62] In the American west gangs of harvest hands used to follow the ripening wheat for two months, from Texas to the Dakotas.

was the theme of *Fleta*, written about 1290: 'At reaping time the servants should not give way to sloth but early in the morning the hayward should have his workers assemble and hasten to send their sickles into the corn and he should make them reap in orderly fashion and continuously without quickening the pace, watching lest in grudging hurry beneath the first handful the crop is laid and left uncut but that on the contrary it is cleanly reaped and the shocks set up in good order so that they may dry the sooner and be conveniently and evenly tied up in small sheaves, for a small sheaf is handier than a large one to cart to rick and to thresh, to be safely carried and lodged in the barn as soon as the weather is suitable.'[63] Wheat was cut with a sickle half way or more up the stalk and the reapers cut the spears of differing length in handfuls and laid them on the ground. Then came binders to gather the spears and tie them in sheaves, which were then set in shocks to dry. Fitzherbert describes the process: 'Set four sheves on one syde and iiij sheves on the other syde and ii sheves above . . . and they wolde be set on the rydge of the lande, and the sayde sheves to leane together in the toppes, and wyde at the grounde, that the winde may go through, to drye them.' One binder was needed for four reapers.[64] To bind spears together in sheaves without some loss was impossible and more would be lost as the sheaves were set in shocks. Gleaners, then, were required no less than reapers and binders. Oats and barley were mown with a scythe close to the ground, but the stalks were short and much remained to be gleaned after the sheaves were gathered. In the peak days of harvest every able-bodied man and woman would be in demand as reaper or binder. A man or woman able to wield a sickle or swing a scythe dawn to dark through a long summer's day needed to be at full strength. Children and grown-ups too old or too feeble for such heavy labour might glean; there was work for everyone. The days when grain is ripe enough to cut but not too ripe are few; if cut too soon it will spoil; if over-ripe some kernels will be knocked out in handling and fall to the ground.

The competition for harvest hands was keen and the lord of the manor had an advantage. His prime source perhaps were the members of his own 'family', his staff of farm hands, and even household servants not urgently needed for other tasks. Then there was the labour service owed by his tenants. The thirteenth-century virgaters of the Priory of Canterbury were obliged to reap half a day five days a week with one man, or a whole day if the lord furnished food; besides this, two boon-works must be done whenever the lord asked, each of three days with food at the lord's expense.[65] It would be with some difficulty that such

---

[63] Vol. 2, *loc. cit.*
[64] *The Book of Husbandry*, ed. W. W. Skeate (1882).
[65] *Rotuli Hundredorum* II, 761–763.

tenants could garner their own grain, especially if it was ripening fast. Customary tenants of Ramsey Abbey owed five days' work, half-days really perhaps, in each week at harvest with two men; also three boon-works on days of the lord's choosing. And at the first or 'great' boon-day they must bring all the family.[66] The obligation of harvest work is one of the most familiar features of the manorial system and further illustration is not needed. Boon-works were the last labour service to be commuted. Further, landlords commonly had priority in the hiring of the casual labourers of the village. In the manor of Cockerham, Lancs., in 1326, tenants were forbidden under heavy penalty to take into their service as reapers or binders men or women 'resident in the lordship... until the warden of the manor has expressed a wish to have them or not'.[67] In the lands of Fountains Abbey it was 'enjoined on all the labourers of the town under pain of 2s. 4d., that they must work for their wages first with the lord and afterwards with the tenants whenever necessary, and they shall not leave town'.[68] At Kingsbury, Warw., in 1320, the messor was accused of having taken a bribe from the men to withhold them from autumn service, to the lord's hurt,[69] and in Chalgrave, Beds., in 1383, a tenant was fined because he kept a reaper from the lord's service in autumn.[70]

Garnered and gleaned, the lord's grain had to be safeguarded against theft at every stage. The rolls of manor courts are peppered with fines levied for sheaf stealing in the field, and a close watch had to be kept in the barn, as well. Walter of Henley wrote, 'The reeve must take care that no thresher or winnower shall take corn to carry it away in his bosom or in tunic or boots or pockets or socklets hidden near the grange.'[71]

The landlords were well able to gather and guard their grain, but how did the villagers deal with the problems of harvest? They acted in communal fashion. Let us look again at some of the early agrarian by-laws, noting that these were recorded in late June or early July, on the eve of harvest and that infractions were reported in mid-September or early October.

A by-law of Newton Longville, Bucks., in 1290: 'It is granted and ordered by the community of the vill that no one henceforth shall be allowed to glean who is able to earn a penny a day with food or two pence without food if there be any who want to hire him.'[72] And simi-

---

[66] N. Neilson, *Economic Conditions on the Manors of Ramsay Abbey* (1898), 42 ff. Extents of about 1250.
[67] *Transactions of the Lancashire and Cheshire Antiquarian Society*, loc. cit.
[68] Cited in *Open-Field Husbandry*, 13.
[69] *Ibid.*
[70] *Ibid.*
[71] *Le Dite de Nosebondrie*, ed. E. Lamonde (1890), 99.
[72] Doc. 8.

larly at Great Horwood, there was 'an agreement of the community of the vill in the lord's presence that no man or woman among them shall be allowed to glean who is able to earn for his labour a penny a day and food'.[73] When reaping and binding were done by hand, gleaning was essential as we have seen. One authority estimates that a gleaner could earn almost as much in a day as a reaper.[74] But no one able to reap might glean. To keep competition for reapers within limits a wage was fixed which no one might exceed. Do these rules apply to the members of a man's own household? May he not set some of them to gleaning his acres even if a neighbour wanted to hire them as reapers? The implication, clearly, is that he may not. Gleaning can wait but not reaping. Later by-laws are to the same effect. 'It is ordained by the consent of the whole homage that no one shall go gleaning in autumn when the lord or any one else wants to give him a penny a day with food for his labour.'[75] 'No one shall gather ears in autumn if any one wants him to work for a penny a day and food.'[76]

How regulations such as these worked in practice may be observed at Newington, Oxon. The four tithingmen of the hamlet of Berwick, in 1332, presented John Gryce 'for harbouring Alice King who transgressed in gleaning'. He was found guilty and fined 6d. Alice was not then and there proceeded against, but her husband, Robert King, responsible no doubt for the misdeeds of his wife, gave the lord 6d. to have an inquest as to whether Alice had reaped, first, with him and for him, and then with others who wished to hire her, as the by-laws required her to do. The jury said she had reaped with her husband but afterwards when the messor called upon her to reap for others she refused. The record concludes: 'And John Gryce is warrentor for the said Alice till the next court if perchance anyone wishes to make a complaint against her.'[77] Plainly, John Gryce in his concern that every spear of his grain be garnered had unlawfully set an able-bodied reaper to gleaning, to the possible hurt of his fellow tenants. He was fined accordingly. And Alice could have been fined too, if any one had wanted to proceed against her.

Was there ever a doubt about who was able-bodied? In 1282 this instruction was given the reeves of some royal manors: 'Let it be established that the young, the old, and those who are decrepit and unable to work shall glean in autumn after the sheaves have been taken away, but those who are able if they wish to work for wages will not be allowed to

[73] Doc. 36. 1319.
[74] M. le Duc, *Mémoires d'Agriculture* (1787), 117. Cited by Degrully, *Le Droit de Glanage* (1912), 117.
[75] Doc. 92. 1388.
[76] Doc. 103. 1395.
[77] P.R.O., Eccl., 26–50, *m*. 2. Cited in *English Historical Review*, Vol. 45, 217.

glean.'[78] At Brightwaltham, Berks., in 1340 'all the tenants agree that none of the inhabitants may glean corn unless they be under age or over age'.[79] A decision would have to be made of course in case after case as to who was too young to reap and who was too old and decrepit. This could be a crucial matter both for the worker involved and for the one who wished to hire him. Here is the way it was done at Basingstoke, Hants.: 'The impotent passed by view of the bailiff and constable with the assent of two or three of the tenants may commence gleaning from the beginning of harvest.'[80] Doubtless some such provision as this was made in other villages but it is a little surprising that no other example has been found. Nor has there been seen in the roll of any manor court the record of a dispute in such a matter.

Blackstone wrote, 'By the common law and custom of England the poor are allowed to enter and glean upon another's ground after the harvest without being guilty of trespass.'[81] In not one of the very numerous by-laws of gleaning is there a reference to such a right, nor is there a single mention of the poor as gleaners in any of the thirteenth-century treatises on agriculture. Piers Plowman in the fourteenth century said, 'Ac whoso helpeth me to erie [plow] or sowen here ere I wende shall have leave by our lord to lese [glean] here in harvest.'[82] There is no suggestion here that the poor as such had a right to glean. In medieval times the landless were generally classified as 'the poor' and all who were able-bodied would be under pressure to work for their wages as reapers. At a time when the yield of grain to the acre was about one-third to one-half the modern average gleaning made up a significant part of the harvest. When anyone was received as a gleaner in those days it was by consent of the landholder and on his terms. At Islip, Oxon.: 'It was ordered by the steward that none of the tenants nor any other person shall glean grain or peas pods in any land after it has been reaped except by permission of him or her who holds the land or owns the grain under penalty of losing the grain he had gathered and 12d. to the lord.'[83] At Bellington, Beds., in the same century, 'It was ordered and established by the lord's steward by the consent of the lord's tenants that no one shall gather pods or glean in the field of Bellington except in his own grain before the Feast of St Michael next to come under pain of 3s. 4d.'[84] It may be added that Blackstone's *dictum* was set aside in 1788 in the case of Steel vs. Houghton *et uxor*.[85]

[78] Cambridge University Library, Ee I. 1, *f.* 223 *v.*
[79] Doc. 61.
[80] F. J. Baigent and J. E. Millard, *History of Basingstoke* (1889), 217. 1389.
[81] *Commentary on the Laws of England* (1772), Vol. 3, 212.
[82] Book VI.
[83] *Oxfordshire Record Society*, XL (1959), 108. 1462.
[84] Bedfordshire Record Office, D. K. – 619, *m.* 24 *r.* 1470.
[85] The English Reports, Vol. 126, 32–39.

Gleaning, then, along with reaping and binding, was an integral part of harvest. Gleaners must work quickly, for the landholders were waiting to turn their beasts on to the stubble. At Basingstoke, Hants., six days were allowed for gleaning wheat fields, three for other corn, 'by ancient custom'.[86] At Wellingham, Norfolk, 'henceforth no inhabitant shall leave in his fields any rakings more than seven days after the sheaves are removed'.[87] At Littleport, Cambs., 'the Brothers Hospitalers pastured their sheep before the gleaners, contrary to the by-law'.[88] But gleaners need not wait until the entire area of a great field had been cleared of sheaves. At Ramsey, 'it is ordered by the consent of the lord and the whole community that henceforth none shall go gleaning until all the grain of one furlong be carried away under pain of half a mark'.[89] At Leighton Buzzard, Beds., no one was allowed to glean until a ten acre area had been cleared of sheaves.[90] At Elmley Castle, Worcs., in 1411, gleaners were excluded until the grain of all the selions had been gathered, shocked and carried away; but in 1439 an area of 12 selions was deemed safe when cleared, and much later, if an entire furlong was cleared, gleaners might enter it provided it was not within twenty 'lands' of a plot not yet cleared.[91] Sheaf stealing was a temptation to which gleaners were especially susceptible. They must be kept at a safe distance from the sheaves and this distance might have to be increased.

Thirteenth-century by-laws, such as have been found, set the wages of reapers at 1d. a day with food or 2d. without, and this may well have been the market price. Walter of Henley says reapers received 2d. a day, women reapers being accounted half-men.[92] The Statute of Labourers (1351) stipulated that reapers of corn were to be paid 2d. in the first week of August, 3d. in the second week, 'and so till the end of August, and less in the country where less is commonly given, without meat or drink or other courtesie'.[93] A century later Parliament set the wages of reapers and carters at 3d. and women and other workers, $2\frac{1}{2}$d. a day with food or 2d. more without food. Local communities, however, so far as the records of the manor courts reveal, paid no heed to this statutory regulation but continued to set rates of their own, after the Great Mortality as well as before. At Halton, Bucks., in 1330, the stipulation was, 'A penny a day and food at least (*ad minus*)'.[94]

The able-bodied sometimes had to be kept from leaving town for

[86] The English Reports, *loc. cit.*
[87] Holkham Papers, Bdle. 6, No. 55a. 1579.
[88] F. W. Maitland, *The Court Baron* (1891), 128.
[89] 1376. Cited in *Open-Field Husbandry*, 14.
[90] Doc. 160. 1469.
[91] Docs. 121, 147 and 207.
[92] *Op cit.*, 69.
[93] *Statutes of the Realm*, Vol. 1, 211.
[94] Cited in *Open-Field Husbandry*, 15, *m.* 39.

higher pay. At Littleport, Cambs., in 1325, a woman was fined 2d. because 'she absented herself from harvest and would not reap the corn of her lord and her neighbours for her wages but quitted the vill contrary to the ordinance of the by-law'.[95] Neither this nor any other by-law is ever seen in the records of this court. In all the manors of the bishop of Durham it was enjoined in 1375 that 'none of the cottagers shall go forth from town while any tenant had work for them to do'.[96] At Ramsey in 1379 seventeen men and women were fined 3d. each for leaving town in autumn. At Baslow in Derbyshire in 1392 'it was ordered as well by the lord's council as by the village community that if any labourer departed from the demesne in summer and did not return by the Feast of the Assumption [97] for the measuring of the growing crops he should give 12d. to the lord for each offence'.[98]

At Burwell, Cambs., in 1405 a by-law reads, 'It is ordered at this court as well by the lord as by the whole homage that no one shall leave town for gain who is able to earn a penny a day and food under pain of 20d.' [99] Similar by-laws can be found in the rolls of other manor courts of Ramsey Abbey in this period. A like provision is seen in the by-laws of Wimeswold, Leics., *c.* 1425, a vill shared by three lords. There it was enacted 'by the common consent of the whole township that all manner of labourers that dwell in the town and have common among us shall work harvest work and other works for their hire reasonable as custom is and not go to other towns but if they have no work or else no man speak to them so that they may be excused or if they do they shall be chastised as the law will'.[100]

Of course a village community could keep harvest hands at home by offering wages as high as they could get elsewhere. This is what was done at Great Horwood, Bucks. There had been a by-law on the books for a century or more that no one should glean who was able to earn a penny a day and food. On July 26, 1406, the eve of harvest, 'it was ordered at this court by all the tenants as well free as native that no one who is able to earn 4d. a day next autumn shall leave this town to work elsewhere under pain of 4s. 6d.' [101] This is twice the old rate. The fine was exceptionally high.

A provision of the Statute of Labourers was that reapers, mowers, carters, ploughmen and shepherds should not leave the town where they

[95] *The Court Baron*, 46.
[96] *Durham Halmotes*, 126.
[97] Forty days after Easter.
[98] *Derbyshire Archaeological and Natural History Society Transactions*, Vol. 231, 11.
[99] P.R.O., S.C., 2–179–49, *m.* 3.
[100] Hist. MSS. Commission, *Report on Manuscripts of Lord Middleton*, 106–109.
[101] Doc. 113.

dwelt in winter to serve in summer if they might serve in the same town.[102] Re-enacted over and over, this provision came to be enforced by the justices of the peace. Doubtless this is the reason there were no village by-laws on the subject after 1425.

SHEAF STEALING

Sheaf stealing no doubt is as old as open-field farming. The medieval sheaf, bound with a twist of spears, was small; it took twenty sheaves of oats, threshed, to fill a bushel basket.[103] In a field of a few hundred acres stretching for half a mile in every direction it must have been a constant temptation for a would-be thief to tuck a sheaf under his arm and quietly fade from view. And strong indeed must have been the temptation of the landless poor for whom the cereals supplied substantially all their food and drink.

Inevitably in a field full of folk many pairs of eyes would be fixed on suspicious characters. Nonetheless sheaves were stolen and some thieves were caught. Two women at Chalgrave, Beds., in 1278, were charged with stealing sheaves of oats, but their fines were remitted because they were poor.[104] At Malden, Essex, in 1289, the free and customary tenants swore that all was well except that 'the reeve's daughter took a sheaf of oats when the reapers were returning from their work in the evening'.[105] At Ripton Regis, Hunts., a thief, said the jury, was taken by night with the goods—one sheaf of oats.[106] At Hanworth, Norfolk, a thief took from the field in autumn two sheaves of wheat, two pence, and four sheaves of barley worth two pence.[107] These items are all from thirteenth-century rolls. At Newington, Oxon., in 1326, a jury of inquest said that Henry the baker had seven sheaves wrongfully come by, contrary to the statutes of autumn, fine 12d., and that John Goszoseyr harboured him, fine 12d. Also, John Porcar the rector, they said, had three sheaves wrongfully come by against the statutes of autumn. He and his harbourer were fined 12d. each.[108] At Barton, Staffs., in 1344, several women and two men were fined 1d., 2d., and 3d. each 'because they were common thieves of sheaves in autumn'; and in the following year eight women, including two found guilty in 1334, were fined 3d. or 6d. each for the same offence.[109] All through the

---

[102] *Statutes of the Realm*, Vol. I, 312.
[103] At Warboys, Hunts., in 1294. Br. Mus. Add. Ch. 39597.
[104] *Bedfordshire Historical Record Society*, Vol. 28 (1958), 5.
[105] Merton College Muniments, 4715. 1289.
[106] *Court Rolls of Ramsey Abbey*, 217. 1294.
[107] Norfolk Record Society, MS. 12177-32, A 1. 1290.
[108] Doc. 40.
[109] *History of Tatenhill*, Vol. 2, 31, 39.

medieval centuries the story is the same: sheaves of grain were stolen, and now and then some thieves were caught.

Village communities tried to check sheaf stealing in a number of ways. One rule was, the landholders themselves must take their sheaves from the field, or cause them to be taken. A man was fined at Broughton, Hunts., in 1288, 'because he paid with sheaves in the field contrary to the common statute of the villagers'.[110] The by-law is not quoted in the rolls of Broughton but it can be found in the records of a good many manors, for example, Halton, Bucks.: 'No one shall pay anyone with sheaves in the field.' [111] The number of landholders were comparatively small. They were well-known. Harvest hands should be paid their wages in sheaves at the barn door, not in the field. Anyone seen in the field with a sheaf in his possession, unless he were well known to be its owner, would be under strong suspicion.

Here and there, in this village or that, exceptions were made to this rule. At Chalgrave, Beds., 'No one shall pay with sheaves for any service in autumn except it be to some outsider.' [112] And at Halton the rule was, 'No one shall pay anyone with sheaves in the field unless he reap for sheaves.' [113] These exceptions would add some but not too many persons to the list of those authorized to have sheaves in their possession in the field. One notes, however, in a Compotus Roll for Halton, dated 1379, that a carter and four ploughmen were paid with sheaves in the field.[114] The wages of each of these manorial servants was, for eight weeks, a quarter. Newington, Oxon., also tried the experiment of allowing landholders to pay their reapers with sheaves in the field. But we observe a few years later that 'the steward ordered that no one shall pay with sheaves in the field under pain of half a mark', a very heavy penalty indeed.[115] And still later the villagers themselves added emphasis to the new rule, ordering that 'no one shall give out sheaves in the field, neither as a gift nor as wages, unless they are herdsmen'.[116]

In the fifteenth century sheaf stealing was as much a problem as before. At Elmley Castle, Worcs., 'no one ought to give sheaves in the field in autumn time either to gleaners or to any man'.[117] And in the next century we find this item at Scotter, Lincs., 'yt is ordered that none dwellinge within the parishe of Scotter shall gyve any sheves of corn in

---

[110] Doc. 7.
[111] Halton Rolls, Cathedral Library, Canterbury, 1–16–44, *m*. 11. 1325. See also Doc. 36. 1319.
[112] *Bedfordshire Historical Record Society*, Vol. 28, 47. 1303.
[113] Halton Rolls, *loc. cit.*, 1–16–45. 1330.
[114] Compotus Rolls of Halton, III Richard II. Cathedral Library, Canterbury.
[115] Newington Rolls, Canterbury Cathedral Library, 1–27–32. 1343.
[116] Doc. 69. 1348.
[117] Doc. 145. 1439.

harvest for bynding of corne but only at the layth [barn] dore, and not in the feild, upon paine of every sheif 12d.' [118]

The general rule was, let no one take sheaves from the field unless he is well known to be their rightful owner. But this could well be a matter for doubt. One landholder might have leased an acre, or several acres, from another, generally for two-thirds of the crop. A plot of six acres in Martham, Norfolk, was held jointly by ten tenants and they divided the sheaves on the spot.[119] Some of the sheaves belonged to the rector, for it was usual for each landholder to set aside the tenth sheaf, or shock, in the field where it was carried away by the rector's servants. At Halton, Bucks., in 1329, 'the wardens of the statutes of autumn present that fifteen sheaves of wheat were taken from the lord's grain in the East Field by Richard Beauchamp, servant of the rector of Halton', but the sheaves, as it happened, had been set aside by the tithers.[120] The confusion of the wardens may have been due to the fact that a different procedure was observed in Halton's other fields. At Holywell, Hunts., tithe sheaves were laid out in the South Field but those of the West Field were delivered at the barn door.[121] But suppose a landholder paid his harvest hands with sheaves in the field, as was the case at times in some villages. Were 'God and the Church' entitled to one-tenth of the sheaves that were left, or one-tenth of *all* the sheaves? A landholder of Belsington, Kent, paid some of his reapers in cash but others in sheaves, one in ten reaped, and of the sheaves that were left gave one-tenth to the rector. The matter was settled, eventually, in the rector's favour, but in the meantime there was a doubt, in the case of some sheaves, as to who was the lawful owner.[122]

Another safeguard against the theft of sheaves was that all carting and carrying must be done by the light of day. 'Let there be no carting by night,' was one of the by-laws of 1290 at Newington.[123] This prohibition was phrased in a number of ways. At Chalgrave, in 1303, 'it was provided by the whole court that no one shall cart through the whole of autumn except by day and not at night, and if such an one shall be found he shall give 12d. to the use of the church and 12d. to the lord'.[124] At Great Horwood, in 1319, 'none of them shall have his grain carted from the field by night'.[125] At Halton, in 1324, 'no one shall cart by night but only between sunrise and sunset'.[126] At Newington, Oxon., 'no one

---

[118] *Archaeologia*, Vol. 46, 378. 1556.
[119] Cited by G. C. Coulton, *The Medieval Village* (1925), 41.
[120] Halton Rolls, *loc. cit.*, 1–16–45, *m.* 4.
[121] *Cartularium Monasterii de Rameseia* (1894–95) I, 294. 1252.
[122] *Archaeologia Cantiana*, xxxii, 152. 1292.
[123] Doc. 8.
[124] *Bedfordshire Historical Record Society*, Vol. 28, 46. July 25th.
[125] Doc. 36.
[126] Halton Rolls, *loc. cit.*, 1–16–44, *m.* 11.

shall cart by night unless his cart was in the field by day time'.¹²⁷ Working late in harvest time and caught by darkness with his cart loaded or partly loaded, a villager might legitimately drive it home. An especially emphatic by-law is that of the village of Burwell, Cambs., in 1411.¹²⁸ To prevent sheaf stealing by night must have been a matter of special difficulty in this village. It might not be easy to fix the precise moment when day had dawned and night had fallen in a time of heavy cloud, so there must have been someone with authority to give the word. At Wimeswold the signal was the ringing of the church bell, on the authority of the parson, perhaps. Many by-laws specified that sheaves must be taken from the field by cart only.¹²⁹ At Therfield, Herts., in 1294, a man was fined 'because he carried grain in sheaves on his horse without a cart'.¹³⁰

As a means of preventing sheaf stealing this makes a good deal of sense. Each inhabitant would know by sight every cart, carthorse and driver in town, and carting by night without detection would be impossible. In some villages, however, it was lawful to load the sheaves on the back of a horse, but in so doing one must not trespass on his neighbour's land. At Wimeswold, Leics., for example, 'for ich a fote pay a peny to the kyrke'.¹³¹ At Great Horwood harvest hands were allowed to carry sheaves from the field in their arms if they were for the use of their masters.¹³² This exceptional provision has not been seen elsewhere nor is it repeated in the rolls of Great Horwood. It would have been difficult to administer.

Here is another sensible precaution. At Hesleden, County Durham, 'it is ordered by common consent that none shall enter the fields except by the town roads and whatever they gather in the field they shall take out by the same exit, that nothing be hidden', and further, 'all things gathered in the field whether green crops or grain shall be carried forth openly through the middle of the town and not by way of the back lot in secret'.¹³³ Not many by-laws of this kind are seen; conformity in such a matter went without saying, perhaps; it was ancient custom. A sixteenth-century by-law reads, 'At this court it is ordered that the tenants of the town shall have but four gates open between the town and its own fields until the grain has been entirely removed, under pain each one of using any other gate 6s. 8d.' ¹³⁴ Gleaners again were given special attention.

---

¹²⁷ Doc. 48. 1331.
¹²⁸ Doc. 122. A similar by-law with like penalty at Upwood, Hunts. P.R.O., S.C., 2–179–47, *m.* 2.
¹²⁹ E.g., Chalgrave, Beds., in 1303. *Loc. cit.*
¹³⁰ Doc. 15.
¹³¹ *Loc. cit.*
¹³² Doc. 38. 1322.
¹³³ *Durham Halmotes*, 126–131. *c.* 1370.
¹³⁴ Washford, Somerset. Cited in *Open-Field Husbandry*, 19.

They must not leave the field except by the four principal roads;[135] they shall not come into town with their gleanings by any road except the King's way; and not through gaps.[136] Gleaners were still a problem in the seventeenth century. 'It is laid in payne that noe person whatsoever gleane corne . . . any way but by eare and eare and not to take corne unlawfully and carry itt home in sheffe but carry itt home in gleanes.'[137]

The medieval harvester was a man, not a machine. One plan was to have four reapers in echelon followed by a binder who gathered the spears into sheaves and set them in shocks. The daily stint of this gang of five was two acres. A mechanical reaper of sorts had been invented in Roman Gaul in the fourth century. It consisted of a wheeled vehicle with two scythes pushed across a field of grain by an ox between shafts. 'In a day an ox can get in the whole harvest.'[138] Some idea of this contraption can be gained from a fragment of sculpture.[139] Nothing came of this. It is obvious that it would not work. Very few of the stems would be severed by the fixed scythes; the rest would be pushed to the ground. What was needed was a cutting board with scissors or knives attached to it. These could be activated with suitable gearing by the wheels of the vehicle on which the cutting board was mounted. The Rev. Patrick Bell, a Scotsman brought up on a farm, produced such a machine in 1826, using scissors, but this was displaced in 1831 by the famous machine of Cyrus McCormack who used knives. McCormack's first reaper still called for considerable man-power but it did reap cleanly; no more gleaning. Half a century later a much improved model delivered sheaves bound with twine in lots of six or eight, ready to be set in shocks. Three or four men with this reaper could account for twelve to fourteen acres a day with a labour output of one-tenth the medieval figure. Nowadays a 'combine' of header and thresher cutting a swath of up to forty feet reduces manual labour to the vanishing point. Developed for use in regions of high heat and low humidity, the combine can be employed in a cool damp climate if an oven is used to reduce the moisture content of the grain to the required level.

PEAS AND BEANS

The nutritive value of peas and beans and related legumes as food for man is little less than that of wheat, and they are prime feed for cattle as

[135] Doc. 77. 1357.

[136] Doc. 115. 1407.

[137] Ulceby, Lincs. Lincolnshire Archives Committee, Misc. Deeds 69 (i). 1677.

[138] Palladius, *De Re Rustica*, book VII.

[139] L. C. Matthews, 'Harvesting by the Gauls: The Forerunner of the Combine Harvester', *Agricultural History Review*, Vol. 70 (1920), 52-3.

well. They came into general use rather slowly. As late as the thirteenth century some manors did not grow them at all and in others the percentage of the arable sown to legumes was small.[140] by the sixteenth century the sowing of peas and beans was more general and in some counties they constituted a large proportion of the total acreage under crop.[141]

As food for man peas and beans are ready for use without milling and unlike cereals in another way they can be picked and eaten green,[142] though they are at their best for a few days only. Every family would relish a mess of these tasty legumes, green or ripe, and in a matter of minutes enough could be gathered in the field for a meal. Field peas grow tall, however; a grown-up could conceal himself among them with care and a child with ease. It is evident that it would be difficult, in fact impossible, to restrict the picking of peas and beans in the field to those who had planted them. Three of the thirteen by-laws recorded at Newton Longville in 1290 were directed to this problem. They suggest that the growing of legumes was a new thing in this village. One by-law directed that anyone who wished to gather peas, beans or vetches in the fields must do so between sunrise and prime; another that the poor (that is, landless persons) must not gather them inside a ploughstrip but at the end and along the sides. The third by-law provided that landholders who had lands sown with peas, beans and vetches must gather them from the lands they had sown and not elsewhere. There were twenty-nine virgaters in the village according to an Extent of 1310 and forty-two half-virgaters. The holdings of the four freeholders were not large and there were five cottagers who had no arable at all. How many of the landholders had acres sown to peas or beans we are not told, but we note that only three of thirty-eight parcels of the demesne land under crop that year were sown to peas. It seems probable therefore that quite a number of the inhabitants, landed or landless, had no peas of their own to pick.

The regulations of other villages were similar. Codding, as it was called, must all be done at a certain hour of the day, and even on certain days. All must enter the field and leave it at the same time.[143] The by-laws of Wimeswold, *c.* 1425, are comprehensive. 'Also, all manner of men that have any peas in the field when codding time comes, let them cod on their own lands and on no other man's lands. And other men or women that have no peas of their own growing, let them gather them twice in the week on Wednesday and on Friday, reasonably going in the land furrows and gathering them with their hands and with no sickles,

---

[140] J. Z. Titow, *English Rural Society*, 1200–1350 (1969), 41–42.
[141] In Leics., about 1500, 43 per cent. W. G. Hoskins, *The Medieval Peasant* (1957), 154–155.
[142] E.g., Doc. 44. 1329.
[143] See Index of By-Laws.

once before noon and no more, for if any man or woman other that has any peas of his own and goes into any other for each time [he shall] pay a penny to the church and lose his cods, and they that have none and go oftener than it is before said with sickle or without, shall lose the vessel they gather them in and the cods and a penny to the church.'[144]

By restricting pea picking time to certain days or hours of the day or both a maximum of communal surveillance was ensured. It must have been effective; instances of infraction of the law, so far as the records reveal, were rare.

Some sixteenth-century by-laws make a different point. 'Let no man gleane anie beanes or pease anie time but of ther owne';[145] and 'let no persone gather any peacods onles it be upon ther owne grounde'.[146] It may be that by this time all the landholders in such villages sowed some of their arable to the legumes. And it may be that the more general sowing of peas and beans was due to the discovery that the fertility of the soil was increased thereby. (Anyone who examines the roots of these and other legumes will observe nodules of nitrates on the roots.)

We may assume, I think, that villagers who had no lands at all to sow, that is, the poor, were permitted to gather peas and beans to eat, under the conditions prescribed, even where specific mention is not made of this, which is very seldom. At Launton, Oxon., in the late sixteenth century, it was ordered by all the tenants that everyone who held a virgate of land or more 'shall sowe one rydge of pease . . . any ware within the corne ffeild to be gathered by the inhabitants without contradicon of the owner thereof'.[147] This provision accords well with the care of the poor which was the subject of so much Tudor legislation.

PASTURE

The produce of his fields for the most part was consumed by man, and it provided for his drink as well. Grain was fed to animals sparingly, on an emergency basis. Fodder was never plentiful, and the advent of spring and the first bite was anxiously awaited. Throughout most of the year medieval flocks and herds pastured ceaselessly.

The meadows after hay time were of prime value and it was with some difficulty that neighbours were restrained from turning in their cattle before the hay had all been carted away. A by-law of Great Horwood prohibited the pasturing of beasts in any meadow 'before the hay is

---

[144] A version in Modern English, by S. P. Bland, P. A. Brown and R. H. Towney, *English Economic History* (1925), 76–77.
[145] Scotter, Lincs., *Archaeologia*, Vol. 46, 384. 1578.
[146] Brigstock, Northants. *Northamptonshire Record Society*, X, 367. (1553).
[147] Westminster Abbey Muniments, 15572.

lifted',[148] and at Chalgrave, Beds., two centuries later there was a similar provision: 'No person shall kepe any cattell in the meade among the hay cocks untill the haye be carried awaye.'[149] Some time must elapse after mowing before a meadow is fit for pasture, an interval of three or four weeks during which a second growth takes place. By that time all hay cocks should have been removed. In many villages in the midlands and to the south meadows were declared open to pasture at Lammas, that is, August 1st, hay-making having ended a month before. At Elmley Castle, the date, except for oxen and plough horses, was July 25th.[150] In an exceptionally favourable season a second crop of hay might be harvested, and this would impose a further delay in 'breaking' the meadows for pasture; or severe flooding might stop pasturing altogether.

Some animals were barred from the meadows: pigs in Chalgrave,[151] calves at Abbot's Ripton,[152] and sheep at Houghton.[153] All these were of low priority in an age when good pasture was in such demand. Restricted to the 'great beasts', pasturing the meadows might go on for three months or more. The Orwins say it was the duty of the pinder to 'drive' the meadows on November 1st.[154] There would be little further growth after that, and during the rainy months of winter the naturally soggy ground along the banks of streams would be seriously damaged by the heavy feet of horses and the sharp hooves of cattle. The few by-laws that have been seen do not assign so early a date as November 1st. At Launton, pasturing ended on December 29th.[155] In one of the Yorkshire manors of Fountains Abbey, 'no one shall pasture his beasts in the lord's meadow without common consent from February 2nd each year until haying time'.[156]

Gathering straw for the lord's use was a routine service in some manors. It was used for the bedding of cattle, for thatch and for fuel. The stealing of stubble by the landless poor is reported in some of the earliest rolls of manor courts.[157] An early by-law provided that 'no one shall gather straw in the fields except from his own land'.[158] A few years later this was amended to read, 'no one shall gather stubble from another man's land before the Feast of St Martin' (November 11th).[159]

---

[148] Doc. 65. 1343.
[149] Bedfordshire Record Society, DD–MC 4. 1561.
[150] The Feast of St James. Doc. 151.
[151] 1302. *Bedfordshire Historical Records Society*, Vol. 28, 43.
[152] 1429. Br. Mus. Add. Ch. 39480.
[153] Hunts. P.R.O., S.C.2-179-50, *m*. 1 *d*. 1405.
[154] *Open Fields*, 3rd ed. (1967), 159.
[155] Westminster Abbey Muniments, 15565, 15586.
[156] Br. Mus. Add. Ch. 40010, f. 13. 1305–1430.
[157] E.g., at Ripton Regis, Hunts., in 1276. Br. Mus. Add. Ch. 14305.
[158] Great Horwood, Bucks., Doc. 24. (1306).
[159] Doc. 46. (1330).

This provision assured the landholders a long season for pasturing the stubble for their cattle. After that the inhabitants could go about collecting what they could. Note that the fine for breaking this by-law was only half that for breaking others, but even so a poor person might not be able to pay it.

Village landholders could hardly wait to turn their cattle into the field. 'No one shall pasture the stubble until all the grain of the whole village is brought in' is the way one by-law read. Another said, 'No horse, bull, steer, heiffer, cow or calf shall be fed or feed on the stubble of the fields until the corn is entirely carried away unless they are securely tethered or watched.'[160] The men of Wimeswold were agreed that there should be no cattle either in the wheat field or the pea field until the whole crop had been gathered and carted away; then the cattle 'may go togeder as thei schuld do, in peyn of ech a beast a peny to the kyrke'.[161] But if all must wait until the last sheaf has been carted away should there not be a time fixed for the field to be cleared? In many midland villages a date was set, the Feast of the Nativity of the Blessed Virgin.[162] The Feast of St Michael was the day elsewhere.[163] In certain other villages no precise date was set but 'the consent of all the tenants', or 'the reasonable assent of all' was stipulated. Some such flexibility was desirable, one might suppose, for the season of harvest varied from year to year. On the day appointed a 'shack' bell was sounded, or announcement was made from the pulpit on the nearest Sunday.

Before the grand opening a man might pasture his own acres. This called for careful regulation, however, if damage to the grain, in sheaves or still standing, was to be avoided. The number of by-laws on this matter, and they are among the earliest recorded, attests the urgent need for pasturing the stubble. Let us see how the village of Newton Longville tried to solve the problem of assuring the right of one man while securing that of his neighbours. It was provided in 1290 that no one should pasture his beasts in any 'culture' until the grain of at least one adjacent acre had been wholly removed.[164] This by-law was re-enacted from time to time without change. In 1320 the words 'one acre on both sides' were added.[165] In 1331 a space two acres wide was stipulated.[166] In 1387 it was declared that a space of ten acres must be cleared unless the beasts were tethered.[167] In the following year the space cleared must be

[160] Cited in *Open-Field Husbandry*, 21.
[161] *Loc. cit.*, 108.
[162] September 8th. Docs. 122, 139, 140.
[163] September 29th. Doc. 109.
[164] Doc. 8.
[165] Doc. 42.
[166] Doc. 49.
[167] Doc. 90.

fourteen acres in the case of the larger animals and twenty acres in the case of sheep or hogs.[168] In 1406 'no one this autumn shall pasture beasts, sheep or pigs on his own grain by a space of ten acres'.[169]

Experience taught that a space of ten acres, at least, was needed for the safe herding of cattle, while a larger area was needed for sheep or hogs. It is unlikely that all the acres of the cleared space would be held by one man; it would be the right of each of the owners to begin pasturing there. Cattle are easy to herd; a cow will not look far afield if there is good grazing under her nose. Sheep and hogs present difficulties.[170] At Great Horwood the minimum space was ten acres.[171] At Elmley Castle, in 1391, it was fifteen acres;[172] thirty in 1411;[173] and forty in 1454.[174] Sheep must wait till the end of autumn.[175]

Preliminary pasturing was sometimes allowed for tethered animals before a field was declared open to general grazing. Available for this purpose were headlands, roadsides and other bits of ground left unploughed, as well as the acres from which the produce had been removed. In the numerous by-laws about tethering, horses are frequently mentioned but oxen never. 'No man shall tie his horses in the fields where there is grain, whether in sheaves or still standing, in such a way that damage can be done,' was a by-law of Halton, in 1329.[176] At Elmley Castle tethering was allowed on each furlong as soon as all the grain of that furlong had been carried.[177] At Wimeswold if any one tied his horse on headland or syke and it trespassed on the growing grain, he must 'make amendes to hym that hass the harme, and for ich a fote that iss withine korn a peny to the kyrke'.[178]

From sixteenth-century by-laws we select the following: at Poddington, Beds., '... non shall stake eny horses amongst heycocks untyll ye hey be caryed away but uppon there one gronds ...;[179] at Buckland, Berks., horses might be tethered on the lanes and headlands in the grain fields, from March 25th to August 1st, if 'they be fast tied with good cordes'.[180] In another village tethering must be with a head stall and a tether five fathoms long.[181]

---

[168] Doc. 92.
[169] Doc. 114.
[170] See below.
[171] Doc. 51. 1332; Doc. 80. 1389.
[172] Doc. 101.
[173] Doc. 121.
[174] Doc. 153.
[175] Doc. 170. 1498.
[176] Doc. 44.
[177] Doc. 83. 1373.
[178] *Loc. cit.*
[179] Bedfordshire Record Office, DD. OR. 505, 23r.
[180] Shakespeare's Birthplace Library, Buckland, C. 11.
[181] Horncastle, Lincs., Lincs. Arch., Merc. Dep. 36 *m.* 2. 1673.

Hardly any matter was the subject of more by-laws than that of tethering a mare with foal. A day or two only need elapse after she has brought forth her young before a mare is available for work. She will be in special need of good pasture for a time since she will be suckling her colt. Mobile from birth, the foal will stay close to the mare during the first few weeks of its life but it could make destructive forays. Keeping it within bounds then and later may seem a small problem but it bristled with difficulties. At Great Horwood the earliest by-law on this subject is dated 1305 and the last 1521.[182] The first provided that a mare must not be tethered before August 1st where her foal could trespass on a neighbour's grain. Another specified that a mare must never be tethered at the side of any land but only at the end. After August 1st, when a mare will be in the field drawing a cart her foal must be tied to her harness if it is three weeks old or more—a younger foal will cling to its mother.

Sixteen-century villagers had the same problem. At Launton, in 1571, it was ordered 'that no colt beying in sucke shall folo any cart or carts from May day ontill all harvest be home and also neither horse nor mare but to tye them to their harness . . .'[183] At Salford, Oxon., 'nonne shall cepe any colts loose in the fields before harvest be inned'.[184]

Pasturing the stubble had to stop well before the onset of winter if the field in question was to be sown to winter wheat, for it must first be ploughed. Sowing had to be carefully timed lest there be too much growth before the first hard frost, or else the green shoots would grow too tall and joint. There was some pasturing of the herbage of winter wheat, but Tusser thought this a doubtful practice.

> 'The flocks of the lords of the soil
> Do yearly the winter corn wrong
> The same in the summer they spoil
> With feeding so low and so long
> And therefore the champion field
> Does seldom good winter corn yield.[185]

Only a few references have been found to this kind of grazing. At Ackley, Norfolk, all beasts had to be withdrawn by Christmas.[186]

It was inevitable that individual cultivators would challenge the village-wide control of fallow and pasture. In one of the earliest of manor court rolls at Malden, Essex, June 18, 1290, we find this record: 'The court says on oath that the field of Adam of Charlesham by ancient custom ought to be fallow and common every third year like the other

---

[182] See Index of By-Laws.
[183] Westminster Abbey Court Rolls, 15551 d.
[184] Codrington Library, Salford, No. 363. 1592.
[185] Cited by G. Slater, *English Peasantry*, 82–83.
[186] *Durham Halmotes*, 41. 1365.

INTRODUCTION 45

lands of the villagers and he ought not to till [*hechiare*] it unless by leave of the lords and unless the other villagers till their fallow by getting leave of the lords in the matter. And because the fields ought to have been sown this year as they say and lie fallow the following year therefore it is ordered that it be in defence until the first of next August. The rest of the year and in the following year it shall be fallow and common.[187] All the landholders must conform to the three-course system of crop rotation at Malden unless, with the approval of the lords, all agreed to a change. Neither Adam nor any other might till his acres in a field lying fallow. When it was the turn of a great field to be under crop Adam's acres, if now sown, must be in defence, that is, closed to pasturing like all the rest; he may sow them or not as he pleases but he cannot pasture them before August 1st. Harvest will have begun by that time, and the by-laws of pasture in time of harvest will come into force.

In the roll of the manor court of Broughton, Hunts., the same year: 'These are the names of those who sowed in the fallow where the free and customary tenants ought to have their common pasture [nine names, each the tenant of one or two acres]. And because it was affirmed by the freeholders and by the whole township that the aforesaid lands were sown while the fields were fallow for the past twenty years and more it is granted the said men that they shall appeal to the lord abbot before the next court or be amerced.'[188] A family man with one or two acres, scratching for a living, would be sorely tempted to keep them under crop every year. The total acreage of the nine offenders was a tiny fraction of a great field; but the right of communal pasture of the fallow, village wide, must not be curtailed in the slightest. The men were fined for their nonconformity, but advised to appeal to the lord of the manor, who might well condone the fine. These instances of the enforcement of communal rights over fallow are not unique.[189]

At Barkby, Leics., in 1596 a tenant was charged with having enclosed a seven-acre plot with a ditch and hedge in a field 'in which all the tenants from time immemorial had common appurtenant with their beasts'. The jury held that the villagers had right of common as follows: 'When the aforesaid field is lying fallow then the entire time of fallow until the field is reseeded. And when the aforesaid field is reseeded with wheat, rye, oats, peas or beans then from the Feast of St Peter in Chains (August 1st) to the Feast of the Purification of the Blessed Virgin Mary (February 2nd) the said close shall be held in severalty and the tenants of the manor shall not have their common there.'[190] Under the terms of

[187] Merton College Muniments, 4706. Cited in *Open-Field Husbandry*, 22.
[188] Br. Mus. Add. Ch. 39754. Cited, *ibid*.
[189] See *Open-Field Husbandry*, 22–23.
[190] Merton College Muniments, 6653.

this compromise the villagers would be excluded from their right of pasturing the stubble of this seven-acre plot after harvest.

At Methley, Yorks., the partial breakdown of the open-field system in the sixteenth century had unfortunate consequences. Methley was a town of 2,000 acres, mostly arable, held of a lay lord by some sixty tenants, free and customary. Some of the arable was already enclosed but most of it lay in four open fields. In any one field, in a given year, some landholders sowed their acres with corn, some allowed them to lie fallow, and still others turned them to grass. As a result, we are told, 'there hath bene much misorder and destrucon of corne by men's cattel that wolde put the same to eat their grasse landes and besides that the land for lack of good husbandrie and fallowing brought forth little or no corne'. After several failures articles of agreement were drafted and recorded in a document dated November 19, 1563. 'The freeholders, tenants and inhabitants of Methley in the County of York for the good order of their corne and fallow fields agree' that each of the four fields shall be sown with corn or lie fallow as a whole in its turn. The agreement was to stand for twelve years but if at the end of eight years, that is two full rotations, 'it shall appear the same not to be profitable and commodious for the husbandmen and good for the increase of corne and so allowed by the most part of the husbandmen there with the assent of the lord or his steward then they ordered to be voyde and of none effect'.[191]

SHEEP

Sheep were not much used for food by medieval man, but were valued chiefly for their wool. The dung suitably concentrated on a field-course was an important fertilizer, worth a third as much as the wool. Their skin, suitably prepared, was used for records, as legible today as when they were written centuries ago and with a reasonable certainty of surviving as many centuries more. The ownership of sheep was widely distributed, from the landed magnate with flocks of thousands to the cotter who, with neither horse nor ox, could yet support a few sheep in his croft. Sheep, however, have to be tended with care. They cannot defend themselves against predators nor can they adjust as well to changes in the weather as other domestic animals.

In competing for pasture sheep have a natural advantage over other animals. They crop so closely that cows who have no upper incisors and even horses who have can find little to bite. This was the basis of the war between sheep and cattle raisers in the American West. The by-law at Halton, in 1424, is typical: 'No one may enter the stubble with his sheep

---

[191] John Rylands Library, Lat. MS. 249 *passim*.

INTRODUCTION 47

before it has been pastured by the other cattle, namely, horses, oxen and cows.'[192] In 1329, also at Halton, another by-law stipulated that none should enter the stubble with their sheep before it was pastured by the beasts of the plough.[193] At Newington in 1331, sheep must not go before the greater beasts.[194] The rolls of Newington continue in almost unbroken series in this period for nearly a century, but no such by-law was found, again, until 1410.[195] Without doubt this was a deep-rooted and generally accepted custom. There would be no need to rehearse the by-law very often.

A few other by-laws of particular interest may be cited. At Ramsey, Hunts., shepherds were strictly forbidden to pasture the sheep on sown land at any time between seed time and harvest.[196] At Charlton, Wilts., sheep were allowed to pasture in the wheat field after it was first sown but they must have a shepherd over them and they must be out of the field by October 17th.[197] The shepherd at first would keep his sheep on the headlands, droveways and other areas of untilled land. By October 17th, however, the tender shoots would be showing above ground and these might tempt the sheep beyond the shepherd's power of control. At Hemingford, Hunts., in 1424 the meadow was closed to sheep the year round for a term of six years.[198] Perhaps this meadow had been over-pastured. At Cressingham, Norfolk, the villagers sought to reserve their crofts for their own sheep for forty days after harvest, excluding the flock of their lord, and they caused an ordinance to that effect to be recorded in the rolls of the manor court, with half of the fine to the lord and half to the church. But the scribe wrote in the margin, 'cancelled, because the lord is unwilling to confirm'.[199] Even in an enclosure such as a croft the communal right of grazing was not extinguished, as we have seen, and the lord of course was a great commoner.

It is commonly accepted that sheep-raising was more important in England's economy in the later Middle Ages than in earlier centuries. It might be assumed that village by-laws would reflect this. Before the sixteenth century however only a single ordinance has been found which fixed a stint of sheep. This was at Newton Longville in 1426, where it was stipulated that no virgater should keep more than 100 sheep,[200] not a very severe restriction. In 1509 the figure was set at thirty for each

---

[192] Halton Rolls, *loc. cit.* 1-16-44, *m.* 11. This was repeated in substance in 1326. *Ibid.*, *m.* 16 *d.*
[193] Doc. 44.
[194] Doc. 48. 1331.
[195] Doc. 119.
[196] Br. Mus. Add. Ch. 3/636. 1396.
[197] Cited in *Open-Field Husbandry*, 26.
[198] P.R.O., Eccl., 2/179/37, *m.* 3.
[199] *Rolls of Cressingham*, 66-69. 1490.
[200] Doc. 134.

virgater, and this figure remained constant until 1608 when it was reduced to twenty.[201] Fixing stints of sheep was routine in sixteenth-century villages. One, one and a half or two sheep to the acre of arable were the figures most frequently cited. A lamb was to be accounted a sheep on and after the Feast of St Michael. If a tenant with right of pasture had no sheep of his own or fewer than the law allowed he must offer his pasture rights, for a price, to his neighbours, not to 'foreners'.[202]

All the sheep of a village must be kept in one flock without by-herds. There might, otherwise, be an unseemly scramble for pasturage by the various villagers, each with his own flock. This ordinance is found in the sixteenth century but not before. At Elton, Hunts., for example, in 1527, sheep might graze in the fallow field provided they were put with the main flock under the common shepherds.[203] At Ramsey, Hunts., in 1531, 'there shall be no by-herd any time of year'.[204] Town shepherds and their wages are frequently referred to in the rolls of the halmotes of the priory of Durham. In one village the tenants were enjoined to assemble together and collect among themselves the wages of the town shepherd. In another, 'it is ordained by common consent that each of them shall pay the shepherd his wages within a fortnight of being summoned'; and in still another village the tenants tended the sheep themselves, in turn, at the rate of one day for every five sheep.[205] At Wimbledon, Middlesex, in 1553, it was agreed by the whole homage that 'no boy shall keep any sheep henceforth in any of the common fields and commons ... unless he is sixteen years old under pain of every owner of the said sheep 3s. 4d.' [206] Full responsibility came at an earlier age then than now.

Walter of Henley wrote that the shepherd 'ought not to leave his sheep to go to fairs or markets or wrestling matches or wakes or to a tavern without taking leave or asking it or without putting a good keeper in his place to keep his sheep'.[207] It would seem that a good many regulations might be needed to insure that the keeper of the town flock was a good shepherd to his sheep, but no such by-laws have been found.

PIGS

Pigs were raised for food. They are brought forth in litters, two a year, of half a dozen or more, and they can be eaten profitably in the second

---

[201] Doc. 175.
[202] See *Open-Field Husbandry*, 27.
[203] Doc. 187.
[204] Br. Mus. Add. Ch. 39659.
[205] *Durham Halmote Rolls*, 101, 161, 184.
[206] *Wimbledon Court Rolls*, 102.
[207] *Seneschaucie*, 115.

year. Their meat supplied much of the fat which was so scarce an item in the medieval diet.

Nowadays pigs are grain fed for the most part, in pens, but in medieval times they had to forage for their food. Horses, oxen and milk cows might get some grain now and then to supplement their winter fodder and grain might be scattered to the chickens along with the kitchen scraps, but pigs stood at the end of the line. However, pigs can and will eat anything and they have an irresistible digestion. Their choicest foods, when and where available, were acorns and mast, from oaks and beeches respectively, and these trees, whole forests of them, were far more plentiful in medieval times than now.

It is very difficult to prevent pigs from going anywhere they please in their search for food. They can squirm through a hedge or fence that will stop other animals, or root their way under it. Therefore pigs must be herded. 'None of the tenants may have his pigs, large or small, outside his home unless they are in good keeping.' [208] Another by-law said that none should have their pigs in any field unless they were put with the common hogherd.[209] Herding pigs in the woods might not be too taxing, but herding in open fields was a different matter. Pigs were firmly excluded from all fields in harvest time. At Sevenhampton, Wilts., for example, in 1276, a man was fined because his pigs were in the grain in autumn time. He had to make good the damage in sheaves.[210] At Castleacre, Norfolk, a number of tenants were fined because 'they did damage with their pigs in the grain of their neighbours in summer'.[211] At Dedyngton, Oxon., 'it was ordered that no one henceforth shall pasture his pigs among the shocks of grain'.[212]

It might seem that because of their known proclivity for doing damage pigs would be penned up after dark, but nothing is seen of this in the by-laws until the sixteenth century. 'Every tenant shall cot his hogg in the nyght time . . .'; [213] 'Every man shall kepe his hoggs in his stye untyll such tyme as the hoggerd shall goe'; [214] '. . . every man shall have their swine cotes sufficiently made and their swine . . . to be styed up before sonne sett and so to kepe them styed till sonne rise.' [215] Tenants who did not have sufficient houses for their hogs must make them.[216] The law was being broken in the sixteenth century and that,

---

[208] Doc. 64. 1332.
[209] Doc. 119. 1410.
[210] P.R.O., Eccl., 1-209-49.
[211] Holkham Papers, Bdle. 3, No. 27. 1399.
[212] Codrington Library, X 21-395. 1490.
[213] Poddington, Beds. See *n*. 179. above.
[214] Burbage, Beds., *Bedfordshire Record Society*, L 26/1046.
[215] Scotter, Lincs., *Archaeologia*, Vol. 46, 384. 1578.
[216] Kilworth, Leics. Merton College Muniments 6442. 1539.

perhaps, is why we find out what it was; or it may be that men were much more prone to put their customs in writing.

A further means of restricting the damage that a pig can do is to place one or more iron rings in the rooting edge of his nose. These rings, so-called, were curved bits of wire with sharp points which were firmly clinched in the nose. If properly placed they will effectively discourage the pig from destructive rooting. More by-laws deal with this matter than with any other means of restraint. They are among the earliest of all by-laws and they are found throughout the medieval period. At Eynsham, Oxon., in 1296, three men were fined 'because they left their pigs unringed with iron contrary to the by-laws made in the preceding court'.[217] Items of this sort are very numerous in the extensive rolls of Eynsham over the two centuries that follow. In 1475, it was ordered that 'the ancient by-laws of pigs with the usual penalties be kept and that they hold good for the future'.[218] No by-laws were ever recorded; they were immemorial custom at Eynsham, reaching back to a period much earlier than the first recorded punishment of offenders. At Ealing, in Middlesex, two men whose pigs had uprooted the land of the lord and his tenants were ordered to ring their pigs, 'by which ringing the said pigs will not be able to uproot the aforesaid land'.[219] At South Hamingfield, Essex, 'all and sundry tenants of the manor having pigs at pasture are warned that from henceforth they shall ring their pigs so that they shall not damage or uproot the soil of the lord and his tenants in the common'.[220] In the light of this evidence and of common sense, we may find it surprising that a current authority on medieval agriculture says that pigs had rings in their noses to make them easier to catch!

Specific dates were fixed by which all pigs large and small must be ringed—Michaelmas or October 15, or October 18th, or October 28th in different villages. Hog-ringers were appointed too. When they found pigs unringed they might either warn the owners or impound the pigs or ring them themselves and charge it up to the owners. 'Pigs as the most perverse of animals required the firmest and most rigorous handling.'[221] But the perversity of medieval pigs derived not so much from the nature of the animal as of the times. Pigs are docile when grain-fed in pens, as they are today. (One hears, even, of battery pigs.)

---

[217] Br. Mus. Harl. E. 17.
[218] *Ibid.*, G. 1.
[219] Middlesex Record Office, Eb. 205–10, *m.* 1. 1492.
[220] Essex County Record Office, D-Dp-M, 878. 1501.
[221] John Harland, *Manchester Court Leet Records*, Chatham Society, Vol. 63, viii.

FENCES

Herded by day and penned at night farm animals nonetheless will go astray, so crofts and even open fields had to be hedged or fenced. In medieval Braunston, Northants., 'the length of the croft ran back from the house. In a simple village plan it ran as far as the edge of the field. At the meeting place of croft and open-field strips there was often a back-lane.... This was bounded on one side by a ditch and fence which kept domestic animals from straying on the arable fields, and on the other side by the croft hedges which helped to keep fox and wolf from the geese and hens'.[222] The crofts of Braunston with a lane at the back are still extant. In some villages there were crofts on both sides of the road. Thus there might be two back lanes 'each turning back from the main street at the village end, forming an envelope inside which the houses, the church, the manse, the green and the gardens lay'.[223] If domestic animals are to be kept from straying from the croft night or day it must be completely surrounded by a stout fence or a sufficient ditch. At Newton Longville, in 1290, every man must have the stiles and lanes nearest his neighbours kept securely lest anyone suffer damage.[224] This by-law was repeated later on with the amendment that if any damage occurred whoever was nearest must answer for it.[225] At Great Horwood, no one may have his gaps open on the edge of a sown field.[226] In a Yorkshire manor of Fountains Abbey it was ordered that 'everyone shall close the gates of his garden so that animals may not enter the field'.[227] Fences helped to keep out wrongdoers. At Great Horwood, every man must keep all lanes and fences on the edge of a field in good repair so would-be malefactors would be obliged to come in by the main road where they could be seen.[228] It is evident that between crofts and fields in Great Horwood there was a lane and that each tenant was obliged to maintain along his section of it on both sides a fence or hedge tight enough to turn both man and beast. At Rowley, Massachusetts, in 1649, 'It is ordered and agreed that all common Gates and particular mens ffences ioyning upon any Corne feild shall be mentened against Great Catle ... at any time when Catle may doe hurte upon Corne.'[229]

---

[222] W. W. Beresford and J. K. S. St. Joseph, *op. cit.*, 62, and fig. 23, an aerial photograph.
[223] W. W. Beresford, *The Lost Villages of England* (1954), 54 and Plate 6, an aerial photograph of Sunderlandwyck, Yorkshire.
[224] Doc. 8.
[225] Doc. 43.
[226] Doc. 76.
[227] Cited in *Open-Field Husbandry*, 130.
[228] Doc. 42. 1327. See also Docs. 46, 51, 74 and 77.
[229] *Rowley Town Records*, Vol. 1, 55.

It was essential of course that an open field be protected by a fence from cattle straying from adjoining crofts. To fence a great field on all sides, however, might seem to be a work of too great magnitude, yet there are suggestions that this was sometimes done. Something like this is indicated in one of the provisions of the laws of King Ine.[230] It is not until six centuries later that we find a reference to such a fence in a local record. At Alreways, Staffs., in 1259, 'Robert Forester, in mercy, 3d., because he took his fence away before the appointed time.' And in the following year 'Gilbert son of Geoffrey is in mercy 2s. because he "broke" a certain fence before time and trampled down the grain of Reginald son of Alice wrongly, and therefore it is considered that he shall make rightful compensation to the said Reginald according to the custom of the neighbours.'[231] There was in the village of Alreways, apparently, a fence around a field of grain, or partly around it, which the neighbours were bound to make, each his own share, and leave in place for a prescribed period of time. Such a fence could be made of hurdles set in place and readily removed. At Pennington, Lancs., one of the villages of Fountains Abbey, a by-law provided that 'every tenant who has lands in the fields shall make his fence along his acres within one week at the sowing of the grain under pain, each one, of 6d.'[232] Open fields varied considerably in extent; some it would be practicable to fence about, others not. Besides, a fence on every side might not be called for.

METES AND BOUNDS

A major problem of open-field farming was the maintenance of boundaries. Every ploughstrip was individually owned and it would need to be plainly demarcated from the strips on either side of it, and from the headlands at either end. Stones and stakes were much in use. Inevitably some of these were displaced in ploughing and they would have to be reset, normally by a jury of neighbours appointed for the purpose. We do not find any early by-laws dealing with this subject; it was too obvious for emphasis. What we do find is a great many examples of the unneighbourly stealing of furrows, 'a major sin in rural society'.[233] At Barkby, Leics., in 1296, a tenant was amerced 12d., rather a heavy fine, 'because he unjustly ploughed the land of his neighbour'.[234] At Great Horwood, in 1306, William Bayhote, virgater, was convicted by the jury of having ploughed a part of the land of Alice Asculf, half-virgater, both 'natives'; 'wherefore the said Alice shall recover her land,

---

[230] See above.
[231] *William Salt Archaeological Society*, N. S., Vol. 10, 285.
[232] Cited in *Open-Field Husbandry*, 30.
[233] M. W. Beresford, *Studies in Leicestershire Agrarian History* (1949), 93.
[234] Merton College Muniments, 6567.

unjustly taken, by view of the jurors and she shall have six sheaves of beans for her damages. And the said William is in mercy 12d.'[235] At Castleacre, Norfolk, in 1305, a ploughman encroached on balks on both sides of a strip of arable, the whole length of the furrow, half a foot wide; fine for each of the encroachments, 2s.[236] This gives us some idea of the width of the medieval ploughshare. At Houghton, Hunts., in 1308, the jury found that 'William, Emma's son, had taken to himself in ploughing a furrow of land of William Catalyne to his damage 3d. which he has paid'. He was fined 12d. 'And it is ordered that he restore the said furrow to him by the view of the jurors.'[237] At Mapledurham, Hants., two neighbours became so involved in taking furrows from each other back and forth that the whole homage laid down the law to them: 'whoever makes the first move hereafter shall pay the other half a mark and the lord half a mark', a fine to bring financial ruin. At the next court it was reported that one of the two had broken down the door of the other and slandered him.[238] These examples show us how important it was to maintain exact boundary lines, and how difficult.

And yet it is not until the sixteenth century that we come across a by-law on boundaries. It is in the records of Great Horwood, in 1552; three days were set aside on which all the tenants of the manor must go about the fields setting stones and stakes.[239] At Launton, '. . . it is ordered that on Sunday next being the ffyrst days of October all the lord's tenants of this manor shall assemble themselves together and make a view throughe all the fields of this lordship of all encroachments made by any tenant upon others lande by carying or removinge of meres, bounds or markes betweene lord and tenant, freeholder and copyholder, or any other, and to agre upon the reformacion thereof and that everie tenant founde offendinge shall refourme his fault according to the agreement of the resydue of the said tenants uppon payne to forfyte for everie default therein 12d.'[240]

This was the procedure at Broughton, Northants., as recorded in 1555: 'It is ordeyned by the full court that Truman Hoyte, Humphreye Lyjunde, Thomas Wright, Henry Samson shall see encroachments in erynge [ploughing] in the fallow field and also for erynge and sowinge in the sonnday nexte comming uppon pain of every of them in defalt xij d.

'Item if any person doe after that eyre eny further than the said iiij men shall lymite and marke the same, then the same accrocher to forfeite for every defalt iij s. iiij d.

[235] Cited in *Open-Field Husbandry*, 36.
[236] Holkham Papers Bdle. 3, No. 14.
[237] Cited in *Court Rolls of Ramsey Abbey*, 245.
[238] Br. Mus. Add. Ch. 28034 and 28035. 1337–1338.
[239] New College Court Rolls, G. H. III, 2, 3.
[240] Westminster Abbey Muniments, 15562.

'Item that where every persone hath accroched in large erynge & sowinge yt is agreed that the partie whose land is encroched shall have the corne growynge uppon his owne grounde this croppe as yt shall be marked oute by the saide iiij men uppon payne that he that denyeth the same to forfeite to the lorde iij s. iij d.'[241] The procedure in many open-field villages must have been along these lines.

Not before the sixteenth century, either, do we find any mention made of the kind of markers used. The villagers of Kibworth were ordered 'to fix stones on the metes and bounds'.[242] At Aylsham, Norfolk, the markers were to be of wood or stone.[243] At Great Horwood, the tenants were ordered to 'sett stones or other marks'.[244] At Elmley Castle, stones were used; no mention is made of stakes.[245] At Salford, Oxon., also 'mere stones' were used and apparently nothing else.[246] At Down Ampney, Wiltshire, stakes alone were used.[247] But at Brokfound, also in Wiltshire, mere stones only were specified.[248] The most detailed specifications are found in New England. Each landholder of Rowley, Massachusetts, was ordered on pain of 5s. to bound his lands 'with steaks and stones at the corners and at the said corners a hole shall bee made about a footwidde into which the ston shall be laid and the steak being about the thicknes of a man's legg shall be stuck into the said hole....'[249]

Why must we wait till the sixteenth century for boundary by-laws? In the close-knit villages of earlier times everyone knew the rules by heart; the need to rehearse them would come with the increase of mobility. Furthermore, by the sixteenth century some of the laity could read and write.

ROADS AND WAYS

To enable an open-field village to function well, or at all, there would have to be ways of access to the fields for ploughs, carts and the teams and those who drove them; also, droveways for the cattle on their way to pasture, a road to the mill and a network of footpaths. Every village community would be constantly concerned to maintain all of these as rights of way, free from obstructions, and in serviceable repair. Further,

---

[241] Northamptonshire Record Office, X, 386.
[242] Merton College Muniments, 6441. 1525.
[243] *Norfolk Record Society*, 12131–27, B4. 1560.
[244] 1552. See *n.* 239.
[245] *Worcestershire Record Society*, 899–95–4–65. 1583.
[246] Codrington Library, Salford, No. 363. 1592.
[247] *Wiltshire Record Society Court Book of Latin* Atton, 75 *d.* 1594.
[248] Wiltshire Record Office Sav. P. H. 4-392, *m.* 4 *v*, and *m.* 51. 1615.
[249] *Rowley Town Records*, 1639–1672, Vol. 1, 90. 1687.

INTRODUCTION 55

the villagers would have to be constrained to use the accustomed ways and paths and no others.

There was always the temptation to take a short cut, and when this was done over standing grain the damage could be considerable. At Ickham, Kent, in 1298, a tenant was amerced because his servants without right made passageways through the lord's grain.[250] Two men were called to account in Lewisham, Surrey, in 1299, because they made a path through the villagers' grain and made use of it day and night.[251] Trampling the spears of grain was an offence so patent and so rank that it went without saying, apparently. No by-law has been found before 1324 that deals with it. Sixteenth-century by-laws of trespass are plentiful. The whole problem was depicted in this one: 'No manner of person or persons shall drive or lead any horse, carriage or ploughs or any foote folkes goe over any lands or downe any lands sowen or unsowen to or from the milne or merkett without the consent of him who owns the lands that is soe gated but only use those ways as be knowne to be highways upon paine of every draught or carriage taken on defaulte for every time 12d. and for every horse 6d. and every one going afoote 2d.' [252]

A theorist might assume that an unhindered right of ingress and egress would be a right appurtenant to every plot of land. A freeholder of the manor of Notleigh, Hants., had a plot of twenty-two acres that lay in the midst of the demesne. Having been denied access to his plot by the lady of the manor, the tenant took his case to the king's court which held that 'The tenant had free access in cultivating his land through fallow and ploughland and other land as by right he ought to have'. This was in 1229.[253] A customary tenant of Newington, unable to take his case to the king's court, complained before the manor court that his right of way had been blocked by a neighbour. The jury found in his favour; the plaintiff had a right 'to carry grain, manure and stubble at will over the aforesaid land to and fro but in opening and closing the way he shall save his neighbour harmless'. The defendant was amerced for obstructing the claimant. This was in 1301.[254] Thus, access to his land was declared to be the natural right of any tenant both in a royal and a manorial court. We have to wait for the sixteenth century, however, to find the principle laid down in a village by-law: 'We doe present that every tenant shall have free ingress and egress to his ground.' [255]

Tenants sometimes claimed a limited right of way over the land of a

[250] P.R.O., Eccl. 18–19, *m.* 9 *d.* Cited in *Open-Field Husbandry*, 37.
[251] *Ibid.*
[252] *The Geologist's Magazine*, Vol. 4, 83.
[253] *Curia Regis Roll*, Vol. 13, Nos. 1225 and 2084.
[254] Cited in *Open-Field Husbandry*, 38.
[255] Court Book of Ashton Veynes. Wiltshire Record Society, 102.

neighbour at certain seasons of the year. Five tenants of Newington complained that one of their neighbours had blocked the use of a right of way 'which they have been accustomed to have going and coming with their horses and wagons in the field, namely from the Feast of St Peter ad Vincula [August 1st] until their Lenten seed had been sown'. A jury of thirteen vindicated the claimants, and the defendant was fined 2s. for his unlawful act. One of the five claimants was fined 2d. because he opened the way before judgment and two others were fined 3d. each for advising the defendant to close the right of way.[256] At Broughton, Hunts., in 1320, the jury said that Richard de Long had closed a certain way next his house, 'which ought to be common the whole time between the Gules of August [August 1st] and the Feast of St Martin [November 11th] so that all may drive their wagons over it for the reaping and the carting of the grain'.[257]

The sixteenth century brings further illustrations of limited rights of way. At Harrow, Middlesex, in 1552 the manor court settled a dispute between two tenants this way: the one 'shall have and enjoy from hensfforth one waye wyth carte and cattell under his close throwe the ground' of the other; and when the latter sows and harrows his land he 'shall leve hym a suffycent waye wythin the seyde close where lest harme shalbe done'.[258] At Winterbourne Stoke, Wiltshire, in 1576, a custumal included the following item: 'Our Custome is that when Shortsbill Field is sowed with wheat or barley tennants have a harvest way through the Parsonage Ground above the Barn and the Backside.' [259] At Whitchurch, Hants., the jury said that a certain lane was a part of the lord's waste. The tenants of the manor and other inhabitants of the town have the right of driving their cattle to and fro in the said lane but they may not allow them to stay and pasture there. Moreover, the lane must be kept safe for the inhabitants in going to church.[260] The need to define, adjust and rehearse a limited right of access must have been perennial. Of the process we know only a little for most of it, we may be sure, went unrecorded.

All roads should be maintained in usable condition of course, but by whom? In some villages the answer was, by the abutters. At Fulstow, Lancashire, in 1277, a tenant was fined 6d. because 'he did not make his way at his house by reason of which the road was in poor shape to the harm of the whole town'.[261] At Crowelthorpe, Lincs., 'it was ordered that each tenant shall maintain the way in front of his tenement to the

[256] Cited in *Open-Field Husbandry*, 38–39.
[257] *Ibid.*
[258] Middlesex Record Office, Acc. 76, Ha. 2423.
[259] *Wiltshire Archaeological and Natural History Magazine*, Vol. 34, 214.
[260] Br. Mus. Add. Ch. 44628. 1600.
[261] Cited in *Open-Field Husbandry*, 39.

middle of the road'.²⁶² At Great Horwood, in 1348, 'it was agreed among all the tenants free and customary that each of them shall make the royal road next to their own place so that carts shall not be hindered, on pain of 6d.' ²⁶³ At Wistow, Hunts., on July 17, 1410, it was ordered that each tenant mend the road leading to his holding with stone before September 20th, under pain of 12d.²⁶⁴ And at Beeston Regis, Norfolk, the rector was ordered to repair the common way along his land at the end of town before the next court under pain of 2s.²⁶⁵

In other villages communal responsibility was the rule. 'It is ordered that all tenants of the town be prepared to make and mend the causeway which leads to the marsh before the Feast of St Martin next under pain of 10s.' ²⁶⁶ At Launton, all the customary tenants were ordered to mend the road which led through the middle of the town before the next court.²⁶⁷ At Elmley Castle, all the tenants and inhabitants were obliged to work on Parsons Lane for two days and on Wood Lane for one day and on the common way whenever needed. Those having carts must haul stone.²⁶⁸ At Houghton, Hunts., 'every man shall be prepared when summoned by the bailiff to mend the road to Huntingdon on the day of the Nativity of St John the Baptist' (June 24th).²⁶⁹ At Warboys, Hunts., 'every inhabitant of this town who has a cart of his own shall be ready on the day appointed by the bailiff and the chief pledges to repair the roads of the town before the next court under pain each one of 12d.' ²⁷⁰ One even sees examples in village by-laws of the election of overseers of the roads, as for instance at Wistow, Hunts., where all the tenants were ordered to do their part in repairing certain roads of the town and two of their number were elected overseers whose orders all must obey.²⁷¹

The Highway Act of 1555 provided that every landholder must supply a horse and cart and two able-bodied men, and that cotters and others without carts must give their labour. They must work a maximum of four days a year, directed by two overseers elected by the villagers. Thus were procedures that had been evolved at the local level given statutory authority, which was the way with many Acts of Parliament.

---

²⁶² *Ibid.*
²⁶³ *Ibid.*
²⁶⁴ Doc. 118.
²⁶⁵ P.R.O., D.L. 102–108, *m*. 7 *d*. 1495.
²⁶⁶ Holywood, Hunts. P.R.O. Court Rolls, S.C. 2–179–79, *m*. 3. 1372.
²⁶⁷ Doc. 95. 1389.
²⁶⁸ Doc. 152. 1453.
²⁶⁹ P.R.O., S.C. 2–179–71, *m*. 5. 1469.
²⁷⁰ *Ibid.*, S.C. 2–179–82, *m*. 7 *d*. 1513.
²⁷¹ Br. Mus. Add. Ch. 39661. 1534.

COMMON CONSENT

When by-laws were recorded the scribe wrote, 'ex commune consensu' or 'per communitatiem totius villate', and he referred to a by-law as 'ordinacio vicinorum ville', or 'commune statutum ville', or 'plebiscitum'. Now and again the phrase was, 'Agreed and ordered by the lord and the community of the town'. 'Community of the whole township', 'the neighbours of the town', and 'common consent', the words used more often than any others—whom did the clerk have in mind when he wrote these words? Maitland has warned us that the 'communitas villate' was made up of serfs; freeholders would not be bound by 'restrictive customs and by-laws'.[272] In many cases, however, the consent of the freeholders to a by-law is specifically recorded by the scribe. In other instances it can be shown that the community of the township included the freeholders. The interest of a freeholder in a by-law to conserve the produce of the field would be dictated by his economic interest, not his legal status. He was quit of the more onerous labour services and he could resort to the king's court for justice; but in a great many instances he was not a principal landholder of his village. As Miss Neilson wrote, 'Perhaps we exaggerate the importance of the part played by legal status. It probably meant less to the medieval peasant than his economic rights and privileges.' [273] To test this thesis let us consider two of the by-laws recorded in the roll of the manor court of Great Horwood in 1319: 'An agreement of the community of the vill ... agreed and ordered by the whole homage of the vill ... in the presence of the lord.' The first is, 'none of them shall permit their hired hands to carry grain away from the field for their own use'; that is, if you pay your hands in sheaves, do not pay them in the field. All owners of sheaves were concerned about this, without distinction of status. The other regulation was that every man and woman able of body must reap and not glean. This by-law would be of special interest to those with acres to reap and the more acres the greater the interest. By-laws like these make up a very large proportion of all agrarian by-laws. The principal landholders must have been the predominant group in 'the community of the vill'. Landless labourers would not account for anything, even share-croppers had little voice. In a village assembly in medieval times 'there was almost certainly no counting of heads'.[274]

One of the more important members of the farming community was the parson. His holding, the glebe, was equal to that of a rich peasant, and it was freehold, with economic advantages which lay landholders

---

[272] *History of English Law*, 2nd ed. (1898) 1, 64, 67.
[273] *Cambridge Economic History*, Vol. 1, 446.
[274] B. Wilkinson, *Constitutional History of England*, Vol. 3, 188-189.

did not have. His arable acres, the 'church furlongs', lay intermingled with those of the laity. Their tithes were stored in his barns; their mortuaries were added to his own beasts and pastured with the village flocks and herds. Many a parson acquired added lands of his own and engaged in the cattle trade. His voice in communal affairs owed something, too, to the fact that he was the ghostly father of his fellow villagers. In village meetings the parson's assent or dissent must have been crucial. The intervention of the lord of the manor alone could have been more decisive.

The lord of the manor did not depend on communal by-laws to conserve his crops, even when he held the demesne in his own hands and his acres lay commingled with those of his tenants. Manorial officers watched out for trespassers and reported them to the manor court. Nonetheless it was to the advantage of a lord that there should be good order among his tenants. In the court roll of a manor of Fountains Abbey is this item: 'It is ordered that all tenants shall be ready to come to the plebiscite when summoned and obey the by-laws established and ordered by them'; and, 'all the tenants shall hold their plebiscites once a year as they are wont to do'. Elsewhere in these manor court rolls we find, 'it is commanded in court at the request of the whole homage that they shall order and establish among themselves laws and customs in their plebiscites and that none of them shall be rebellious against them under pain of 3s. 4d. to the lord'. And in still another entry the plebiscites of the villagers are said to be 'for their mutual good will and profit'.[275] It would seem, then, that it was customary for these villagers to assemble together regularly to draft by-laws for the common good, but sometimes they failed to do so, or the attendance was poor, or some villagers were disobedient. The authority of the lord and his court was asserted to secure greater regularity and better conformity.

The fourteenth-century records of the halmotes of the priory of Durham support this view. 'It is enjoined upon all the tenants of the town that each of them come at the call of the reeve to treat of common matters of profit touching the town,' and 'It is ordered by common consent that each of the tenants shall come at the reeve's summons to treat of common affairs and that each shall hold to whatever shall be agreed upon among themselves.' In some vills a committee of four or six was named, some of them freeholders, and commanded to draft by-laws before the meeting of the villagers. Some of the priory's manors included a number of vills, each an economic unit. The prior and his steward were at pains to have the inhabitants of each vill draft regulations for the common good; the by-laws themselves were not recorded.

[275] Br. Mus. Add. Ch. 60010. 1305–1430.

ENFORCEMENT

When by-laws were recorded the entry sometimes concluded with the names of the 'wardens of autumn'. These men (once only was there a woman), elected by the same authority that enacted the by-laws, were put on their oath to watch out for infractions and report offenders. More often than not, however, no mention was made of the election of wardens; at Great Horwood, wardens were named one-third of the time; at Newton Longville, eighteen times out of thirty-five. Allowance must be made for the scribe's failure to note that an election of wardens had taken place but one gets the impression that wardens were elected only when it was considered that there was need for a special means of enforcement. Regulations of field and pasture were a part of village custom, which in a tightly knit community was binding. There was also a compulsion, economic as well as social, to be a good neighbour, and this was supplemented by the argus-eye of communal surveillance.

The election of wardens was recorded in one of the earliest rolls now extant,[276] and there can be little doubt that the practice was still older. It continued to be quite general in the fourteenth century, but in the fifteenth century it ceased altogether. The last election at Great Horwood, as recorded, was in 1433; at Newton Longville in 1406, at Newington in 1416, at Halton in 1425, and at Launton in 1476.

We can learn a good deal about the wardens of Great Horwood. Until 1385 elections took place in late July or early August, invariably, that is, on the eve of harvest. A list of seven or eight wardens was the rule but once there were nine. After 1385 elections took place, or were recorded, in April or May. Problems of pasture were more pressing than those of harvest by this time, and the number fell to four, three, or even two. In 1433 two 'plebiscites' were recorded with two elected to enforce the one, and one, the other.[277] Nearly all wardens were villeins, virgaters or half-virgaters in equal measure; no cottager was ever chosen.

Among the wardens at Great Horwood in 1290 was John Frank. A freeholder, his tenement was a messuage and one virgate of arable. His son and namesake was elected warden in 1330, 1340, 1341, 1342, and 1348. He was a chief pledge also, making presentments with his fellows from 1322 to 1332. In 1332 he was one of the ale-tasters and in 1334 a juror. Richard le Rous, freeman, held a messuage and three-quarters of a virgate. He was elected warden of the by-laws in 1339, 1340, and 1341. In 1343 he was one of the chief pledges and an ale-taster. John Gerard, villein, was a virgater, owing rent and labour services. In 1322 he was the reeve and in the same year served as one of the taxers of a royal levy on the vill of Great Horwood. Between 1330 and 1342 he was elected

[276] Doc. 2. 1273.   [277] Doc. 142.

warden five times and he was also, from time to time, a chief pledge and an ale-taster. Once, though not in the year that he was warden, he was fined for harbouring wrong-doers in autumn.[278] Hugh the Reeve, 'nativus', was warden in 1322 and, with John Gerard, a taxer. He was fined on one occasion for allowing his calves to enter the field of grain and once he was fined for paying his workers with sheaves in the field 'contrary to the will of the community of the vill'. Most of the other wardens at Great Horwood were busy in the service of the lord of the manor and his court. In looking through the rolls one becomes familiar with their names as chief pledges, reeves, constables, ale-tasters, wood-wardens and messors. Evidently they were among the more substantial and responsible members of the community.

At Newton Longville the number of wardens might be anything from four to eight, and once there were nine. One might suppose that it would make some difference in the effective surveillance of the fields in harvest whether many or few were engaged in the task. For the years 1329 to 1333 inclusive there is a record of five elections in as many years but in no instance was the identical group elected two years in succession, though one man served four times and two others three times each.

Not much can be learned about the wardens of Newton Longville; no Extent of the manor has been found but a few details can be gleaned from the rolls of the manor court. Two wardens were referred to as 'native'. None was called 'freeman' and it is possible that there were no freeholders in this vill. The names of the various wardens appear in the list of trespassers against the by-laws, from time to time, but never in the year when they held office. One warden, while in office, took some sheaves he had found near the town, left there by a thief apparently, and carted them away 'contrary to the order of the messor', a case of conflict of jurisdiction perhaps.[279]

In the earlier years at Halton six wardens were named at a time, but in 1370 the number was reduced to four, in 1404 to three, and in 1415 to one. This reflects an important change of balance in the village economy, but this can be seen just as clearly in the by-laws themselves. No Extent of the manor is available. One of the wardens of 1337 held a virgate in villenage;[280] three of the wardens of 1343 were chief pledges at the time.[281] The sworn duty of the wardens is thus described: 'to see to the observance of these ordinances, to attach wrongdoers if any are found, and to present offenders'.[282]

At Newington there were two wardens for each of the four hamlets of

---

[278] New College Court Rolls G. H. I., 3–5.
[279] New College Court Rolls N. L. I. 1. 1. 1290.
[280] Halton Rolls, *loc. cit.* 1–16–45.
[281] *Ibid.*, 1–16–46.
[282] *Ibid.*, 1–16–44, *m.* 11.

the manor, as a rule. The court record for July, 1334, gives us a glimpse behind the scenes. Among the various items noted by the scribe was the election of eight wardens, one of whom was Henry at the Hedge. Among the entry fines we see this: 'Henry at the Hedge who held one-half virgate of customary land of the lord has gone the way of all flesh, and the lord has for a heriot one ox worth 11s. 6d., and Margery at the Hedge his wife . . . comes and does fealty.' [283] Evidently the election of Henry and his fellow wardens had taken place some time before the court was held. This item from the roll of 1416 is significant: 'Berwick. The homage there presents that William Erleche and John Chilledy were chosen keepers of the by-laws there.' [284] It would seem that each of the four farming communities chose their own wardens and reported the names to the steward at the next meeting of the manor court. Whenever it is possible to establish the status of a warden in Newington, using the extent of 1310 or the Hundred Rolls and chance references in the rolls of the manor court, it is found, invariably, that he was a virgater or half-virgater, owing rent and villein services.

In the Ramsey manor of Broughton, Hunts., in 1288, offenders against 'the common statute of the town' were presented by the chief pledges.[285] Later on, in this and other manors of the abbey special wardens of autumn were elected, though by-laws were seldom noted before the fifteenth century. At Houghton, Hunts., there were eleven wardens in 1307, but only four a century later. At Warboys, Hunts., there were nine in 1378, four in 1440.

Like the enrolment of by-laws and the election of wardens the presentment of offenders was never a routine item in the agenda of a manor court. Only forty-two presentments were noted at Great Horwood between 1290 (the first), and 1423 (the last), and these were between 1324 and 1354. At many an autumn court in a year when wardens were elected, no presentments were made, not even *omnia bene*. Presentments in other manor courts, Newton Longville, Newington, Halton, Launton and the manors of Ramsey Abbey, likewise were infrequent and irregular. One can only conclude that the enforcement of the by-laws, like the election of wardens and the by-laws themselves, was not a manorial matter.

From the enforcement items recorded, however, some conclusions can be drawn. Before 1350 harvest offenders predominated: they gleaned when able to reap, they carted by night, they paid with sheaves in the field, or they harboured harvest offenders. Presentments such as these were made at courts held in September or October. After 1350 it was trespassers against the by-laws of pasture who were most frequently

[283] Cited in *Open-Field Husbandry*, 45.
[284] *Ibid*.
[285] See *n*. 237, above.

presented: they trampled the grain of the neighbours with their calves or their foals; they put their sheep in the stubble before the great beasts; they sent their beasts into a field of grain before it had been cleared. Those who gleaned when they could reap were landless labourers, mostly; virgaters and half-virgaters were prominent in the other categories.[286]

In most manors there was an officer who was responsible for defending the lord's arable and pasture from trespassers. He was called messor or hayward and he was paid with a parcel of arable, an allotment of sheaves, or a share of the fines. His presentment of trespassers was a routine item on the agenda of the lord's court. Normally he was elected by his fellow tenants who were thus held responsible for his deeds, and an official enquiry was made into his conduct at regular intervals. The wardens of autumn on the other hand performed no services for the lord of the manor as such, nor were they ever the subject of an enquiry as to the discharge of their sworn duty. They were not officers of the manor and they were not paid.

HALF THE FINE TO THE VILLAGE CHURCH

Fines for the infraction of by-laws went to the lord of the manor; it was his court. In the fifteenth century, however, and only in the fifteenth century, there was a widespread practice of assigning half the fines to the village church. Instances of this have been found in the rolls of forty-eight manors in thirteen different counties.[287] It is significant that the practice was limited (with rare exceptions) to agrarian by-laws. At Warboys, Hunts., for example, in 1405, 'it was ordered at this court by the lord and the whole homage that no one shall pasture any of his beasts in the grain stubble before the Feast of St Michael under pain to the lord of 40d.' This by-law was re-enacted word for word in 1411; the penalty, still to the lord, was 12d. In 1430, however, the fine was 20d. to the lord and 20d. to the church, and in 1440, 12d. to the lord and 12d. to the church.

To understand why the village church got half the fine we must bear in mind that the community of the vill was also a community of parishioners. In the less populous north several vills might be included in the same parish, but in most cases the two communities were the same persons. As parishioners they were charged collectively with maintaining the fabric of the church, that is, they must keep the walls of the nave and its windows in good repair with a tight roof, and they must provide a belfry with bell and bell ropes. The parishioners must also provide most of the necessaries of worship. The enclosure of the churchyard was

---

[286] See *Open-Field Husbandry*, 46–49.
[287] W. O. Ault, 'Manor Court and Parish Church in Fifteenth Century England'. *Speculum*, Vol. XLII (1967), 53–67.

their responsibility also. The rector, for his part, must provide a full schedule of divine services and give his parishioners pastoral care, cradle to grave; he must also maintain the chancel. Records of the collective acts of parishioners begin about 1350. In the earliest of these the churchwarden appears as a fully developed officer; indeed his responsibilities and duties have varied but little from that day to this. Churchwardens were elected 'by the whole body of parishioners'.[288] They had charge of the goods of the church (vessels, ornaments, books and vestments); they made repairs; they administered for the church's profit its land and livestock. At the end of their year in office they made an accounting to their co-parishioners and handed over to their successors. Once a year, therefore, the community of parishioners assembled for a view of accounts and a fresh election. The word most commonly used by medieval scribes for churchwardes was 'custodes', the word commonly used for wardens of the agrarian by-laws. Both sets of officers were elected, in most cases by the same group of villagers.

In the fifteenth century the naves of village churches were being enlarged and embellished. Half the fines for infractions of the by-laws was an item of some importance. Let us look again at Warboys, a village of 8,500 acres on the eastern edge of Huntingtonshire. Manor, vill and parish were co-terminous. At the time of the Hundred Rolls there were four freeholders, no more important, however, than some of the virgaters, of whom there were forty. There were sixty half-virgaters also and a few acremen and cotters. The parson held two virgates and a messuage and much livestock with special rights of pasture, a man of weight. The twelfth-century church, which replaced an earlier structure, had a nave fifty feet long, with aisles on both sides and a tower at the end. In the fifteenth century the parishioners raised the walls of the nave to provide a clerestory, with large windows of stained glass. A timbered roof, finely carved, completed the work of reconstruction. All this was expensive, and it probably took a number of years to complete. The fine for breaking a harvest law at Warboys was 12d. to 40d. in the fifteenth century, and as many as a dozen offenders were presented each year by the wardens of autumn. Skilled stone masons were paid 6d. a day in those days. No accounts of the churchwardens for Warboys survive, but it seems probable that they spent the share of fines allotted to the parish church for its embellishment.[289]

VILL AND MANOR

The court of a manor was an assembly of all the tenants of the lord. Suit of court was an incident of their tenure, though individuals some-

---

[288] G. C. Cox, *Churchwarden's Accounts* (1913), 5.
[289] *Speculum XLII*, 62.

times bargained to be excused. The records of a manor court are filled with matters pertaining to the lord's estate: whether all those who owed suit of court had come; whether the officers of the manor had been faithful in the discharge of their duties; whether the lord's demesne had been well cultivated, his meadows and woods conserved; whether any had trespassed in his grain or his pasture; whether any had put their sons to clergy or allowed their daughters to marry without leave; and all other matters that pertained to the proprietary interests of the lord. Where vill and manor coincided it would appear to the casual reader of manor court rolls that the vill, with such responsibilities and initiatives as it once had, was dead, its life snuffed out by a thick overlay of manorialism. But if we turn over enough rolls and are on the alert we catch a glimpse here and there of the community of the vill acting on its own initiative and in its own interest.

In 1303 the two woodwards of Great Horwood, in the manor court, demanded as of right that each tenant of the manor pay them a quota of grain. The villagers assembled in court denied this and an inquisition was ordered. The 'jury of freemen and others said that the township (*villata*) had never given the woodwards anything unless by the common consent of the whole town'.[290] Woodwards, like reeves and messors, were paid officers of the manor. Their duty was to see that no tree was cut down or limb lopped off without leave and that there was no other unlawful trespass in the lord's wood by man or beast. We learn from the roll of the court that the woodwards of Great Horwood, as elsewhere, were elected by the villagers, who were thus made liable for any default in service. Twenty years later the lord appointed the woodwards out of hand and demanded that the customary tenants contribute to their sustenance. They on their oath declared that the woodwards were always elected by them, that they were chosen from the tenants in villeinage who held half-virgates, and that during their term of office they had remission of half their rent and the verdure of a bit of meadow called woodmead. Further that they, the customary tenants, had never contributed to the sustenance of the woodwards except once, when one of them was unable to work and that on that occasion each virgater had given one bushel of wheat and each half-virgater one-half bushel. Since that time six different woodwards had been elected, and their names were recited, to whom the customary tenants had given nothing.[291] Here the record ends. It is clear that the customary tenants were accustomed to act collectively, at times independently, of the manor court and its lord, but not without difficulty.

The following is from the roll of the manor court of Warboys, Hunts.: 'The whole homage as well free as others ask that no one of the com-

[290] New College Court Rolls, G. H., I, 1.
[291] *Ibid.*

munity shall be permitted henceforth to sell or give away any reeds or fern from the marsh of Warboys until he has carried it to his house and bunched it, under pain of paying half a mark to the lord as often as he breaks the said ordinance in any way. And it is granted in full court in the aforesaid form.' [292] This by-law was designed to keep unauthorized persons from taking reeds and fern from the marsh; it is similar to the ordinance providing that no sheaves were to be given out in the field, but only at the barn door. Rights in the marsh of Warboys were vested in the tenants, free and customary. The better to guard against theft, they drafted on their own initiative, apparently, a rule for their own self-government and requested the steward to have it recorded in the roll of the manor court. The fine, a stiff one indeed, was allotted wholly to the lord; in the fifteenth century the community of tenants would have stipulated that half the fine go to the reconstruction fund of the parish church.[293]

Wakefield, Yorks., was a large manor with a number of vills and hamlets under its jurisdiction. The following entry is from the roll of 1297: 'Stanley. German Filcok against Robert, son of Robert the Grave, Walter son of Adam, Robert son of Geoffrey, and William Tagge, for unjustly taking his horse on his own ground and detaining it against gage and pledge. They say that the seizure was made for 5d. awarded to them by the community of the plebiscite [*per communitatem plebisciti*] for trespass committed by it in the fields of Stanley. German says they took the horse off his own ground, and not in the fields of Stanley put in defence. An inquisition is ordered.' [294] The vill of Stanley had its own set of fields and they were closed to pasture at certain times of the year by an ordinance of the community of the vill. The four men named by the plaintiff were wardens elected by the community to seize trespassing animals and impound them until the owner paid the fine which the ordinance specified for trespass, in this case, 5d. Filcok alleged that the seizure of his horse was not made while it was trespassing in the field but on his own ground, his close perhaps, and his suit against the wardens in the manor court turned on that question of fact. The authority of the 'community of the plebiscite' of Stanley to impose a penalty for violating its by-laws and to proceed with its enforcement was not called in question. We are not told the verdict of the manor court.

In another case from the roll of the same manor for the year 1316 three men of Holme sued Adam son of John of the same village for 8s. due from Adam as his father's executor. John 'did trespass by his cattle in the corn and meadow' of the three men, and damages in the sum of 8s. had been awarded them 'by judgment of the plebiscite'. John died with

[292] Br. Mus. Add. Ch. 39760. 1346.
[293] See above.
[294] *Wakefield Court Rolls*, I, 279.

the debt unpaid and his son and executor refused to carry out the judgment of the village 'court', hence this appeal to the court of the lord of the manor. We may surmise, then, that the village communities within the manor of Wakefield enacted by-laws with fines specified for their infraction and elected wardens with authority to make distraint for exaction of the fines. But beyond that the community could not go. Cases of stubborn, unneighbourly resistance had to be carried to the court of the manor.[295]

Examples of villagers settling matters among themselves and then going to the manor court to record and enforce their regulations are especially numerous in the sixteenth century. No doubt seigniorial authority had lessened and, of course, documents of all sorts were more numerous. At Glatton, Northants., 'it was ordered by the assent of the whole homage there ... that every tenant of this manor who has a virgate of land in his tenure shall come to the church of Glatton when the great bell sounds twice or thrice ... and they shall stay there until the matters of principal interest of the aforesaid town shall be determined and ordered by the inhabitants there under pain for each delinquent to forfeit 20s.' [296] Here the villagers resorted to the authority of the manor court to enforce the attendance at the village assembly of the principal landholders; no by-laws were recorded on the rolls of the court. At Framfield, Sussex, an agreement was reached 'by the hole homage or the moore parte of the same' with respect to the election of the town constable, and it was ordered that 'the ordinance be brought into the court and the steward ... cause the same to be inrolled in the court rolles there to remayne matters of record'. Eight villagers appended their seals to the document and eighteen others signed by mark.[297]

At Shrewton, Wilts., in 1596, there was no longer a manor court; the manor had been dismembered by the sale of the lands, to the inhabitants themselves for the most part. After three years during which 'divers disorders have been committed ... in breache of Christian charitie and peace of the neighborhode' the inhabitants 'at thernest persuasion' of the vicar drafted a 'code' of nineteen by-laws, to be 'unviolably kept and observed bindin ourselves our heyres and assignes to the due observation thereof' from thenceforth forever. 'And for the better corroboration hereof we have caused these orders to be Ingrossed in this register booke to remayne in perpetuell record.' Appended were the signatures of the vicar and twenty-two inhabitants.[298]

[295] The Rolls of Halesowen, Shropshire, contain similar examples. *Court Rolls of the Manor of Heles*, Pt. II, 419, 423, 431, 432. 1301, ff. Cf. Ruyton, Shropshire. *Shropshire Archaeological and Natural History Society*, 3rd Series, II, 133.
[296] Br. Mus. Add. Ch. 26836, *m*. 5.
[297] Cited in *Speculum*, XXIX, 393. 1506.
[298] *Wiltshire Archaeological and Natural History Society Magazine*, XXIII, 36, ff. See *Speculum*, XXIX, 393–394.

A vill established itself as an entity separate from the manor with which it coincided when it leased the manor from the lord of whom 'the men of the town' were individually tenants. In 1320 the lord of Great Horwood leased to his tenants all his demesne land, 'together with the pastures, the labour services and all pasture rights pertaining to the aforesaid town excepting rents of the town, pleas, and perquisites and suits of court, fines of land, sales of men and marriage of women, heriots and tallages, the whole of the wood and the rent of cocks'. The lease was for eight marks nine shillings four pence a year. A copy of the lease was to remain in the hands of the tenants. The lease was for twelve years and renewable; the last renewal on record was in 1432. We may wonder who got the better of the bargain. If we add the value per annum as set down in the Extent of 1320 [299] of the demesne lands, meadows and pasture and include the rent of the capital messuage and the mill plus the works of the customers and cottagers, we arrive at a sum which lacks a few pence only of equalling the stipulated farm. For their profit the villagers would have the produce of the lord's arable and the rent of his pastures. How the men of Great Horwood managed their joint affairs under the terms of the law we are left to imagine.

A close parallel is the lease of the manor of Hemingford, Hunts., to the men of the vill, and about this we can learn more. The manor and vill had been held by the abbey of Ramsey of the king since the time of the Confessor. It was larger than average in the county, having about three square miles (2,000 acres) of arable, with meadow, wood and waste lands. Five of the twenty hides were in demesne. The earl of Oxford held a sub-manor of two hides and the holdings of seven other free tenants added up to two more and there were three virgates (one-half hide) of glebe land. Fifty-six virgaters held one-half, one or one and a half virgates each and there were twenty-four crofters, each the tenant of a few acres of arable.[300] There may have been a few landless cotters but they were not listed in the Extent of *c.* 1255, and there were doubtless a few carters, ploughmen, shepherds and maid servants attached to the household. An overall population of about 400 is a safe estimate for the vill of Hemingford in mid-thirteenth century.

The manor was first leased in 1265, for a seven-year term, and the lease was renewed septennially until the eve of the Dissolution. The rent was forty pounds sterling, but a bonus (*gersum*) of ten and a half marks was payable at each renewal, which in effect added one pound a year to the rent. 'Know ye that we have demised at farm to our men of Hemingford our manor of Hemingford.... Our men shall have the aforesaid manor with all its appurtenances except the church, a fishery and a mill; and they shall have all the profits of the town, except tallage, sheriff's

[299] Doc. 204.
[300] *Cartularium Monasterii de Rameseia*, II, 350–392.

aid and hundred aid, wardpenny, scutage, the issues of causes that cannot be decided without us or our bailiffs, of the issues of which they shall have half, view of frankpledge, the Maundy acre and the acres of the reeve of Ramsey.' The granary was stocked with grain, the equivalent of which must be returned at the termination of the lease, 'with the land well ploughed twice'. No mention was made of livestock.[301]

The men of Hemingford were to have the manor with its appurtenances, except the church, a fishery and a mill. Included would be the manorial farmstead with its granaries, feed lots and stockyards. The staff of hired hands, men and women, was at their disposal too; they would have to be housed and paid. (Reference is made in the reeve's accounts of 'the natives of the land who dwell in the town to the use of the tenants of the town'.) There was a demesne meadow which the men of the town had leased before they took over the manor; this was worth 30s. Outweighing all else was the demesne arable, the acres lying intermingled with those of the virgaters and crofters. Some furlongs had been rented to individual cultivators, at a total rental of 17s. per annum, but there remained 350 acres from whose produce the men of the town could profit; and to these acres belonged the right of pasture in stubble and fallow. Available for the ploughing, sowing, weeding and harvesting of the demesne acres was the labour service of the virgaters, three days a week, year round, and the crofters, one day.

'All the profits of the town' were demised to the men of Hemingford, as well as the manor and its appurtenances. The list of profits of the town that were reserved has several items which according to our lights did not pertain to the town as such. Tallage was a tax levied by a lord on his servile tenants; scutage was, at least in origin, strictly feudal. Wardpenny, sheriff's and hundred aid and the view of frankpledge are clearly not manorial, but the Maundy acre is just as clearly an ecclesiastical item and the reeve's acres are a manorial matter. But thirteenth-century men did not always distinguish manorial from villar, private from public. In a series of reeve's accounts which, as extant, begin in 1311 and run with many gaps to Henry VIII, the farm of forty pounds was always called 'the farm of the town'; in a seventh year, 'the whole township owes the lord ten and one-half marks in *gersum* for the farm of the town' (*Tota villata debit domino . . . pro firma ville*). In their accounts the various items—manorial rent, profits of the town and rental of the free-holders—are listed by the reeves in an order quite without pattern. A credit item which was earmarked, 'to the use of the customers of the said vill in aid of their farm' (*ad opus custumariorum ejusdem ville in auxilio firme sue*) seems to say that 'the men of Hemingford' consisted of the virgaters and crofters only.

---

[301] *Ibid.*, II, 244. Translation in Bland, Brown and Tawney, *op. cit.*, 79–80.

It is not easy to see that much would be left of the profits of the town once the long list of exceptions was subtracted. We learn from the accounts, however, that the reeves paid a lump sum that never varied for some items. For example, each virgater and crofter owed a farthing per annum, by the Extent of *c.* 1255, for wardpenny, or if he had livestock worth 30d., a half-penny. With pigs worth 42d. each and lambs 12d.,[302] the poorest tenant might have 30d. worth of livestock and more. And so the sum of 49d. would be due; the added payment for livestock suggests that cattle theft was still rife. The surplus went to the farm, no doubt. It was the statutory duty of the lords of manors to enforce the watch. In the case of Hemingford it would seem that the abbot in return for a fixed sum allowed the townsmen to carry out the provisions of the statute in any way they pleased.

Among the profits of the town were 'issues of causes that cannot be settled without us or our bailiff of which issues they shall have half'. The manor courts of Ramsey Abbey met at least twice a year, a view of frankpledge and an autumn court. Matters manorial, that is, enforcement of services, punishment of trespassers in the lord's arable or pasture by man or beast, levying of heriots and transfer of land, were dealt with in the autumn court, though not exclusively; matters pertaining to the 'View', at the view of frankpledge court, but at times at the autumn court too. No autumn court was held at Hemingford during the period of the lease, so far as extant records go. Manorial items at a view were few; the record of the court of a neighbouring manor held by the same steward a few days later was twice as long.[303] The reeves of Hemingford faithfully accounted for the proceeds of the view of frankpledge, year by year. Now and again the item, 'Perquisites of the court' is seen along with proceeds of the view and one wonders whether this was the abbot's share of the proceeds of cases which, unable to settle among themselves, the men took to the court of the manor. This may be the record of such a case: 'The jury say that William Belond a native of the lord is in rebellion against his neighbours and will not submit to the judgment of his fellows, to the injury of the community.... In mercy 6d.'[304] This passage seems to imply that there was at Hemingford, on occasion, an assembly of the villagers which could make a 'judgment' but, in some cases, lacked full authority to enforce it.

Bearing on the same point is this record from the view of frankpledge

---

[302] At Downton, Wilts., in 1324–1325. J. Z. Titow, *Op. cit.*, 120. But note that the lambs sold were 'feeble'.

[303] Compare Hemingford with Elton. F. W. Maitland, *Select Pleas in Manorial and other Seigniorial Courts*, Selden Society, Vol. II (1890), 88 ff. (1278); also Hemingford and Houghton, W. O. Ault, *Court Rolls of the Abbey of Ramsey* (1928), 219–221, 226–229.

[304] Hemingford, Manor Court Roll, P.R.O., S.C. 2-179-43, *m.* 2, 1391.

INTRODUCTION 71

at Hemingford in 1326: 'And they (the jury) say that Simon atte Style, Henry Barber, and Simon Euerard hindered the taxers elected by the whole community of the town so they could not collect a *collectio ad arma* etc. but they interfered and collected the aforesaid payment themselves and they refuse to render an account of it. Therefore they are in mercy, 3s. Pledge, each the other.' [305] In the following year, 'They say that Simon atte Style, Simon Euerard and Henry Barber refuse to act justly in the matter of rendering an accounting of their collections in the town to the community of the town as was ordered in the last view. Therefore they are amerced 18d. And they have a day to render an accounting next Sunday.' [306] This view was held on a Monday. Simon at the Style and Simon Euerard had been the reeves in 1318–1319,[307] and the former with another were reeves in 1326–1327; both were removed from office for being 'useless both to the lord and the community'. Henry Barber cannot be traced.

The *collectio ad arma* was for the expedition to Scotland in 1325. The military service of peasants as a personal, not a tenurial, obligation had never died out even in the period of high feudalism and the vill continued to be the unit in the exacting of this service, each vill being assigned a quota of foot soldiers. The sheriff, or the lord of the manor, was held responsible by the state but the men of the vill in some cases were free to produce the men in whatever way they chose. It was usual for men to be 'elected' to go by their fellow villagers who sometimes made an assessment to pay the soldiers. This was what the men of Hemingford did in 1323 when required to supply their quota of soldiers to go with the king to Scotland; they voted an assessment on the property owners, basing it on the number of cattle perhaps, and elected taxers to collect it. In the ordinary course the taxers would collect the individual assessments, in cash or kind, pay out to the soldiers the sums agreed on, and make an accounting to the community of the town. But all did not go smoothly in Hemingford this time. Three men, the two Simons and Henry, brushed aside the taxers and made the rounds themselves, and this is what they had done with regard to others (*divers*) collections as well, and then they refused an accounting; at least they were so accused. One supposes that the community had done all it could to compel the three men to make an accounting of the sums they had collected and, unable to settle the case themselves, had turned to the court of the manor. There the accused were found guilty not of brushing aside the official taxers but of refusing to make an accounting of what they had collected. For this they were fined and ordered to make an account. This was in 1326. Still recalcitrant a year later they were fined

[305] P.R.O., S.C. 2-179-22, m. 3.
[306] *Ibid.*, m. 7 d.
[307] Min. Accts., 876/30.

in court once more and ordered to make their account to the community of the town on the following Sunday. Ramsey's manor courts always met on weekdays; attendance was a substitute for the labour service of the day. It is clear from the context that the accounting was to be made before an assembly. Churchwardens were making annual accountings in this period in the parish church with the parson in the chair. The 'divers collections in the town' for which these three men were ordered to account may have included sums due for wardpenny, sherriff aid and hundred aid. They were payable by individuals as part of their tenurial obligations, the reeves compounding with the abbot for a fixed sum.[308]

Did the reeves of Hemingford make an annual account to 'the men of the town', their fellow villagers? When the demesne of a manor was not at farm a reeve's account set forth the proceeds of the various manorial properties in considerable detail with a statement of expenses incurred to the last farthing. The account for Downton, Wilts., for 1324–1325 covers twenty-one printed pages.[309] By the terms of their lease the men of Hemingford held all the manorial properties except a fishery and a mill. The reeves were the administrators of the properties under lease and we are entitled to suppose, I think, that the men of the town would require an accounting, and that this would follow the lines of the account made to the abbot before the manor was leased. No record of such an account has survived, but perhaps none was ever made. Every one of consequence in the town knew what the reeve ought to have done and pretty well what he had done. Some townsmen had themselves been reeves and others would be. If all was in balance at the accounting and straight answers had been given to all questions no one but an archivist would want to make a record of what had transpired.

The last accounting of the reeves to the officials of the abbey was in 1533.[310] The men of the village had been managing their joint affairs under the lease for two centuries and a half.

KINGSTHORP

The men of Kingsthorp, Northants., lessees of the manor of which they were all tenants, made and kept records. The manor lay on the edge of Northampton and is now part of that city. It was a small manor of about a thousand acres, rated in Domesday Book at four hides and three virgates. Its economy was agrarian and the lands of the tenants lay intermingled in the open fields, which were unenclosed until the seventeenth century.

---

[308] See above.
[309] J. Z. Titow, *op. cit.*, 115–136.
[310] P.R.O., Min. Accts., Henry VIII, 1657, 50.

Thorp, alias Kingsthorp, was part of the royal demesne and sometime in the reign of King John it was leased to its 'men and tenants' for successive terms of forty years. Nothing was reserved, not even view of frankpledge.[311] The village had a seal, and its records were found by a nineteenth-century vicar 'in a promiscuous heap in the Church Chest much mutilated, injured by damp and mildew and likely in a short time to perish altogether'. The vicar printed a description and calendar of the documents he found and arranged for their future care.[312] The principal documents still extant are rolls of the manor court beginning in 1350 and continuing, with many gaps, to the seventeenth century; the seal, *Sigillum Commune de Kyngesthorp*, which probably dates from the time of Richard II, and a custumal of thirty-three items dated 1483 and another of seventy-nine items dated 1547. The earliest headings of the manor court read 'Court of Kingsthorp' or 'Kingsthorp: View of Frankpledge with Court'. No lord of the manor was ever mentioned, not even the king as lord. Later on the scribe wrote 'Kingsthorp: court of the inhabitants and tenants of the lord king'. The enactment clause of the custumal of 1482 is missing but that of 1547 begins, 'Ordinances and Statutes made by the consent of all the inhabitants of the Towne of Kingsthorp'.

The officers of the town were a bailiff, two constables, four ale-tasters and six 'thurborowes'. There was also a group called 'the twelve', the jurors, apparently, from whose ranks the bailiff and other officers were chosen by the bailiff for the time being and the 'community of the town' in turn, in a typically complicated medieval process. Elections were held annually in the 'court house', on a Sunday. Anyone who 'reviled, rebuked or disobeyed' an official was subject to a fine. Two courts were held each year and attendance was compulsory. The familiar 'articles' of a view of frankpledge were ticked off at each session; it was from the authority of this franchise that the authority of the village assembly of Kingsthorp was derived.

One sees at once why the community of the vill made and preserved a record of its proceedings: transfers of land by inheritance, sale or gift were numerous and continuous. 'This roll witnesses that Richard Day of Kingsthorp gave to John Peck his heirs and assigns in full court before a large number of people [*multitudo copiosa*] a part of a croft in le Ryrzerles to be held according to the custom of the manor and town.' [313] Wills, too, were recorded. The town owned four water mills at which the villagers must grind their grain. 'The bailiff of the town and

---

[311] *Victoria County History, Northamptonshire*, IV, 83.

[312] J. H. Glover, *Kingsthorpiana* (1883). By courtesy of Canon Andrews and P. I. King, Archivist of the Northamptonshire Record Society, I was able to examine the contents of the chest.

[313] *Kingsthorpiana*, 25. 1402.

his two constables and the whole community of the town by unanimous consent and assent grant to William Branfeld of Kingsthorp their four water mills . . . for 7 marks of good money . . . and a cask containing 26 gallons of ale when the meadow is mowed, or 2s. 2d. in money.' [314] Twenty-six gallons would supply a good many pints for thirsty hay hands. As elsewhere, the agricultural community of Kingsthorp had rules of order. 'If any man reaps or mows any land before the bailiff and the community be agreed, to forfeit 6d.' [315] A man can do with his own what he likes, but not, in an open-field village, when he likes. 'It is ordered by the twelve that if any one plough a headland more than he ought he shall forfeit 12d., of which 4d. to the bailiff, 4d. to the man who discovers the default, and 4d. to the poor box.' [316] This was in 1553 when the Church had become 'a department of the state', and the churchwardens were included along with the bailiff and the constables in the list of officers of the town. 'And the more part of the twelve be ready to place mere stones . . . in the fields where they seem to be needed on Thursday in the week of Pentecost next under pain of 12d. each one who is delinquent without good reason.' [317] Stints were established according to 'olde custome', one horse and one cow for every ten acres of arable; two sheep to the acre. Mares with foal, as 'hinderers and harmdoers in the corn and pasture of the neighbours' must be in the paddock at all times; fine 40d.[318] Kingsthorp was a run-of-the-mill agricultural village, but it had and exercised all the self-governing authority of a royal borough.

The earliest rental of Kingsthorp now extant is dated 1570. Some ninety tenements are listed. Three tenants head the list, each denominated Esquire. One of them paid £4. 8s. 3d. a year, but the others 5s. and 10½d. each. Most of the other tenants paid a few shillings, or a few pence; one as little as a penny.

There was a chapel there, the mother church being St Peter, Northampton. Dependent chapels were usually built at the expense of the parishioners and their friends and consisted of a nave only, there being no rectorial chancel. Thus the maintenance of the fabric rested on the inhabitants, according to the rule laid down by a thirteenth-century synod that the burden belonged 'wholly to the parishioners of the chapel since it was for their advantage and convenience that it was built'.[319] The wages of the chaplain, also, were the responsibility of the inhabitants. It should follow as a logical consequence that the chapel com-

---

[314] *Ibid.*, 36–37.
[315] *Ibid.*, 44. 1377.
[316] *Ibid.*, 30–31.
[317] *Ibid.*, 32. 1550.
[318] MS. in Church Chest. 1377.
[319] *Register Brantingham*, 23.

INTRODUCTION 75

municants would nominate the chaplain, and instances of this have been found. The records of Kingsthorp have nothing to say on this point.

VILLS OF DIVIDED LORDSHIP

In a good many vills, as many as one-third in some regions of England, the landholders were not all tenants of the same lord and there was, therefore, no one manor court which all must attend. Inasmuch as local records were exclusively manorial, or nearly so, it is well-nigh impossible to find out how the inhabitants of a vill of divided lordship managed their affairs under an open-field system of agriculture. They must have held village meetings; as Maitland remarked, 'the total absence of written records of such meetings hardly makes the fact less probable'.[320]

The lack of records is not quite total. The village of Harlestone, Northants., was divided among six lords. A change had been made from a two to a three course plan of crop rotation, but one field was made too small. A document of 1410 recites that by the assent and consent of the six lords, six named inhabitants, and 'other good men and of the whole of the villagers' an arrangement had been made to enlarge the smallest field; certain lands had to be fenced, a few roads widened and others newly laid out. Two of the lords conveyed parcels of land 'to the men of the village and to the community of the aforesaid village for the widening of the roads'. At a meeting of the villagers a standing committee of nine was elected to relocate boundary lines, measure roads, superintend cultivation, and settle disputes. Provision was made for the continued life of this committee through fresh elections. 'The nine good men of Harlstone,' as they were called, were to act by majority vote. Finally, 'if it shall seem to a majority of the men of the aforesaid village . . . at the end of six or eight years that the aforesaid arrangement is to the common disadvantage and damage of the aforesaid villagers then the arrangement shall altogether cease'. On the back of the manuscript on which this arrangement is inscribed there is the record of successive elections of the committee of nine, one as late as 1505.[321] If the men of Harlestone with the help of their lords could deal with a problem as difficult as this they could certainly draft by-laws for the common profit.

In a document unique so far as I know we have the actual text of by-laws adopted by the inhabitants of another village of divided lordship. This was Wimeswold, Leics., and the date of the document is *c.* 1425. It begins as follows: 'Be it remembered that it was enacted at Wimeswold on Tuesday before the Feast of St Dunstan the Bishop, before Sir John

---

[320] Pollock and Maitland, *op. cit.*, I, 42.
[321] Joan Wake, 'Communitas Villae', *English Historical Review*, Vol. 37, 406–411.

Nevill, Hugh de Willoughby and William of Radcliffe, proctor of the Abbot and Convent of Beauchief, and by the common consent of the whole township that all the statutes written below be kept and observed on the aforesaid penalties.' Nevill, Willoughby and the abbey of Beauchief each had a manor in this vill. Fines for the breach of the by-laws were to go to no one of them, however, in a whole or in part, but to the village church. There are nineteen by-laws in the list, six dealing with the rules of harvest and thirteen with rights of pasture. The by-laws are in 'bucolic English', but the enactment clause is in Latin. The stipulations of the by-laws are familiar; some of them may be as old as open-field farming itself. Codes similar to this must have been common in open-field villages of divided lordship, but if any others were written down they have not survived.[322]

Another vill of divided lordship was Walsoken, in Norfolk, near the Wash. Its lands were divided more or less equally among three lords, the abbot of Ramsey, the bishop of Ely and the prior of Lewes. Each may have held a court for his own tenants; the abbot of Ramsey certainly did. The authority and the profits of the view of frankpledge had long been in dispute and a compromise was arranged: the three stewards to preside jointly, a fine to be allotted to the lord of the guilty man. Custody of the roll of the court was in the hands of the bishop's steward. The records of two sessions are extant, March, 1295, and June, 1299.[323] A jury of twelve was sworn, the tithings were checked, the assize of bread and beer enforced, those who harboured strangers against the statute fined, and other articles of the view ticked off. No manorial items such as enforcement of labour services and transfer of lands are in the record. What we do find are items of community concern. Men who 'destroy the grain of the neighbours to the common nuisance' were fined; women guilty of 'wrong-doing in autumn' were dealt with, though the pertinent by-laws were not recorded. Three men were elected hog-reeves to see to it that all the pigs of the town were suitably ringed in season. Four men were elected to be 'reeves of the sea dike'; their names appear in the lists of jurors, chief pledges and ale-tasters, also; they were important men, it would seem, and maintenance of the sea dike was crucial. And there was another item about the dike: The jury 'presents that Adam de Marham, John son of Kym' and Walter de ... (illegible) entered the dwelling of Thomas Raysun and against his will took away his cow for a tax levied for widening the dike from Welles to Elm. And they also took a cow from the close of Emma of Gloucester for the same tax for which cause the said Thomas Rayson and Emma raised the hue against them, whether justly or unjustly, they know

---

[322] The text is in Hist. MSS. Comm., *Middleton Report*, 106–109.
[323] *Court Rolls of the Abbey of Ramsey*, 173–179.

INTRODUCTION 77

not at present'. Reading between the lines we conclude that a decision to widen the dike was made and a tax voted by common consent of the villagers, and that the three men (Adam de Marham was a juror in the following year) were elected to be the taxers. It was a common practice to measure the wealth position of a villager by the number of his cattle. The tax on each principal landholder in this case was one cow. Thomas and Emma resisted when the taxers came to collect and when the taxers seized the cows by force (note that they took Thomas's cow from his dwelling), raised the hue. This brought the matter within the jurisdiction of the view of frankpledge, but there the record ends. A village assembly which can levy a tax and make provision for its collection and expenditure is in a mature stage of development.

Another item from the record of the view gives us another look at the community of the vill of Walsoken. Six men, four the abbot's and two the bishop's, 'common fishers, sold fish outside the town contrary to the prohibition. Therefore they are in mercy (fine 3d. or 6d.). Accordingly it is provided by common consent that none of the aforesaid fishermen nor any other fisher shall sell any fish outside the town henceforth until after he has taken his fish to the church (the market nearby perhaps) to see if any one of the parish wants to buy it, and whoever is found guilty of this henceforth shall be fined half a mark'.[324]

The inhabitants of Walsoken were fortunate in having a view of frankpledge in common to which they could resort as needed. Other villagers of divided lordship had to manage their affairs without assistance; but, 'it seems difficult to avoid the conclusion that from time to time they gathered in village meetings to discuss and regulate their joint interests in the cultivation of the fields and the rights of common.' [325]

THE NEW ENGLAND TOWN

We shall never have a satisfactory knowledge of the village community of medieval England. Most of what we do know is based on evidence that is difficult to interpret and insufficient in amount. We can find out a good deal about a particular village here and there but individual differences are so great that generalities are unsafe.

A helpful analogy is the New England town. Documents are plentiful and they consist largely of town records, not the Extents, accounts and court rolls of manorial overlords. The colonists brought with them 'the ideas with which they had been familiar from childhood'.[326] Some of them came from London and other boroughs of the south and west of

[324] *Ibid.*, 179.
[325] A. L. Poole, *Domesday Book to Magna Carta* (1951), 18.
[326] Edward Channing, *A History of the United States* I (1932), 426.

England; but whatever had been their way of life in the old country and whatever they might aspire to be in the new, the early colonists were perforce tillers of the soil.

Only a bare outline of the New England story can be given here. The settlers usually took up land as a group, a congregation perhaps, led by the minister. Home lots were marked out on the town site, with a churchyard and village green. Settlement beyond the town site was not permitted as long as a lot was vacant. A division was made of a tract of arable ready or nearly ready for cultivation; in a later year a second tract, then a third and a fourth, perhaps. These tracts, of a few hundred acres each, were marked out in strips of nearly equal size, grouped in tiers. In some towns the strips were numbered and distributed by lot. Some householders were allotted more than others; they had more of the tools of agriculture or more cattle and they could hire servants. But most settlers shared alike and tilled their acres with the help of their families.

Co-aration was mandatory. It required from four to eight oxen to draw a plough through root-infested, boulder-strewn ground and a team of ten was not unknown. Pasturing the stubble, also, was practised from the start.[327] In short, the early New England settlers practised open-field husbandry. They elected 'select men', constables, herdsmen and hog-reeves, and they enacted by-laws of fencing, cropping and pasturing, on the principle that 'the greater quantity of town's people shall have power to order the whole'. They built their churches without chancels, on the model of the English chapel, and they named their ministers and paid them, though not in tithes. We can learn a great deal about the villagers of early New England, and we may see in the way they managed their affairs a reflection of the centuries of English experience on which it was based.

[327] See above.

DOCUMENTS

Documents numbered 1 to 195 are village by-laws, mainly agrarian. They were taken from the court rolls of thirty-one different manors in ten English counties. First published in *Open-Field Husbandry and the Village Community*, they are printed here in translation.[1] As a rule only a few by-laws were taken from the rolls of any one manor but all the by-laws recorded at a given session of a court have been included in the excerpt selected. The rolls of Great Horwood, Bucks., Newton Longville, Bucks., and Elmley Castle, Worcs., contain by-laws well distributed from the thirteenth to the sixteenth century and they have all been included to enable the student to observe in detail the changes that took place in farming practice and communal control. All excerpts have been arranged chronologically and listed by manor and county in a special index. Dates by Saints' days or Festivals and regnal years have been converted into the modern form.

The court rolls, numbered 196 to 206, show how by-laws were recorded in the roll of a manor court; they illustrate, too, the ways in which by-laws were enforced. The rolls have been grouped by manors. In view of the large number of by-laws taken from the rolls of Great Horwood an early Extent of that manor has been included (Doc. 204).

[1] The numbering here is the same as in that volume, where references to the source are given.

GLOSSARY

Affeerer	assessor of fines
Agist	to pasture, or to pay for pasture
Amerce	to fine
Codding	gathering of peas, beans, or vetches
Curtilage	stockyard attached to a dwelling
Defence, in	closed to pasture
Drage	mixed cereals
Essoin	lawful excuse
Gersum	a fine, a premium
Heriot	best beast, or the equivalent, accruing to his lord on the death of a tenant
Mainpast	one for whom another is legally responsible
Mercy	an amercement or fine
Messor	hayward, warden of fences
Messuage	dwelling with outbuildings, feed lots and kitchen garden
Native	villein by birth
Seisin	lawful possession
Selion	strip or measure of ploughland
Stint	share of pasture rights, based on size of tenement
Tithing	a mutually responsible group of men
Vetch	bean-like legume
View of frankpledge	held periodically to see that all men who ought to be are in a tithing
Virgater	tenant of a virgate, a measure of land averaging in many cases 30 acres

By-Laws

1270

1 *Newington, Oxon.* Monday, September 15th

Emma, maid-servant of Ella Somer, and others unknown carried grain by night in autumn contrary to the law [*contra defensionem*], namely, in the middle of the night.

Thomas Est put himself in mercy, 4d., for having put his pigs in the Lenten field, against the order of the bailiffs and the ordinance of the neighbours of the town.

John Garleche received Isabella [as a gleaner] contrary to the statutes of autumn. Therefore he is in mercy, 2d.[2]

1273

2 *Chatteris, Cambs.* Sunday, July 9th

Wardens chosen to guard the fields, Godfrey Tector, John Hagun, Andrew Alberd, John Hayse, Robert son of Thomas Gilbert.

1275

3 *Cheddington, Bucks.* Friday, August 9th

It is ordered in court that no one shall harbour anyone male or female [*aliquem aut aliquam*] who is able to reap, under pain of half a mark.

1276

4 *Staines, Middlesex.* A. Monday, July 27th

It is provided and ordered by the community of the whole town that no one whether in town or out shall accept any one, stranger or not, to gather grain in the field what is called *glenyinge* nor shall they pay [anyone] with sheaves in the fields but only at the doors of the granaries, under pain of half a mark.

B. Tuesday, September 15th

Adam in the lane, because he harboured a certain woman, a stranger, who was a malefactor in the grain and meadows, 3d.

[2] Early by-laws are scarce but sometimes they can be inferred from items like this. See Nos. 7, 10, 12, 13 and 15.

Peter Beauchamp for the trespasses of his pigs and sheep in the common field for a whole year, 3d.

Let Christina de Chabsham and William her son be distrained because they were malefactors in the meadows and grain of the whole community.

1286

5 *Newington, Oxon.* Saturday, July 27th

It is granted by the whole court that no one in this manor shall harbour any stranger who is a wrongdoer especially in autumn time under pain of 2s. 6d. to the lord.

And that no one in the aforesaid time shall accept any one as a gleaner who is capable of doing the work of a reaper.

1287

6 *Welwyn Rectory Manor, Herts.* Thursday, August 7th

It is ordered by a judgment of the whole court that men and women who are able to reap be distrained not to glean after the fashion of paupers and that those who harbour them be punished and whatever [they] the gleaners have gathered be seized.

1288

7 *Broughton, Hunts.* Wednesday, November 17th

And they say that William Kataline paid [his workers] with sheaves in the field in autumn contrary to the common statute of the township. Therefore he is in mercy, 12d.

And they say that the wife of Thomas le Hund was a gleaner contrary to the common statute of the township. Therefore he is in mercy; pledge, the reeve.[3]

1290

8 *Newton Longville, Bucks.* Saturday, July 1st

It is granted and ordered by the community of the town that no one henceforth shall gather herbage in another's grain.

Item that no one who holds land of the lord shall gather peas, beans or vetches in the fields except on land that they have sown.

Item that anyone who wants to gather beans, peas or such like shall gather them between sunlight and prime in le Hech' [one of the fields], and this [may be done] after the Feast of the Blessed Virgin Mary.

[3] Five others were fined 2d. each for the same offence.

Item that no one shall allow his calves to be in the fields in the growing grain [*infra segetem*] before the other animals. . . .[4]

Item that no one be allowed to glean who is able to earn a penny a day with food or two pence without food if he finds anyone who wishes to hire him.

Item that no outsider be allowed to glean unless he who harbours him is willing to answer for his deeds.

Item that no pauper be allowed to gather beans between the selions but only at the ends and dividing lines. And if he shall do otherwise he shall lose what he has gathered and he shall not be allowed to enter the fields thenceforth to gather beans.

Item that there shall be no carting by night.

Item that everyone shall see that his stiles and lanes, those nearest his neighbours, are so kept that neither the lord nor any of his tenants incur damage because of the lack of such maintenance.

Item that no one shall have his beasts depasture in any cultivated area until one land [*terra*] is lying wholly cleared [of grain].

Item that no one shall have his beasts depasture in le Hech before . . . [illegible].

Item that no one shall have his beasts depasture in the growing grain in the night time.

Item that no one shall . . . [gather] peas nor shall any grain be taken from the fields by night . . . [illegible].

And if any one shall be found [doing the] contrary he shall give the lord 6d. And if any one shall be found to be delinquent in the premises by night he shall give the lord 12d.

9   *Great Horwood, Bucks.*   Tuesday, July 11th

A day is given to the town messor to report the names at the next [court] of all those who were transgressors against the ordinance made recently forbidding lambs to be pastured in the common grain [fields] of the town.

Ordinance of autumn. It is granted by the whole homage and by the freemen that all the statutes and ordinances of autumn . . . [illegible] in the sixth year [5] be observed. And for the observing of these ordinances and the keeping of these statutes John Fraunk and Richard le Rous [6] . . . are elected.

10   *Newington, Oxon.*   Wednesday, September 20th

Because John le Meister allowed Walter de Ponte of Chaulhampton to

---

[4] A few words are illegible.
[5] 1277. The roll of this year is missing.
[6] Two other names, now indecipherable.

pasture his mare in the meadow of Brockhampton contrary to the form of the law which he cannot do and which is contrary to the statute of the town, therefore the said John is in mercy, 3d.

1291

11 *Newton Longville, Bucks.* Tuesday, June 19th

It is agreed by the lord and the community of the town to observe all the statutes and ordinances of autumn of the preceding years and to keep the aforesaid statutes and ordinances and faithfully to present offenders. There were chosen John Robert, Richard Carlisle, John Gerard, Henry Holden, Geoffrey Hawkins, Henry Robert, Henry le ferrour, Walter H . . . [illegible].

12 *Ripton Regis, Hunts.* Friday, October 31st

The jurors did not present that . . .[7] was a gleaner when she was able to earn half a penny a day and her food. Therefore the said jurors [are in mercy] for concealing this, 10d.

13 *Houghton, Hunts.* Monday, November 10th

From the wife of Peter Wran because she gleaned wrongfully in autumn contrary to the prohibition. She is poor.

Geoffrey of Brinton because he did not bind the lord's grain in autumn as his neighbours did, 6d.

1293

14 *Newington, Oxon.* Wednesday, July 22nd

Robert Tornepeny, Henry atte Hegge [and] Hugh Hobesort are chosen to see to it that no one who does damage in autumn is harboured within the limits of this manor and to see if any women glean who are able to reap, and if any are found guilty of such a thing to notify the bailiff at the next [court].

15 *Therfield, Herts.* Friday, January 30th

From John Aspelon because he carried grain on his horse in bundles without a cart, 6d.

16 *Brightwaltham, Berks.* Wednesday, July 28th

All the lord's tenants are forbidden to pay in the fields with sheaves anyone of the town or any outsider on pain of half a mark.[8]

[7] MS. torn.
[8] No other by-laws enrolled.

1295

17 *Halton, Bucks.* Thursday, June 23rd

It is provided that no one shall look in the fields for beans to eat except between morning and prime, and if anyone looks for them in some other way let him be attached to answer in the lord's court.

18 *Newton Longville, Bucks.* Thursday, August 11th

All the lord's tenants, free and customary, agree to observe all the statutes of autumn which were ordained at the court held on the Saturday next after the Feast of the Apostles Peter and Paul in the eighteenth year of King Edward,[9] and Hugh Robard, John Hervey, John Bouere, Henry Simcan, Ralph Robyns [and] Henry Hakene are elected to see that these statutes are observed and to present [offenders].

1296

19 *Eynsham, Oxon.*[10]

It is ordered that Richard Teofle [11] be distrained because they kept their pigs without iron rings contrary to the by-law in the preceding court.

20 *Hemingford, Hunts.* Tuesday, December 8th

Because it was enacted by the assent of all the customary [tenants] in this village four years ago that if anyone of the aforesaid customers was found guilty of buying beer for more than a halfpenny and [it is found] by inquest that all the customers except William Gargan bought beer for a penny, the sum of which is 8s. And for the present they pay a fine of 20s.

1301

21 *Cuxham, Oxon.* Thursday, June 1st

Robert Waldering to answer to the lord at the next [court] in that against the lord's prohibition he harboured strangers in the lord's pasture contrary to the liberty of the town.

Richard Cook was attached because he harboured a woman, a stranger, who was a malefactor in autumn, contrary to the lord's prohibition.[12]

[9] 1 July 1290. See above, Doc. 8.
[10] Day and month are illegible. There were 26 virgaters and 4 cottagers here; also 20 freeholders, some with tenants of their own. *R.H.*, II, 34 and 859.
[11] And two others.
[12] Robert and Richard were both *nativi*.

1305

22 *Great Horwood, Bucks.* Wednesday, July 28th

It is granted by all the lord's tenants, the free men as well as the villeins, that whoever shall be found guilty of having his mares so tethered that the foals get in the grain of the neighbours shall give the lord 6d. as often as he is found guilty before the Gules of August.[13]

Item it is granted by the same that no one shall go about gathering grain [14] who can earn half a penny a day and his food.

Nor shall anyone harbour such as carry away grain unlawfully.

And to keep and maintain this agreement wardens are elected, namely, Hamon le Brit, William le Franklin, Ralph Margery and Robert Saundres.

1306

23 *Stukeley, Hunts.* Tuesday, February 9th

...[15] chosen as wardens of the field and meadow and sworn to maintain the metes and bounds, in the aforesaid meadow and fields. And to correct defaults of whatever kind that may be found in the aforesaid meadows and fields.

24 *Great Horwood, Bucks.* Wednesday, July 27th

It is granted by the whole township that no one shall accept any outsider as a gleaner in autumn nor any man or woman to glean who is able to earn a penny a day with food.

Nor shall anyone pay in the field with sheaves, only handfuls.

Nor shall anyone reap or cart except by day.

Nor shall anyone allow [his] calves or foals to go into the common [fields of] grain.

Nor shall anyone gather straw in the fields unless [it be] each from his own land.

And if anyone be found guilty in respect of the aforesaid provisions in any way, as often as he is found guilty he shall pay the lord 4d.

And to maintain the aforesaid conservators are chosen, namely, Hamo le Bret, William le Frankelyn, Robert Saundres and Ralph Margery.

1307

25 *Roxhill, Beds.* Wednesday, November 29th

Hugh the merchant was charged with having knowingly harboured ...[16]

[13] August 1st.
[14] i.e. gleaning.
[15] MS. torn.
[16] MS. torn.

the lord's grain and the goods of other men in autumn, contrary to the common ordinance of the whole town, and this he denies and . . . therefore he is in mercy.

1308

26. *Roxhill, Beds.* Saturday, November 16th

Cecilia Pate (1d.) gleaned contrary to the town ordinance and William le Vite (3d.) is surety for her.[17]

1309

27 *Castleacre, Norfolk.* Day and month illegible

Item they present that Margaret Garhole harboured two maid servants who habitually gleaned wrongfully and carried away the grain of the earl and the neighbours in autumn. Therefore she is in mercy, 6d.[18]

1310

28 *Houghton, Hunts.* Thursday, July 9th

Because it appears that in a court held on Thursday, the eve of St Margaret the Virgin in the fifth year of Abbot J[ohn] [19] all the customary tenants mutually bound themselves and undertook on pain of paying 6d. to the lord that none of them would enter the grain of another to root out herbage [*ad herbam eradicandum*]; and if any one was found guilty of this the fine aforesaid would be levied from him. And now at this court all the customers by their own confession are delinquent and guilty [of offending] against the aforesaid ordinance. Therefore it is adjudged that the aforesaid fine be levied from them, namely, from 78 customers and landholders 39s., that is 6d. from each customer.

29 *Great Horwood, Bucks.* Wednesday, July 29th

Alice Baynard for that contrary to the ordinance made by the common consent of the whole township she gathered herbage in the beans of the township and caused it to be gathered she puts herself in mercy, 2d.[20]

---

[17] Four other women and their sureties, identical fines for the same offence.
[18] Six other women were fined 3d., 6d., or 12d. 'because they did the same'.
[19] 19 July 1291.
[20] Thirty others, for the same, 2d., 3d., or 6d. each.

1311

30 *Upwood, Hunts.* Wednesday, November 3rd

And the jurors say that John son of Nicholas reaped his grain by night contrary to the custom of the town, and he took away his grain and the grain of his neighbours, contrary to the ordinance. Therefore etc., 6d.

1314

31 *Great Horwood, Bucks.* Thursday, June 20th

It is agreed and granted by the whole township that no one shall allow [his] calves to go into any grain, meadow etc. henceforth before the Feast of the Annunciation of the Blessed Mary [21] nor shall calves enter into any grain or meadow after the Feast of St Peter in Chains.[22]

And that no one shall gather herbage in any bean [field] henceforth unless in his own etc.

And that no one shall trespass in lotted meadows [*in pratis partibilibus*] etc.

And it is agreed that if anyone shall act against the aforesaid grant etc. he shall straightway pay the lord 4d. for each . . . [illegible].

1315

32 *Cuxham, Oxon.*[23] Friday, August 8th

It is ordered that no sheep shall come into the field sown with wheat this year until the grain has been altogether taken away.

And that no sheep shall come into the field sown with Lenten grain until the Feast of St Michael [24] under pain of 40d.

1316

33 *Great Horwood, Bucks.* Monday, June 28th

It is granted by all the lord's tenants as well free as native that no one of them shall harbour any unknown outsider henceforth under pain of paying 6d. to the lord. And that none of them shall gather beans for his food except between mid-prime and prime on pain of paying 6d. to the same lord, etc.

---

[21] March 25th.
[22] August 1st.
[23] There are very few by-laws to be found in the rolls of Cuxham, which are extensive.
[24] September 29th.

1317

34 *Ripton Abbots, Hunts.* Day and month illegible

From Alice daughter of Stephan because she would not be hired in autumn as was enacted by the by-law [*byrlawe*] 3d.

1318

35 *Newington, Oxon.* Wednesday, September 20th

It is ordered that Thomas Est be distrained to answer to the lord as to why he depastured his pigs in the Lenten field contrary to the lord's prohibition and the ordinance of the neighbours.

1319

36 *Great Horwood, Bucks.* Monday, August 13th

A grant by the community of the town. It is granted and ordered by the whole homage of the town of Great Horwood in the presence of the lord that no one among them male or female be allowed to glean who can earn [his] food and a penny a day for his work.

And also that no one of them shall accept any outsider to glean among them.

And that none of them shall have his grain carted from the field by night.

And that none of them shall pay any one with grain in the field.

And that none of them shall allow his workers to carry any grain from the field as their wages etc.

And that each one of them shall have all openings of all their tenements towards the fields in such a state of repair that wrongdoers cannot enter a field in any part of the town except by the king's highways or the common roads.

And they grant all these on pain of three pence to be paid to the lord for each default etc.

1322

37 *Newton Longville, Bucks.* Wednesday, July 8th

All the customers grant all the autumnal ordinances made in the preceding year with the exception that every one may depasture his beasts between [the selions] of his own growing grain in le Hech'.

And chosen to keep this and present offenders are.[25]

---

[25] No names are recorded.

38 *Great Horwood, Bucks.* Tuesday, August 10th

Ordinance of autumn. It is granted and ordered by the homage of the whole town of Great Horwood in full court that no one of them male or female shall be allowed to glean who is able to earn his food and a penny a day for his work.

And also that none of them shall accept any outsider to glean among them.

And that none of them shall have his grain carted from the field by night.

And that none of them shall pay anyone with grain in the field.

And none of them shall allow his workers to carry any grain from the field on behalf of any one unless it be one of his own *famulae* and this of necessity on behalf of his lord.

And each of them shall have all openings towards the fields of all their tenements [26] so that wrongdoers cannot enter a field anywhere in town except by the royal and common roads.

And all these they grant on pain of 6d. for each default, to be paid to the lord.

And to keep the aforesaid and to present as often as necessary those who break them William Baynard and Hugh the reeve, John Maykyn and John Haryon were chosen by the community of the town and they take oath.[27]

1324

39 *Roxhill, Beds.* Day and month illegible

It is enjoined on all tenants as well free as native that no one shall harbour an outsider or someone known [to him] as a gleaner in autumn who is able to find [employment at] a penny a day and food.

Item that none of them shall harbour an outsider or one known [to him] who damages the grain of the lord or the neighbours.

Item that no one of them shall pay anyone with sheaves in the field under the aforesaid pain.

Item that their beasts shall not enter the stubble until the fields have been cleared [of grain] except on his own land under the pain aforesaid (2s.).

1326

40 *Newington, Oxon.* Thursday, September 4th

The wardens of the statutes of autumn say that, from Newington, Henry

---

[26] i.e., in such a state of repair.
[27] For the by-laws of July 20, 1323, see Doc. 203. In those of July 24, 1325, there are a few minor verbal changes.

le Baker (12d.) has four sheaves [which he] came by in evil manner, contrary to the statute of autumn. And John Costyr' (12d.) harboured the same Henry. Therefore etc. Item they say that John the rector's swineherd (12d.) has four sheaves wrongfully come by, contrary to the statute of autumn, therefore etc. And Isolda . . . (12d.) harboured the same John, therefore etc. Item they say that . . . and his daughter has six sheaves wrongfully come by, therefore etc. And that John . . . (3d.) made default at the great boon day. Therefore etc. And Laurence de Berwick (3d.) harboured the same John. Therefore etc.

41 *Halton, Bucks.* Thursday, July 22nd

Names of the wardens of the statutes of autumn. William West, Thomas Hemmyng, Thomas le Cok, Thomas Godrych, Thomas at the pit, and Robert de Merwell, and the statutes are these.

That no one shall harbour anyone whether an inhabitant or an outsider who is a malefactor in autumn under pain of 6s. 8d.

And that no one shall glean who is able to earn a penny a day and food under the same pain.

And that no one shall have egress over another's ground, and if he has egress over his own ground he shall save his neighbours harmless.

And that no one shall make a way with a cart or otherwise over the grain of another.

And that no one shall cart grain after sunset or before sunrise.

And that none shall enter the stubble with his sheep after harvest before it has been depastured by the other beasts. And all these under the foregoing pains.

And moreover all the aforesaid wardens are charged with the keeping of the autumn works at boon days and with presenting defaults if there are any.

1327

42 *Great Horwood, Bucks.* Wednesday, July 15th

Autumnal ordinance. All the free and customary [tenants] grant all the autumnal ordinances made in the preceding year and under the same pain and adding this, that everyone shall have all his gaps [*brekkas*] and lanes next to the fields by which malefactors can enter repaired, to the end that they will enter by the royal roads so that they can be seen etc.

And John Gerard junior, John Simond, Richard Raynard and John Hiron were chosen to keep these ordinances and present those who break them and they took oath.

1329

43 *Newton Longville, Bucks.* Monday, July 17th

It is granted and ordered by the whole homage of the town of Newington that no one be given leave to glean anything in the said town if he can find any one who wishes to hire him for his food and a penny a day.

Item that no outsider be given leave to glean unless he who harbours him will answer for his deeds.

And that there be no carrying of any grain by night.

And that there be no paying with sheaves in the fields.

And that everyone shall have his stiles and lanes nearest his neighbours so kept that neither the lord nor anyone of his tenants incurs harm because of a defect in the keeping, and if any defect is found they shall answer who are the nearest.

Item that no one shall cause his beasts to pasture in any land under crop before the produce of the acre lying next to it has been wholly removed.

Item that no one shall have any green crop taken from the fields of growing corn after the Gules of August, beans only excepted.

And if anyone shall be found doing anything contrary to the foregoing he shall pay the lord 6d. for each default.

And Robert Hood, Robert Adekynes, John Gerard, John de Stoke are chosen to keep the said ordinances and present those who do the contrary and they take oath etc.

And that no worker shall carry any grain from the fields.[28]

44 *Newton Longville, Bucks.* Wednesday, October 31st

The wardens of the ordinances of autumn present that Alice Dymok (6d.) took grain from the field, contrary to the ordinance.

Walter Cheseman (nil), Walter Vele (nil), Hugh . . . (6d.) paid Margery Frounceys (6d.) with grain in the field, contrary to the ordinance. Therefore they incur the penalty.

Elena Sutor did not take the beans she found in the field to the lord's court [yard] but to her own house. Therefore she is in mercy (3d.).

William de Leighton (1d.) took a sheaf from the field, as was presented by the wardens of autumn. Therefore [he is] in mercy.

1330

45 *Newington, Oxon.* Saturday, January 28th

The wardens of the statutes of autumn present that Roger Martin (6d.)

---

[28] In the margin.

harboured two gleaners [who were] malefactors in autumn. Therefore he is in mercy.

Item Roger Martin (12d.) William atte Touneshende and Alice le Carter (12d.) were malefactors in the pastures with their beasts and depastured the pasture with their sheep contrary to the ordinance of autumn, therefore etc.

Item they present that Alice West (12d.) and John Somer (12d.) depastured the pasture with their sheep, contrary to the statute of autumn. Therefore etc.

Item Ralph le Chapman (6d.) harboured a certain stranger who was a malefactor in autumn, therefore [he is] in mercy.

Item Alice de Sweyns (6d.) and Alice Bert (6d.) harboured strangers wrongfully in autumn.

Item Agnes Wat' (3d.) would not reap and was able to reap, therefore, in mercy, pledge John Price.

46 *Great Horwood, Bucks.* Thursday, August 9th

It is granted and ordered by all the free tenants of the lord of Horwood and also by the whole homage that no one who has lands in the fields sown with beans or peas shall gather the beans or peas of others.

Item that no one shall be allowed to glean who can earn food and a penny or two pence without food if any one wishes so to hire him.

Item that no one of them shall accept an outsider to glean among them.

And that no one of them shall have his grain carted from the fields by night.

Item that no worker shall be allowed to carry grain from the fields.

Item that each one of them shall have suspect gaps and lanes near the fields repaired.

Item that none shall gather stubble in the lands of others until the Feast of St Martin.

And if anyone shall be found transgressing against the foregoing he shall pay the lord 6d. for each default.

And John Gerard, John Asculf, John ffraunk and William Baynard are chosen to present defaulters.

47 *Newton Longville, Bucks.* Monday, August 13th

It is agreed and ordered by the community of the town of Newton that no one who holds land of the lord shall gather beans, peas or vetches in the fields except from land that he has sown. And if anyone is found guilty of acting contrary to this ordinance he shall pay the lord 12d. for each default.

And that every one who wishes to gather beans, peas or such like shall gather them between sunrise and prime.

Item that no one shall cause nor allow his calves to depasture in the fields within the standing grain unherded.

Item that no one shall be accepted as a gleaner who is able to earn food and a penny a day or two pence without food if he finds any one who wants to hire him.

Item that no stranger be accepted as a gleaner unless he who harbours him is willing to answer for his deeds.

Item that no pauper shall gather [beans] inside the selions of beans but only at the ends of the selions and between them. And if they do otherwise they shall lose what they have gathered and not be allowed to go into the fields to gather beans thereafter.

Item that there shall be no carting by night.

Item that no sheaves shall be given in payment in the fields.

Item that each one shall have his stiles and the lanes nearest his neighbours so kept that no damage shall befall the lord or any of the tenants from a default in his upkeep.

Item that no one shall have his beasts depasture in any plot under crop until the produce of one land at least has been wholly removed.

Item that after the Gules of August no one of them shall have herbage taken in the standing grain of others.

And anyone found acting contrary to the [aforesaid] premises shall pay the lord 3d. for each default.

And chosen to attend to these ordinances and to present those who act contrary to them are John Kempe, Robert Hood, Hugh le fferour, William Robin, Robert Carlisle and John Stevenes and they took oath.

1331

48 *Newington, Oxon.* Monday, July 1st

Statutes of Autumn. Brightwell, Robert Coly, Andrew le Smith, Berwick, Thomas Turnepeny, Robert le King, Jr., John Somers, William Appelder'. Brockhampton, John Merson, John Gryce. Newington, Gurm Newman, Tristram Hobeschort, John Goneyr and William Trag.

And the statutes are that no one shall accept any gleaners, male or female, who are able to reap and earn a penny a day and food.

Item no one shall pay anyone with sheaves in the fields unless they reap for sheaves.

Item that sheep shall not go [to pasture] before the larger animals.

And that no one shall have a roadway from his messuages into the common field which causes any one to lose his grain.

Item that no one shall cart by night unless his cart was in the field in the daytime.

And these ordinances are under pain of half a mark.[29]

49 *Newton Longville, Bucks.* Wednesday, July 9th

All the lord's customers grant all the ordinances of autumn made by them in the year preceding with the exception that no one shall have his beasts pasture next to [acres sown with] rye, drage or oats until the produce of a space of two acres has been altogether removed.

And to keep these ordinances and present . . . as often . . . [illegible] Simon Bacon, John Gerard, John Simeon, and William Thomas together with the messor.

50 *Great Horwood, Bucks.* Tuesday, August 6th

All the free tenants together with the customers will and grant all the ordinances ordained for autumn in the year preceding and under the same pain.

And to keep them and to present those who act contrary to them, they choose those who were chosen in the year preceding and they take oath, etc.

1332

51 *Great Horwood, Bucks.* Wednesday, June 26th

It is granted and ordained by the whole township of Horwood that no one shall be allowed to glean who can earn his food and a penny a day if there is any one who wishes to hire him.

And that no stranger be allowed to glean among them.

And that no one of them pay with sheaves in the field nor allow his workers to carry grain from the fields.

Item that every one shall cause all lanes and suspect gaps next to the fields to be stopped up.

Item that no one shall gather stubble in the field from the Feast of St Michael to the Feast of St Martin except in his own land.

Item that no one shall cart in night time.

And if anyone shall be guilty in the foregoing or in any one of them he shall pay the lord 6d. for each default, and chosen to keep these ordinances and to present those who act contrary to them are John Fraunk,

---

[29] On Tuesday, November 20th, the wardens presented two who had broken the first by-law, four, the third, and two, the fifth. Fines 2d. to 12d. Also, a woman was fined 12d. because she was able to reap but gleaned, contrary to the statute.

William Beynard, John Maykin, John Gerrard, Hamund le Crue and Richard son of Ralph. And they take oath.

Item that no one shall go with his beasts into the grain of another unless by the space of ten acres.

Item that no one shall move another's grain to tether his beasts there under the same pain.

52 *Newton Longville, Bucks.* Thursday, July 9th

It is granted and ordered by the homage of the lord of Newton that no one who holds land of the lord shall gather beans, peas, or vetches in a field except from land which he has sown and if anyone is found acting contrary to this ordinance he shall pay the lord 6d. for each default.

And that anyone who wants to gather beans, peas or such like shall gather them between sunrise and the hour of prime.

Item that no one shall have or allow his calves to pasture in the standing grain in the fields without a herdsman.

Item that no one be allowed to glean who is able to earn a penny a day and food, if any one is found who wishes to hire him thus.

Item that no stranger be allowed to glean.

Item that no pauper shall gather beans inside the selions of beans but only at the ends and along the dividing lines of the selions and if they do otherwise they shall lose whatever they have gathered and they shall not be allowed in the fields any more to gather beans in this way.

And that there be no carting at night.

Item that there be no paying with sheaves in the field.

And that everyone shall cause his stiles and lanes nearest his neighbours to be so kept that neither the lord nor any of his tenants suffer damage on this account.

Item that no one of them from now until the end of August shall gather herbage in the standing grain of another.

Item that no one shall cause stubble to be gathered after the grain has been carried from the land until the Feast of St Martin except in his own land.[30]

And if any one shall err against the foregoing he shall pay the lord 6d. for each default except the item on stubble for which each delinquent shall give the lord for each default 3d.

And chosen to watch over these ordinances and present those who act against them are Lyman Bacon, William son of Ivetta, John Walter, John Robsaunt, John Simeon, John Gerard, and the two messors, that is to say, the lord's messor and the messor of the community of the town. And they took oath.

---

[30] This by-law does not appear in previous Newton Longville lists.

1333

53 *Newton Longville, Bucks.* Wednesday, June 30th

All the lord's tenants grant all the autumnal ordinances made in the preceding year, this excepted, that no one shall gather stubble except in his own lands between the Feast of St Michael and the Feast of St Martin next following.

And to keep these ordinances there are elected and sworn the messors Robert Hood, John Walter, John Simeon, and John Gerard.

1335

54 *Newton Longville, Bucks.* Tuesday, July 18th

It is granted and ordained by the community of the township of Newton that all the autumnal ordinances of former times be granted by all the customers by unanimous consent and by the same pain.

And chosen to watch over these ordinances and to present those who act against them are John Walter, John Symon, Henry le fferour, William Cheseman, Robin Hod, William Robyn, John Gerard, and they took oath.

55 *Great Horwood, Bucks.* Friday, August 11th

It was granted by all the free tenants of Horwood and by the whole homage as well that no one shall gather beans in the lands of others who has land in the field sown with peas or beans.

Item that no one shall be allowed to glean who is able to earn food and 1d. or 2d. without food if there is any one who wishes to hire him thus.

Item that no one shall pay with grain in the fields.

Item that no worker be allowed to take grain away from the fields.

Item that each one shall cause suspect stiles and lanes nearest the fields to be repaired.

Item that no one shall gather stubble in the lands of another before the Feast of St Martin.

If anyone shall be found delinquent in regard to the foregoing he shall pay the lord 6d. for each default.

Item it was ordained by the community of the vill on the aforesaid pain that no one shall cause calves or young oxen to pasture in the grain. About this ordinance let the reason de diligently enquired. [*Super quem articulum diligenter inquiratur aliqua de causa.*]

And to keep these ordinances and present defaults there are chosen John Gerard, John Asculf, John Frank, and Richard Rous who did not take oath and did not swear to present.

56 *Newton Longville, Bucks.* Wednesday, October 25th

It was agreed by all the lord's tenants, free and customary, that no one henceforth shall pasture his sheep in another's grain under pain of 12d. for each time it happens.[31]

1337

57 *Great Horwood, Bucks.* Wednesday, July 16th

It is agreed by all the tenants, free and customary, to observe all the statutes of autumn that were ordained in the sixth year [32] and to watch over them John Franklyn, Philip Gerard, Richard Halron and Nicholas Stevens were elected wardens.

1338

58 *Cuxham, Oxon.* Friday, February 6th

It is ordained at this court by the whole homage that every man in the town of Cuxham, free and native, shall tether his horses in the pastures, meadows and fields with ropes from the beginning of the mowing of the meadows until the end of autumn under pain of 2s. for each one of them not tethered.

1339

59 *Newton Longville, Bucks.* Wednesday, July 21st

Ordinance of autumn. It is granted by the lord and his tenants that no one shall pay with sheaves or any grain in the fields in autumn.

And that no one shall be allowed to glean in autumn who is able to earn 1d. a day and food.

And that no one shall cause the grain to be carted before sunrise and after sunset.

And that all stiles roundabout the town be altogether laid aside during autumn under pain of 12d.[33]

And to attend to the aforesaid ordinance there were chosen Hugo Robert, John Gerard, William Thomas, Henry le fferour, William Robyns, Simon Dymmoc.

60 *Great Horwood, Bucks.* Friday, July 3rd

All the lord's tenants, free and customary, agree to keep all the statutes of autumn ordained in the sixth year of the present king and to attend to them there were elected namely John Franklyn, Robert Saunders,

[31] Not previously seen in Newton Longville rolls.
[32] June 26, 1332, see above, Doc. 51.
[33] A very selective list of by-laws. Were they the ones most difficult to enforce?

Richard Rous, Thomas Denys, John Gerard, Nicholas Stevenes, together with William Dyne and John Hildryc the messors.[34]

1340

61 *Brightwaltham, Berks.*   Day and month missing.

At this court all the tenants granted that no inhabitant [*intrinsecus*] shall glean grain within this liberty unless he be under age or over age.

Item that no worker shall go outside this liberty to work without leave.

1341

62 *Newton Longville, Bucks.*   Thursday, July 26th

All the lord's tenants as well free as customary agree to keep the autumnal statutes ordained at the court held on the Monday next before the Feast of St Lawrence in the fourth year of the reign of Edward third from the Conquest [35] and to watch over the aforesaid statutes there were chosen Henry le fferour, Henry Roberd, John le Taylour, John Gerard, William Robyn, John Robank, Robert Carlyl, Edmund le Streete, Richard le Zouge, and they took oath.

63 *Great Horwood, Bucks.*   Friday, July 27th

All the lord's tenants free and customary agree to observe all the autumnal statutes ordained in the sixth year [36] on pain of 6d. for each time anyone is found guilty.

And they add that no one shall come with his sheep into the sown field before the time of reaping under the same pain.

Item that no one shall pasture his beasts in the stubble before it has been reaped to the width of three acres.

Item that no one shall have his animals going into the field without a herdsman under the same penalty.

Item that no one shall cause anyone to glean the grain of another under the same penalty.

Item that if any one of whatever condition shall be found with stolen grain he shall incur the aforesaid pain and the said grain shall be taken from the same and be safely kept in a specified place for the benefit of the church.

And if any offender against the aforesaid ordinances is unable to pay the aforesaid pain let his harbourer answer for him.

---

[34] For July 27, 1340, the entry is the same as the above and the first five wardens are identical with the first five named above; then were added Richard Stevens together with William Cok, messor.

[35] Monday, August 13, 1330. See above, Doc. 47.

[36] June 26, 1332. See above, Doc. 51.

And to well and truly keep the aforesaid statutes there were chosen Richard le Rous, John ffraunc, John Simound, Hamo Baroun, Thomas Denys, John Gerard, together with the two messors, that is to say, William Cok and Richard Bret and Hugh Kyng and they took oath.

1342

64 *Newton Longville, Bucks.* Thursday, April 4th

It is ordained by the lord that no one of his tenants shall have his pigs or piglets outside of his house except under good custody and if any one of them shall not observe the said ordinance that he shall lose his pig together with a substantial amercement.[37]

1343

65 *Great Horwood, Bucks.* Thursday, June 19th

It is granted by all the tenants of the lord as well free as villein that no one shall pasture with his beasts in the meadow of Radmord before the Feast of Pentecost in no year unless they are tethered to stakes and that each shall pasture in his own strip and if he pastures elsewhere he shall pay the lord 6d. for each time he shall happen to be found.

And that at the carting of marl and manure they shall go with their carts in the way they have been accustomed to go from of old.

And that no one who has headlands next to the meadow of Aldern nor anyone else shall pasture there with his beasts before the time that hay has been taken away under the aforesaid pain.

Item that no one shall have his calves in the grain of another under the aforesaid pain nor in the meadow of Alderne.

66 *Great Horwood, Bucks.* Saturday, September 20th [38]

Similarly they present that Rosa Steucele (3d.) Alice Steucele (3d.) and Alice Hayroun (3d.) took stubble in the field of another without paying for it. Therefore they are in mercy because they acted against the ordinance therein. And a day is given the homage to inquire better concerning the aforesaid provision.

And that henceforth no one shall gather stubble unless from his own property unless he shall have bought it, under pain of 2s.

And similarly it is ordered and agreed that no one shall gather the dung of oxen and cows and other animals in the meadow which is called Aldemede under the aforesaid pain.

---

[37] This by-law has not been seen previously at Newton Longville.

[38] The conservators first present a list of twenty-one who 'broke the common ordinance'.

1345

67 *Newington, Oxon.* Wednesday, August 10th

The homage charged under various articles presents that all is well. Item they elect Tristram Hobbeshort, William Trag, John Samuel, John Spark, Robert Kyng, John West, William Sawyer, Philip Proute to keep the autumnal ordinances and it is ordained by the steward that no one shall pay with sheaves in the field nor shall he harbour any malefactor in the foresaid town nor shall he allow anyone, male or female, to glean who is able to earn 1d. a day and food, nor shall he cart at night under pain of half a mark.[39]

68 *Newton Longville, Bucks.* Thursday, August 3rd

All natives are ordered not to make any default of works in autumn when summoned and this under penalty for the first day of 5d. and for the second day of 12d.

Item it is ordered that none of the tenants of the lord shall gather herbage in the lord's grain under pain of 12d. and that they shall not have their beasts pasture in the lord's meadow before the hay in the said meadow has been lifted nor in any of the lord's plots sown with grain before the lord's grain has been carted and this under the aforesaid pain.

It is granted by the lord and also by the free [men] and by the villeins that all the autumnal statutes be observed and also the statutes and ordinances of the eighteenth year of the present king [40] and faithfully to watch over the aforesaid ordinances and present those who are delinquent against them there are chosen Hugh Robert, Henry fferour, John Kente, Walter Hawkins, John Robert and they took oath.[41]

1348

69 *Newington, Oxon.* July 14th

Thomas Turnepeny, Philip atte Grene, John West, Currus Newman, William James, John Spark, William James [*sic*], John Samuel, William Sawyer, Philip Proute were chosen to keep the ordinances of autumn and it is ordained that no one shall cart by night unless on feast days nor shall he hand out sheaves in the field neither as a gift nor as the wages of the messor or the herdsman of the animals nor shall he harbour any

---

[39] Seven of the wardens here named were among those chosen on July 28, 1343. The list of by-laws in 1343 does not include the last one of 1345.

[40] The record of this year is missing.

[41] Note the contrast between items beginning 'it is ordered' and the formula introducing the autumnal statutes.

stranger who is a malefactor or a gleaner who is able to earn 1d. a day and food nor shall he have an open path from his close under pain of half a mark.

70 *Great Horwood, Bucks.* Tuesday, July 15th

All the lord's tenants, free and customary, agree to observe all the autumnal statutes ordained in the year [42] and to attend to these statutes and present those who are delinquent against them there were chosen John ffraunk,[43] . . . John Simond, Thomas Denys, John Gerard, and William Kyng and William Cok, the messor, and they took oath.

71 *Newton Longville, Bucks.* Wednesday, July 16th [44]

All the lord's tenants, free and customary, agreed that if anyone of them shall lead his neighbours away to a tavern outside town that he shall incur the penalty of 12d. for each time anyone of them shall be delinquent against the aforesaid ordinance which is to last for one year.[45]

1349

72 *Great Horwood, Bucks.* Wednesday, April 29th

It is agreed by all the lord's tenants free and customary that none of them shall go gleaning who is able to earn food and 1d. a day under pain of 40d.

Item that no one shall pasture his beasts in the grain unless the grain has been removed by a space of ten acres under the aforesaid pain.

1351

73 *Great Horwood, Bucks.* Tuesday, July 19th

The homage present that Ralph Ricardessone, John Hawkins, John Harris, Thomas Clark, John Isende, Henry le Arblester, John Thorneton, John Baynard and Richard Bikon and William de Berddale are all malefactors with their colts in the grain. Therefore they are in mercy (3d.). And it is ordered that henceforth they shall place their beasts of every kind under good custody both they and all other neighbours under pain of half a mark.

[42] Blotted out. [43] MS. torn.
[44] The former ordinances of autumn were ratified. Robert Carlyl, Richard Palfreyman, John Walter and Walter Bonar with John the messor were elected conservators.
[45] Harvest was impending. It was important for workers not to leave town for any purpose.

1353

74 *Great Horwood, Bucks.*   Tuesday, September 24th

It is agreed by all the lord's tenants as well free as customary that each of them under pain of 40d. shall close all his gaps next to the sown field and in his lanes before the next court.

And that no one shall cause his beasts to be herded in the field under the same pain.

1354

75 *Great Horwood, Bucks.*   Monday, April 28th

All the lord's tenants free and customary agree under pain of 40d. that none of them shall cause his beast of the plough with following foal to be tethered in the grain of a meadow so that it does harm to his neighbours.

Item said tenants agree that no one of them shall have his own herdsman for his beasts but that they will be kept with the common herdsman and if any of them act contrary to this ordinance he shall incur the penalty of half a mark.

Item they agree under the same penalty that none of them shall have calves, foals or any other animal in the field untethered.

1356

76 *Great Horwood, Bucks.*   Monday, April 28th

Autumnal ordinance. It is agreed among all the lord's tenants free and customary that no one among them shall go gleaning who is able to earn a penny and a half or 2d. without food under pain of 2s.

Item that no one shall have his gaps open near the common sown field under the same pain.

Item that no one shall cart his grain nor cause his grain to be carted in autumn in the night time under the same pain.

Item that no one shall allow his colts under one year old to go into the field untethered under the same pain.

1357

77. *Great Horwood, Bucks.*   Thursday, July 7th

It is agreed by all the lord's tenants free and customary that no one in the coming autumn shall go gleaning who is able to earn 1d. a day and food or 2d. without food under pain of 12d. every time he is found trespassing against this ordinance.

Item that no gleaner shall leave the field except by the four highways under the same pain.

Item that no stranger shall be received within the lordship as a gleaner under the same pain.

Item animals of every kind shall be kept in the town after the arrival of the common herdsman from the fields or the wood and they shall be put securely in a house or close to the end that they commit no damage in the fields under the same pain as often as anyone of them is found trespassing.

Item that no one shall cart nor cause his grain to be carted from the field by night.

Item that no one shall allow his colts, horses or beasts of the plough to go into the fields untethered under the same pain.

And to attend to this same ordinance well and faithfully there were elected as wardens Roger Bedford, John Philip, William Zordele, and John Hawkins and they took oath.

1362

78 *Great Horwood, Bucks.*   Monday, May 30th

All the lord's tenants free and customary agree that no one of them shall have any of his animals pasturing in the sown field other than his beasts of the plough until the common meadows are mown, to the end that the common herdsman can go into these same meadows with his beasts under pain of 2s.

And that no one shall have a colt under one year of age in the sown field untethered or unguarded under the same pain to the end that his neighbours suffer no damage.

And that no one tether his beasts of the plough with following foal along the side of any land but always at the end of the land or meadow under the same pain.

1363

79 *Wistow, Hunts.*   Friday, July 14th

It is ordered by the assent of the lord and the community that no one shall have his foals going into the fields until all the grain has been housed under pain of paying 40d. to the lord.

And that no one shall allow his beasts to go among the shocks under pain of 40d.

And that no one shall depasture his horses in the meadow of Chenerith before the Feast of St Michael under pain of 40d.

1364

80 *Great Horwood, Bucks.* Thursday, August 8th

It is ordered by the whole homage that no one of them shall enter the meadow of Oldemede with his animals until all the hay has been carted and if anyone shall be found doing this he shall pay the lord 6d. as a pain as often as he does it.

And for this William Gobyn, John Frankelyn, John Smyth, Ralph Richard were elected and the messor likewise.

It was further ordered by the aforesaid homage that none of them shall trespass with foals, calves, oxen, geese, or any other beasts or animals in the sown fields in autumn until ten acres have been carted and if any one is found doing this he shall pay the lord as a pain 12d. and this voluntarily, and the aforesaid were chosen.

1368

81 *Great Horwood, Bucks.* Wednesday, July 26th

It was ordered by the consent and at the request of the whole court that no one who is able to earn at autumn work 1d. with food or 2d. without food shall go gleaning and if he does the contrary he shall pay 6d. as often as he does it.

And that no gleaner under the same pain shall enter with his gleanings by any way except the king's way.

No one shall go forth to gather pods, peas, or beans who has such of his own unless from his own property under the same pain, and this he shall do between sunrise and prime.

And that no one who is hired for autumn work shall carry any grain on his head or in any other way under the same pain.

Item it is ordered that no one shall tether or pasture any beasts in Oldemede before the Feast of St Peter in Cathedra under the same pain.

And to enforce [*sic*] there were chosen John Frankelyn, John Baynard, Walter Hathwey, John Warner and Richard Rede.

1369

82 *Upwood, Hunts.* Saturday, July 21st

Richard Warbush, John Hawkyn, William Hering, John Walle, John Robin, William Alcok, John Angul, Jr. were chosen to keep the autumn and were sworn.

It is ordered by the assent of the lord and of the whole community that no man shall have his beasts in the stubble from the time the grain is beginning to be reaped until three weeks have passed and longer if the lords agree, unless they be plough horses and even so each one shall be tethered under pain of 40d. to be paid to the lord.

1373

83 *Elmley Castle, Worcs.*[46]   Saturday, August 13th

It is ordered by the assent of all the lord's tenants free and native that no one of them shall place his beasts untethered in the field called le Leyre Wyndmillefurlong, ffulardeys furlong and the furlong under Benhull before the grain has been fully removed and carted under pain of 40d.

1374

84 *Great Horwood, Bucks.*   April 26th

By the assent of the whole homage it is ordered for the present that no one shall enter the uncultivated land of the lord to pasture until assignment has been made to each one by reasonable assent and this under pain of each one breaking this ordinance of paying to the lord 12d. etc.

Item it is ordered by the same homage that no one shall depasture the pasture of anyone else nor shall he put his beasts to pasture on the pastures or the uncultivated lands of another without the leave of him to whom the pasture belongs before the Feast of the Nativity of St John the Baptist [47] under pain of 12d. to be paid to the lord.

1376

85 *Elmley Castle, Worcs.*   Friday, July 10th

The wardens of the by-law [*berlawe*] of the town of Elmley, that is to say Thomas White, Walter Hamond, Walter Norton, Adcock de Crediton ... to keep and to present at the next court defaults of the by-law.

1378

86 *Warboys, Hunts.*   Tuesday, July 6th

It is ordered that no one henceforth shall have sheep or foals pasturing in the meadow within the grain under pain of 40d.

Simon Hy', John the Miller, William Baroun, John Wulles, Jr., Henry Norbaggh, William Henry, William Colvyl and John ffoster, Richard Plumbe are chosen ... [*sic*].

And that no one depasture with his beasts in the stubble of the community before the Feast of the Nativity of the Blessed Mary under pain of 40d.

---

[46] The extant rolls of this manor begin in 1347 but this is the first by-law to be recorded. The Earls of Warwick were lords of the manor in the thirteenth century but in 1487 it passed to the crown.

[47] June 24th.

And that no one shall go outside the town in autumn to work for higher pay until all the lord's grain has been fully housed under pain . . . [sic].

1379

87 *Halton, Oxon.* Wednesday, November 16th

John Peygnaunt, Thomas Woodward and Thomas at the pit, wardens of the by-laws [*Belawes*] present that Roger Marewell (2d.) John Chatt (2d.) William Martin (2d.) William Meredene (2d.) have their sheep in the stubble in autumn time before the plough-beasts have depastured it and against the ordinance of autumn. Therefore they are in mercy.

And that Alice servant of Alice Ceram paid Marjorie Haket one sheaf against the said ordinance wherefore she is in mercy (8d.) and that Matilda Trystram (3d.) stole four sheaves in autumn therefore she is in mercy.

1385

88 *Great Horwood, Bucks.* Monday, May 15th

It was ordered by the assent of the whole homage that for the present no one shall depasture the pasture of others nor put his beasts to pasture on the pasture or uncultivated lands of others without the leave of him to whom the pasture belongs before the Feast of the Nativity of St John the Baptist under pain of everyone who breaks this agreement within the demesne paying the lord 4d.

89 *Launton, Oxon.*[48] Wednesday, September 13th

The reeves of autumn, sworn, present that inasmuch as it was ordered in full court by the whole homage that all who work on feast days or by night shall pay the lord, each one of them, 6d., less if in the opinion of the said reeves the trespass has been less, and that the said reeves shall have for their work in this regard the third penny etc. And that the following persons separately have transgressed against the ordinance aforesaid, therefore it is adjudged that each shall pay as appears etc.[49]

---

[48] Given to the abbey of Westminster in 1065 by Edward the Confessor there were $35\frac{3}{4}$ virgates and 9 cotlands in the thirteenth century, all occupied by the customary tenants, there being no freeholder here before the fifteenth century. The two-field system remained unchanged to the end of the sixteenth century apparently. For a detailed study of the manorial economy see the article by Barbara Harvey in *Victoria County History Oxfordshire*, Vol. VI (1959), 234–240.

[49] Twenty-two are named and fines are listed of 2d., 3d., or 6d. each.

1387

90 *Newton Longville, Bucks.* Thursday, August 1st

By the assent of the whole homage it is ordered that no one henceforth shall go gleaning in autumn who is able to earn 1d. a day with food under pain of 2d. for each default.

Item that no one shall tether his beast of the plough with foal except at the side of a plot of grain under the same penalty.

And that no one shall allow any animals to pasture in the fields untethered unless they are herded, under the same pain.

And that no one shall pasture beasts untethered unless at a distance of ten acres from the grain under the aforesaid pain.

And that no one shall enter the stubble with his pigs or sheep while the large animals are pasturing there and anyone who is found a trespasser shall suffer this pain aforesaid as often as he is found and it shall be taken by the wardens of this same pain etc.

Stephen Bacon, Henry Veel, John Robert and William Querndon are chosen wardens of this same pain and sworn.[50]

1388

91 *Great Horwood, Bucks.* May 18th

By the assent of the whole homage it is agreed and ordered that no one shall enter the pasture called Stockyng with pigs or sheep before the Feast of St Peter which is called in Chains under pain for each transgressor of 4d.

Item that no one shall enter any separable pasture which has not already been depastured or broached nor shall he depasture this side the Nativity of St John the Baptist with any beasts before the aforesaid Feast of St Peter under the same pain etc.

Item that no one shall enter the meadow beyond Aldemedebrok with pigs and sheep before the Feast of the aforesaid St Peter under the same pain.

And that if anyone by his own will shall allow any of his animals to pasture in the aforesaid meadow for one continuous day and night before the aforesaid Feast he shall incur the aforesaid penalty.

And for this there are chosen as wardens Richard Bedeford, and William Magge and they are sworn etc.

92 *Newton Longville, Bucks.* Friday, July 24th

It is ordered by the assent of the whole homage that no one shall go

---

[50] At a court held Wednesday, June 27, 1386, the first four of the above by-laws appear almost word for word but the last one does not. In 1386 the wardens were William Hichcock, John Haukyn, John Rous and John Herryes, Sr.

gleaning in autumn so long as the lord or any other wishes to pay him for his labour 1d. a day with food.

And that no one shall tether or cause any work beast with foal to be tethered at the side of any plot of grain but only at the end and if there be only one acre of grain he shall not tether either at the side or at the end and this under pain of 2d. for each default.

That no one shall pasture his great beasts next to the grain unless there be a space of 14 acres in width and this under the same pain etc.

That no one shall pasture nor allow any sheep or pigs to pasture next to any grain unless there be a space of twenty acres in width and this under the aforesaid pain.

And this [sic] as often as any one is found or apprehended trespassing against the aforesaid ordinance by the wardens of the same pain etc.; for which Stephen Bacon, William Hichecok, John Robaunce, John Molle on behalf of Westthorp and John Bryewell, Hugh Bacon, John Coupere and John Hichecoke on behalf of Estthorp were chosen and sworn etc.

1389

93   *Great Horwood, Bucks.*

By assent of the whole homage it is agreed and ordered that no one shall depasture the selions in the fallow field with any animal great or small until the meadow has been mown.

And that everyone may pasture his animals in his separable field and on his own ground until the Feast of the Nativity of St John the Baptist and after the aforesaid Feast every one shall pasture with his animals as has been the manner and custom from of old within this demesne.

And that one-year-old foals and calves shall not pasture in the field or the meadows without good herding.

And that no one shall tether a beast of the plough with foal along the side of a plot but only at the end of the same, and this under pain of each trespasser aforesaid 4d.

And that no one shall enter a certain pasture called le Stokyng with his sheep before the Feast of St Peter which is called *ad Vinculum* [sic] under the aforesaid pain.

And for this there were chosen as wardens John Warin, John Baynard, Richard Churchey and Robert Coupere and they were sworn etc.

94   *Great Horwood, Bucks.*   Tuesday, August 3rd

By assent of the whole homage it was agreed and ordered that no one shall enter the field to reap wheat or rye or oats before the Feast of the Assumption of the Blessed Mary next to come under pain for each default of 40d.

And no one shall go gleaning in autumn who is able to earn 1d. a day with food under the aforesaid pain etc.

95 *Launton, Oxon.*   Saturday, September 25th

All the customary tenants have a day to make and repair their road through the middle of the town before the next court to be held here and this under pain for each man of 12d.

And it is arranged among the customary tenants of this town that le Sladgate be made before the Feast of Easter under pain of 40d.

And that no one shall come with his beasts into Waldfeld before the Feast of Pentecost under pain of 6d.

And that no one shall make a way with his animals or beasts through the middle of his garden before the Feast of St Peter in Chains in such a way that his neighbours suffer damage under pain if it shall happen of 6d. to be levied to the use of the lord etc.

1390

96 *Warboys, Hunts.*   November 1st

And they [the jurors] say that Magota Goffe (3d.) gleaned wrongfully in autumn.

And that Agnes ffree (3d.) left town in August to earn higher pay contrary to the statute.

It is ordered also that no one shall depasture with his beasts in the pathways and roads of the community inside the grain from the Feast of Easter until the Feast of Trinity under pain . . .[51]

It is ordered also in the same way concerning the eastern field of Caldecote through the same period of time and under the same pain.

97 *Elmley Castle, Worcs.*   August 16th

It is ordered by all the tenants free and native that no one shall place cadavers in a certain lane called Parsoneslane under pain for each one so doing of 20d.[52]

Item they present that John Smith (2d.) agisted three geese, Richard Cyryng (2d.) agisted three geese in the brook of the town contrary to the ordinance called Beelawe made therein. Therefore they are in mercy.

---

[51] MS. torn.

[52] The cadaverers reported that 24 sheep, 7 hoggets and 2 pigs had died since the Feast of the Purification (February 2nd)—no one to blame.

1391

98 *Broughton, Hunts.* Tuesday, July 11th

And that William Asbloan, Thomas Thewall, William Everard, and John Schepherd, Sr. were chosen wardens of autumn.

And it is ordered that henceforth no one shall depasture with his animals within the grain of the community until all the grain in one plot has been fully housed under pain of 40d.

99 *Wistow, Hunts.* Tuesday, July 18th

It is ordered that no one shall work in autumn on the days or on the eves of feasts.

Nor shall anyone depasture with his sheep in the stubble before the Feast of the Blessed Mary under pain of 2s.

100 *Warboys, Hunts.* Wednesday, July 19th

It is ordered that no one shall depasture with his sheep within the grain and [sic] in Wodemead and in all other pastures until the grain has been fully housed under pain of 40d.

And that no one shall have his foal in the grain of the community untethered under the same pain.

And that no one shall depasture his beasts in the stubble of the community before the Feast of Michael [sic] under pain of half a mark. William Colvyll, John Brounyng, Jr., Robert Vlynes, Robert Colle, John Willeg, Jr., and Richard Munro, Jr. were chosen wardens of autumn.

101 *Elmley Castle, Worcs.* Saturday, August 1st

It is ordered by all the tenants free and native that no one shall allow his animals of any kind in the wheat fields of the demesne under pain for anyone so doing of paying the lord 12d.

Item it is ordered by the same tenants that no one shall allow his beasts in the fields of the tenants before twenty acres of grain at least have been harvested under pain of each one so doing paying the lord 12d.

Item it is ordered by the same tenants that from now on no pigs shall pasture in the meadows of the lord or of his tenants under pain of each transgressor paying the lord 12d.

Edmund . . .[53] Richard Dyryng, Richard Cole and John Reynard are chosen and sworn to keep the aforesaid bylaw [*bylawes*].

Item it is ordered by all the tenants as well free as native that if any

---

[53] Illegible.

one shall allow his ducks in the town brook which . . . he shall forfeit to the lord through the reeve from now on and for the proceeds . . .[54] to the lord in his account and the reeve is now sworn.

102 *Great Horwood, Bucks.* Wednesday, August 2nd

By the assent of the whole homage it is agreed and ordered that no one shall enter the meadows with pigs or sheep before the end of autumn and this under pain of 4d. from each one in default.

Item that no one shall enter into the field of grain so long as any grain remains in the aforesaid field by the space of one land [*stadium*] and this under the pain aforesaid.

Item that no one shall go gleaning who is able to earn 1d. and food and this under the aforesaid pain etc.

1395

103 *Podington, Beds.* Tuesday, August 1st

It is ordered at this court that no tenant shall have beasts of the plough with foal following them this autumn under pain of 40d. to be paid to the lord.

And that no one shall agist his own beasts of the plough in the lord's grain under the pain aforesaid.

And that no one shall transport any grain outside the fields after the time of carting under the pain aforesaid.

And that no one shall glean [*coligat spicas*] in autumn if there is any one who wants to hire him at 1d. a day and food under the pain aforesaid.

1397

104 *Great Horwood, Bucks.* Thursday, May 31st

By assent of the whole homage it is agreed and ordered that no one of them shall have his beasts or cattle in the meadow, pastures or pathways in the sown field or in the fallow field unless on his own property between this and the Nativity of St John the Baptist.

And that none of them shall have sheep in the sown fields between now and the Gules of August under pain of every transgressor every time 4d.

And there were chosen as wardens William Magge, Richard Twechyn and Richard Banard and they took oath.

---

[54] Illegible.

1398

105 *Elmley Castle, Worcs.* Friday, July 19th

Ordinaces for autumn.

It is ordered by all the tenants of Credeshe that none of them allow their sheep or pigs to go in the fields of the lord during autumn under pain of 2s.

And that no one shall allow his horses to go in the fields day or night in the aforesaid time unless they are tethered under pain of 6d.

And it is ordered by all the tenants of Elmley that if anyone allows any of his beasts to go into the grain of the lord in autumn time he shall pay the lord for each time 6d.

And that if any one breaks or makes a way beyond Eldebery without leave he shall pay the lord for each time 12d.

1401

106 *Newton Longville, Bucks.* Monday, August 1st

Ordinance. It is ordered by the assent of the whole homage for the present that no one shall enter the fields of grain with his sheep by the space of ten acres until the end of autumn.

And that no one shall allow his calves in the aforesaid time to pasture at large without a herdsman unless they be tethered and this under pain of 8d. for each default, 4d. to holy church and 4d. to the lord.

And for this there were chosen as wardens John Bryewell, John Cook, Hugh Bacon, John Haukyn, Richard Crurdy, Richard Zauge, John Bouere and John Godwine and they were sworn.

107 *Launton, Oxon.*[55]

It is ordered by the lord and the tenants that all who work on feast days or by night or who do damage in the grain, the meadows, and the pastures ought to be amerced according to the gravity of the default, of which the third penny belongs to the said reeves and two pennies belong to the lord, and those who work by night shall be amerced at 3d. to the use of the lord.[56]

1403

108 *Halton, Bucks.* Saturday, August 1st

It is ordained by the community of the whole township that no one of

---

[55] Day and month missing.

[56] The four reeves of autumn presented a dozen offenders. In 1410 and in 1411. the same by-law was repeated word for word and the reeves say they have nothing to present 'because none made default'.

them shall pay anyone in the field with any sheaves but if they wish to pay any one with sheaves they shall do so in their own dwelling and not elsewhere under pain of each transgressor 12d.

And that no gleaner [*collector spicarum*] shall carry any grain outside the field before sunrise or after sunset under the aforesaid pain.[57]

1405

109 *Broughton, Hunts.* Tuesday, July 14th

William Ashlond, John Catoun, Jr., William Guerard and John Brenwell, Jr. were elected to the office of reeves of the field and they took oath.

It is ordained by the lord and the whole homage that none shall enter the field to mow, reap or cart any grain henceforth through the whole of autumn neither in the evening nor in the morning so long as it is night under pain for each one of 40d.

And that no one shall trample the stubble of another with any beasts during the whole of autumn until the Feast of St Michael unless it be each one on his own land under the pain aforesaid.

And that none shall pasture with any beasts between the grain in any field until the grain has been removed fully for the space of one land under the aforesaid pain.

110 *Houghton, Hunts.* Tuesday, July 14th

Richard Carter, John Gerard, William Aleyn and Robert Uptoun were elected to the office of reeves of autumn and they were sworn.

It was ordered both by the lord and by the whole homage that no one should gather quisquilias [odds and ends, rubbish] except on his own land under pain of 2s.

And that none shall pasture any beasts in the grain of the lord or his tenants before the grain has been harvested and fully housed by the space of one land under pain of 20d.

And that no one shall pasture with his sheep or his pigs in a certain pasture called heyfurlong before the Feast of St Martin under pain of 40d.

And that no one shall glean [*conspicabit*] through the whole of autumn who is able to earn 1d. a day and food under pain of 12d.

And that no one shall tether or pasture any beasts in the wheat stubble before the Feast of St Michael but every one on his own stubble under pain of 2s.

---

[57] Re-enacted word for word on June 10, 1404.

111 *Upwood, Hunts.*[58]

Thomas Perry, William Chamberlain, Richard Payn and Nicholas Alston were chosen by the whole homage to the office of reeves of autumn and sworn.

It is ordered at this court by the lord and by the whole homage that no one shall pasture or tether any beasts in the lord's wheat stubble until two weeks after [the grain] has been fully housed nor in the stubble of any of the lord's tenants until one week under pain of 12d.

And that no one shall glean through the whole of autumn who is able to earn 1d. a day and food under the aforesaid pain.

112 *Great Horwood, Bucks.* Thursday, November 26th

It is ordered by all the tenants both free and native that no one within the demesne shall brew henceforth when there is a church tavern to the end that no injury or harm can befall the church under pain of 6s. 8d. of which 3s. 4d. to the use of the church and 3s. 4d. to the use of the lord.[59]

And that no one shall drive the draught beasts of his neighbours outside his pasture under pain of 40d.

1406

113 *Great Horwood, Bucks.* Wednesday, July 26th

Ordinance. It is ordained at this court by all the tenants both free and native that no one who is able to earn next autumn 4d. a day and food shall go outside this town to work for any one under pain of 6s. 8d.

That no one shall go about gleaning [*transiet ad spicandum*] who is able to earn 1d. a day and food under the aforesaid pain.

And to observe these ordinances and to present [offenders] at the court next after the Feast of St Michael there were chosen as wardens Robert Tayllour and Richard Tayllour and they took oath.

And that no one shall have his beasts staying on the green [*super le Grene*] henceforth by night on the pain of 6d. for each transgressor.

And to attend to this ordinance there were chosen Richard Churchey and William Hoggs and they took oath.

---

[58] Day and month missing.
[59] This by-law appears again, verbatim, November 26, 1416. On October 29, 1425, and November 12, 1426, it reads as follows: 'Ordinance for the church. It is ordained by all the tenants and commanded by the lord that no one shall brew when there is a church brew under pain of half a mark of which 40d. to the lord and 40d. to the fabric of the church.'

114 *Newton Longville, Bucks.*   Monday, July 26th

Ordinance of Autumn. At this court it was ordered by all the tenants free and native that no one this autumn shall pasture his beasts or sheep or pigs on his own grain by the space of ten acres [*sic*].

Item no one shall tether his mares with foals along the side of any land of the neighbours but at the end of the land.

And that no one who is able to earn 1d. a day and food shall glean under pain of 4d. for each transgressor.

And to keep these ordinances and make presentments at the next court after autumn there were chosen William Hychechoc, Henry Tye, Nicholas Hychecoc and John Harys and they were sworn.

1407

115 *Great Horwood, Bucks.*   Thursday, July 24th

At this [court] it is ordained by all the tenants that no one shall have his beasts staying on the green by night under pain of 4d. And William Hoggeset, John Willyam, Jr., were chosen and sworn to present transgressors.

Item it is ordained that no one who is able to earn 1d. a day and food in autumn shall go gleaning under pain for each transgressor of 3d.

And when they go gleaning they shall enter the town by the royal way and not through gaps.

And they shall not go gleaning before sunrise or after sunset under the aforesaid pain.

And to keep these ordinances there were chosen the constable and John Gaynard, Sr. and they were sworn to present malefactors.

And it is ordained that no one shall tether between the sheaves by a space of three acres under the pain *infra scripta*.

And that no one shall tether his work beasts with foal along the length of any land of the neighbours under the pain aforesaid.

And to keep this ordinance there were chosen John Baynard and William Heyges and they were sworn to present malefactors at the next court.

1408

116 *Great Horwood, Bucks.*   Friday, April 20th

Plebiscite [*plesbiscitum*]. It is ordained by all the tenants free and native that no one shall have beasts or animals to pasture unless tethered in the separable grass of his neighbours before the Feast of St Peter in Chains under pain of each transgressor . . .

And no one shall allow his beasts to be by night in the street unherded nor outside a close until the end of autumn under the aforesaid pain.

And no one shall tether his work beasts with foals along the length of any sown land of his neighbours under the aforesaid pain.

And to keep this ordinance and present transgressors to the next court there were chosen ... John Baynard, John Haukyn, John Wichan Jr., and they took oath.

1409

117   *Hemingford, Hunts.*   Thursday, October 31st

It is ordained by the lord and the whole homage that no one shall pasture his sheep nor place foals in le shepcotefielde between lands that are sown under pain to the lord 20d. and the church 20d.

Item it is ordered also that no skilled labourer [*artificarius laborarius*] shall take more per day than 1d. and food before the Feast of the Purification of the Blessed Mary (February 2nd), under pain of 40d.

1410

118   *Wistow, Hunts.*   Thursday, July 17th

It is ordered by the lord and the whole homage that each tenant shall fill the pits which he made in the low way [*loway*] under pain for each one of 12d.

Item that no one shall let his colts go loose so they are taken in the grain from the Feast of St Peter in Chains (August 1st) to the Nativity of the Blessed Mary (September 8th) under pain of 7d.

And that no sheep shall be allowed in the meadow at Wyldbrigg next to the meadow of the rector before the Feast of the Nativity of the Blessed Mary under pain each one of 4d.

And that each tenant of Wistow shall mend the road next to his land with stones before the Feast of St Michael under pain each one of 12d.

And that no one shall mow or dig in the fen near the boundary ways by a width of three acres under pain each one of 40d.

And that no one shall glean in autumn who is able to earn 1d. a day and food under pain each one of 12d.

And that no one shall tether or pasture beasts in the wheat stubble this side the Feast of the Nativity of the Blessed Mary under pain each one of 12d. The jury of Wistow elect Robert Waryn, John Randolf, William Becker and Thomas ffraunces reeves of autumn and they were sworn.

It is ordained that none of Ravele [60] shall enter the wheat stubble with any animals this side the Feast of the Nativity of the Blessed Mary under pain of 12d.

[60] A hamlet of Wistow.

It is ordered also that no one shall put his foals in the grain this side the Feast of the Nativity of the Blessed Mary.

Item the jurors elect John Owey and John Hysche autumnal reeves and they were sworn.

119 *Newington, Oxon.* Friday, July 25th

John Parmenter and William Teukesbury of Brookhampton, John Vyric and John Champyon of Berwick, Richard Wem, John Benet of Newington were ordained wardens of the statutes of autumn in the aforesaid town, that is to say, that no one shall be allowed to glean who is able to earn 1d. a day nor is any one allowed to have his sheep preceding the great beasts in the stubble nor can any one have pigs going about anywhere in the fields of the said town unless in the keeping of the common swineherd of the said town.

1411

120 *Warboys, Hunts.* Saturday, July 25th

It is ordained that no one shall mow in the meadow from the beginning of autumn until the lord makes an end [of the prohibition] under pain . . .[61]

And that no one shall go forth from town to work before autumn shall end under pain of 40d.

And that no one shall glean in autumn who is able to earn 1d. a day and food under pain of 12d.

And that no one shall go with his animals into the stubble between the shocks before it has been raked under pain of 40d.

And that no one shall send his animals into the wheat stubble except the mares under pain of 2s.

And that no one shall send his foals into the grain loose during autumn under pain of 40d.

121 *Elmley Castle, Worcs.* Tuesday, August 11th

It is ordained by the whole homage that no beasts or pigs shall be kept or pastured in the stubble in the aforesaid fields of Elmley until thirty selions have been cleared under pain of each one doing the contrary as often as he does it, 4d.

Item that no one shall glean [*colliget manipulas*] in the aforesaid field any kind of grain before the tenants shall gather [the sheaves] in ricks [*in tassis*] and clear all the selions under pain of each one doing the contrary 4d. as often as he does it. Wardens of the aforesaid ordinance Thomas Creweman, William Hardy.

[61] Illegible.

122 *Burwell, Cambs.* Day and month illegible.

It is ordered by the lord and by the whole homage that no one henceforth shall have or pasture any foals in the grain or grass of the community whether of the lord or of his tenants under pain for each one of 2s.

And that no one henceforth shall pasture sheep or pigs in the meadows within the grain of the community as above under pain each one of 40d.

And that no one shall pasture with sheep or pigs through the whole of autumn or until the grain shall have been removed and raked by the space of one land under the aforesaid pain.

And that no one shall glean through the whole of autumn who is able to earn 1d. a day and food under the aforesaid pain.

And that no one shall leave town [*deuillabit*] in time of autumn who is able to earn 1d. a day as above.

And that no one shall pasture nor trample any stubble with any animals during autumn before the Feast of the Nativity of the Blessed Mary next to come, under pain of 40d.

Again it is agreed and ordered as appears in the preceding court more fully that no one henceforth through the whole of autumn shall cart any grain away from the field by night nor shall he transport it in any other way neither in the evening nor in the morning while it is still night under pain each one of paying the lord 40d. without mitigation.

1412

123 *Elmley Castle, Worcs.*[62]

Ordinance of By-Laws. [*Belawes*]

It is ordered in court before the steward by the assent of the whole homage that if any one shall pasture any beasts in the stubble in autumn before twenty selions at least have been cleared of sheaves he shall pay the lord 4d. for each transgression.

Item that if any one shall pasture any sheep or pigs in the stubble in autumn time before forty selions at least have been cleared of sheaves he shall pay the lord 4d. for each transgression.

Item that if any one shall tether any horse or work animal in the fields in autumn by night he shall pay the lord 4d. for each transgression.

Item if any one shall tether any work animal with foal in autumn, not tethered, next to the grain by day or by night he shall pay the lord 4d. for each transgression.

Item that no gleaner shall gather grain in autumn who is able to earn 1d. a day and food under pain of each transgressor paying the lord 4d.

Item that no gleaner shall gather grain in autumn until the sheaves

---

[62] Day and month missing.

have been fully carried away from the land under pain each delinquent of paying 4d. to the lord.

The wardens of the aforesaid ordinances namely Walter Chowry, John Monfford, William Handy, John Gallahnay, and Thomas Crewman.

124 *Upwood, Hunts.* Saturday, July 25th

John Onty [63] was chosen to the office of reeve of autumn and took oath.

It is ordained that no one shall pasture with any beasts in the wheat stubble before the Feast of St Michael next to come under pain each one of 12d.

And that no one through the whole of autumn shall pasture his foals in the fields before the grain has been fully gotten in under the aforesaid pain.

And that no one shall glean through the whole of autumn who is able to earn 1d. a day and food under the aforesaid pain.

And that no one shall mow reeds in the marsh of Upwood before the Feast of St Michael next to come under pain each one of 40d.

And that no one shall mow, reap or cart or do any autumnal work on feast days through the whole of autumn under pain each one of 40d.

And that no one shall cart any grain by night during autumn under the aforesaid pain.

125 *Warboys, Hunts.* Tuesday, October 4th

It is ordained that no one shall go forth from town to work for high pay [*pro excessivo salario*] under pain of 40d.

And that no one shall send his cart into the gardens [*ortia*] of the neighbours nor shall he move alestakes under pain of 20s.

And that no one shall mow reeds in the marsh from the Feast of St Michael to the Feast of the Invention of the Holy Cross, under pain of half a mark.

And that no one shall keep any tenant out of his common in the croft in stray time.

126 *Elmley Castle, Worcs.* Friday, October 14th

The wardens present that John Dynby (4d.) and Walter Swan (4d.) Roger Shepharde (4d.) broke the ordinance concerning the clearing of twenty selions in autumn. Therefore they incur the penalty made therein.

Item they present that Edith Mileward (4d.) Alice Depyng (4d.) and Marjorie Colwyle (4d.) common gleaners of grain in autumn broke the

---

[63] And six others.

ordinances as appears in the preceding court. Therefore they incur the pain made therein.

Item they present that Walter Hert (4d.) broke the ordinance concerning the twenty selions as above. Therefore he incurs the penalty made therein.

1415

127 *Great Horwood, Bucks.* Tuesday, June 4th

Pains enacted for pasture. It is ordained by all the tenants free and native that no one within the demesne shall have mares tethered along the side of any sown land under pain of 12d.

And that no one shall tether nor pasture his beasts upon the pasture of any ... [64] before the Feast of the Nativity of St John the Baptist under pain of 4d.

And that no one shall tether nor pasture upon the separable grass of the neighbours before the Feast of St Peter in Chains under the pain aforesaid.

And to attend to these ordinances and present transgressors at the next court there were chosen the messor Robert Churchey and William Cordall'.

128 *Halton, Bucks.* Wednesday, September 25th

The plebiscites of autumn are to be observed this year in manner and form as was the usage before and to attend to this John Haukyn, John Makyn, Jr. were elected and they were sworn to present delinquencies and to be watchful in all things.

1416

129 *Elmley Castle, Worcs.*

It is ordered that no tenant shall have ducks criss-crossing and using the common water in the town of Elmley this year before the Feast of St Michael next to come under pain for each delinquent of 1d. Wardens William Denmell and Nicholas Bonde.

130 *Newington, Oxon.* Saturday, May 23rd

Berwick. The homage there presents that William Erliche and John Chillebury were chosen wardens of the by-laws [*lez bilawes*] there namely to present that if there be anyone who is able to earn 1d. a day and food in autumn time and refuses this and goes about gleaning and

---

[64] Illegible.

if there be any tenant there who has his pigs going about anywhere except in the keeping of the common warden of the same town.

Newington. John Berry and Thomas Chillebury were chosen wardens of the by-laws there.

Brookehampton. The homage there present that all is well.

131 *Elmley Castle, Worcs.* Saturday, July 25th

Ordinances. It is ordained by the assent of the lord's tenants that no one shall pasture his beasts in dyke furlong in autumn before twenty selions shall be cleared of sheaves under pain for each delinquent of 4d.

And that no one of them shall pasture pigs or sheep in a furlong before forty selions shall be cleared of sheaves under pain for each delinquent of 4d.

And that no one of them shall pasture his beasts in the meadow called Hultmede and Brodemede before the hay has been carried from it under pain each one of 4d.

And that no one shall glean [*spicarum coligat granum*] in autumn until the sheaves have been fully carted under pain each one of 4d.

Wardens ... Trewman, William Handy, Thomas Gibe, Thomas ...[65]

1417

132 *Great Horwood, Bucks.* Thursday, November 18th

At this court it is ordered that no one henceforth for the present year shall have his beasts or his work animals pasturing outside of his own pasture before the Feast of St Peter in Chains under pain each transgressor of 4d.

And that no one shall allow his beasts or his work animals nor his sheep to pasture on the roadways next to Olde Mede under the aforesaid pain.

And that the son of John Baynard and John Bedeford are chosen wardens of this ordinance and they took oath.

1422

133 *Newton Longville, Bucks.* Thursday, October 29th

It is ordained by free and natives alike that no one shall pasture nor tether his animals henceforth upon the ways and separable balks within the sown fields before the Feast of Pentecost next to come under pain of 12d.

And that no one shall pasture upon the pasture of another before the Feast of the Nativity of St John the Baptist under the pain aforesaid.

And that each one shall find his food for the herdsman of the beasts as is fitting under the pain aforesaid.

[65] Robert Cole crossed out.

1426

134 *Newton Longville, Bucks.* Wednesday, February 6th

Item it is ordered as well by the lord as by all the tenants that William Harryis nor anyone else henceforth within the demesne shall have or hold more than 100 sheep for one virgate of land and he who holds two virgates of land shall have 200 sheep and he who holds more shall have more and he who holds less shall have less. And he who does the contrary shall lose to the lord as many more as he has. And in the meantime the lord shall have his pleasure of them.

1428

135 *Upwood, Hunts.* Monday, August 2nd

It is placed in pain that no one shall tether mares with loose foals in the field under pain of 12d.

And that no foals shall follow the carts in the fields in autumn under pain of 12d.

And that no pigs or sheep shall come into the field without leave of the reeves of autumn under pain of 12d.

And that no one shall glean who is able to earn 1d. a day and food under pain of 12d.

And that no beasts shall come into the wheat stubble before the Feast of the Nativity of the Blessed Mary under pain of 12d.

And that no one shall come in le ffrith before the hay has been taken away under pain of 40d.

1429

136 *Great Horwood, Bucks.* Saturday, November 26th

At this court a place was assigned as well by the lord as by all the tenants for the making of a pin fold, namely, upon the green opposite the tenement of William Knight namely ten feet between the aforesaid tenement and the aforesaid pin fold and the aforesaid pin fold shall be twenty-eight feet long and as many wide and it shall stay there forever.

1430

137 *Broughton, Hunts.*[66]

It is placed in a pain that no one shall take away grain or herbage from the field of grain under pain of 12d. and 12d. [to the lord and to the church].

And that no one shall trample the grain nor the herbage in leading four or five horses together under pain of 12d. and 12d.

And that no one shall depasture in the wheat stubble before the Feast of St Michael under pain of 20d. to the lord and 20d. to the church.

[66] Day and month missing.

138 *Warboys, Hunts.* Monday, June 12th

It is put in a pain that no one shall tether animals in the wheat stubble before the Feast of St Michael under pain of 20d. to the lord and 20d. to the church.

And that no foals shall follow the carts in autumn under pain of 12d.

And that no one shall tether horses or mares in the fields before the Feast of St Michael under pain of 12d.

And that all ditches within the demesne shall be cleaned before Lent under pain of 20d. to the lord and 20d. to the church.

And that no beasts come into the grain until one land has been cleared under pain of 12d.

And that no one shall glean who is able to earn 1d. a day under pain of 12d.

And that no one shall leave town to earn high pay under pain of 12d.

139 *Wistow, Hunts.* Wednesday, June 14th

It is put in a pain that no foals shall be taken loose into the grain from *ad invincula* [sic] until the Feast of St Michael under pain of 3d.

And that no one shall depasture in the wheat stubble before the Feast of the Nativity of the Blessed Mary under pain of 12d.

And that no sheep shall come into the meadow of Woldeyhus at present under pain of 6d. and 6d.

And that no one shall put anything noxious in the water from Burybyghton to Gerholme under pain of 6d.

Ravele. It is put in a pain that the ditch from Asplondet gerde to the garden of William Hythe shall be cleaned before the Feast of St Martin under pain for each one in default of 6d. to the lord and 6d. to the church.

And that no one shall come into the Halme before the Feast of the Nativity of the Blessed Mary under pain of 6d. to the lord and 6d. to the church.

And that no one shall depasture in the field before one land has been cleared under pain of 6d. to the lord and 6d. to the church.

And that no one shall glean who is able to earn 1d. a day and food under pain of 6d. to the lord and 6d. to the church.

140 *Upwood, Hunts.*[67]

It is put in a pain that no foals shall be taken in the grain loose before the end of autumn under pain [68]. . . .

And that no one shall glean who is able to earn 1d. a day and food under pain of 6d.

---

[67] The date of this court has been torn off but the period is the same as the previous record.

[68] Illegible.

And that no one shall depasture in the wheat stubble before the Feast of the Nativity of the Blessed Mary under pain of 6d.

And that no one shall work in the fields on feast days under pain of 6d. to the lord and 6d. to the church.

Ravele. It is put in a pain that brewers shall brew through the whole of autumn under pain of 12d.

And that no one shall glean who is able to earn 1d. a day and food under pain of 12d.

And that no one shall depasture in the wheat stubble before the Feast of the Nativity of the Blessed Mary under pain of 12d. to the lord and 12d. to the church.

And no one shall depasture in the field until it has been raked under pain of 12d.

1432

141 *Elmley Castle, Worcs.* A. Friday, May 16th

It is ordered that each tenant within Cretases ought to keep his beasts . . .[69] within his own pastures under pain each delinquent of 4d.

And that each one ought not to put his animals into the common pasture there except by the consent of all the tenants there until autumn is completely over under pain each delinquent of 4d. Wardens Thomas Dawbeny and Robert . . .

B. Friday, August 1st

It is ordained that no one shall pasture his beasts in the meadow called Hultmede . . . in the fields of grain except by the consent of all the tenants of the lord under pain each delinquent of 4d.

It is ordered that no one shall pasture his beasts in the meadow called Brodemedowe unless by the assent of all the lord's tenants under pain each delinquent of 4d.

Wardens of these bylaws [*belaworum*] Nicholas . . . William Handy, Robert Cole, Sr. and John Crewman.

1433

142 *Great Horwood, Bucks.* Thursday, July 23rd

Plebiscite. It is ordered by all the tenants that no one shall have his beasts on the green of the town by night until the end of autumn next to come under pain each one of 4d. And there were chosen as wardens John Hayes and Robert Baynard.

Plebiscite. And that every tenant be at Nether forde next Monday

---

[69] MS. torn.

about Vespers with tools to clean the watercourse under pain of 1d. for default and John Baynard of Nether Ende is chosen warden.

1436

143 *Newton Longville, Bucks.* Wednesday, April 25th

It is ordained as well by the lord as by all the tenants that no one henceforth shall lay waste or destroy the separable pasture of his neighbours before the Feast of St Peter in Chains under pain of 2s.

And that no one henceforth shall have any animals or sheep in the stubble in autumn time except beasts that are tethered until the whole field has been housed under pain of 2s.

And that everyone shall share in the wages of the cow herd and the hog herd under pain of 12d.

144 *Great Horwood, Bucks.* Thursday, July 26th

It is ordained as well by the lord as by all the tenants that no one henceforth shall have his beasts standing by night on the green nor out of safekeeping under pain for each transgressor of paying the lord 1d. without abatement.

And chosen wardens of this ordinance were John Hogtes, Robert Wylkyn and Johanna Barbor.

1439

145 *Elmley Castle, Worcs.* A. Tuesday, July 14th

It is ordained that no man dwelling in the town shall pasture his beasts in the meadow called Brodemedowe until autumn is completely at an end under pain each delinquent for each transgression of 4d.

Item it is ordered that no one shall pasture his animals in the fields of grain there until forty selions have been cleared of sheaves and carted under pain each delinquent for each transgression of 4d.

It is ordered that no one shall pasture his sheep in the white [*sic*] stubble in the fields until autumn is completely at an end under pain each delinquent for each transgression of 3d.

Item it is ordered that no one ought to pasture geese in the fields of grain until autumn is completely at an end under pain each delinquent for each transgression of 4d.

Item it is ordered that no one ought to glean in autumn time who is able to earn 1d. a day and food and further he ought not to glean in the field there until twelve selions have been cleared of sheaves and carted under pain each delinquent for each transgression of paying 12d. to the lord.

Item it is ordered that no one ought to cart grain in autumn time after sunset under pain each one of paying the lord for each transgression 4d.

Item it is ordered that no one shall pay with sheaves in the fields there gleaners or any man in autumn time under pain each delinquent for each time of 4d.

Wardens. And to keep the aforesaid ordinances well and faithfully there were elected Thomas Case, Richard Hamond, William Gibbe, Richard Handy, Richard Mountford, Thomas Gilbes, John Creman and John Handy, the messor. And they were sworn and took oath.

B. Tuesday, October 13th

The wardens of the bylaws [*belaworum*] came and presented that John Dawbeny (4d.), of Overende, Thomas Case (2d.), Thomas Spencere (4d.), John Dernell (2d.), John Cole (4d.), Thomas Smyth (4d.), Ralph ffere (4d.), broke the ordinance with their beasts. Therefore, they incur the penalty therein made. John Crewman, 4d., for the same.

Item they present that William Dernell (2d.), broke the ordinance with a cart. Nicholas Huggushunt (3d.), broke the ordinance in carting after sunset. Therefore he incurs the penalty. And Thomas Gibbe (2d.), for the like.

1440

146 *Warboys, Hunts.* Tuesday, July 25th

It is put in the pain that no one shall put his animals in the field of rye until one furlong has been cleared under pain of 12d. to the lord and 12d. to the church.

And that no one shall tether his beasts nor his horses in the wheat field before the Feast of the Nativity of the Blessed Mary under the pain aforesaid.

And that no one shall tether horses in the wheat stubble nor in his own stubble before the Feast of St Michael under the aforesaid pain.

And that no one shall tether his work beasts in those parts where horses are pastured under the aforesaid pain.

And that no one shall have foals following carts or loose in the field under the aforesaid pain.

And that no one henceforth shall tether cows in the field before the end of autumn under the pain aforesaid.

And that no one shall mow reeds or thatch in the marsh henceforth before the end of autumn under the aforesaid pain.

And that no labourer shall work outside the town in autumn who is able to work inside the town [for] 4d. a day with the scythe and 2d. with the ffolner under the pain aforesaid.

And that no one shall sell thatch outside the town while tenants of the township are willing to pay as much etc. under the pain aforesaid. And that the pasture of Humberdale is separable at all times etc. under pain of 6s. 8d.

And they elect John Gerong, Jr. and William Colvyle reeves of autumn for Warboys, Thomas Buntyng and Richard Wylkyns for Caldecote and they are sworn.

1446

147   *Elmley Castle, Worcs.*   Wednesday, April 27th

It is ordered by common consent of all the lord's tenants there that no one of them henceforth shall brew more beer than any of his neighbours and that none of them shall have beer in his house to sell more than four days after the brewing of the beer under pain of paying the lord 3s. 4d.

And that no one of them shall have or keep any greyhound within the town there unless on leash under pain of each one of them paying the lord 4d. as often as he is delinquent.

148   *Launton, Oxon.*   Friday, July 15th

Since it is the custom of this manor that all who are impounded within the lord's demesne with their beasts for trespasses done in the grain and pastures of the tenants ought to be amerced according to the amount [of damage], and now it is reported by the messor that he has nothing to present etc.

John Smyth, William ffreman, Robert Tannere and John ffreman sworn reeves of autumn say that it was ordered by all the tenants that all men within this demesne who work on feast days or by night or do damage in the grain, pastures and pasturages of the tenants ought to be amerced according to the amount of damage done, of which the third penny belongs to the said reeves and 2d. to the lord, the which reeves with the messor, on oath, say they have nothing to present on this day, etc.

1449

149   *Elmley Castle, Worcs.*   Saturday, April 19th

It is an order to all tenants that each tenant and resident of the age of twelve and over without exception shall be in the parish church there at the hour of six in the morning on the Feast of St George the Martyr next to come [Wednesday, April 23rd] for this reason, that the said tenants and residents in a body shall go about this demesne to inspect and make new all metes and bounds of this demesne, and also to look over all inhokes within this demesne under pain for each one of them in default of paying 12d. to the lord.[70]

[70] *Inhokum*, 'any corner or part of a common field, ploughed up and sown . . . in that year wherein the rest of the same field lies fallow and common'. (C. T. Martin, *The Record Interpreter*, 2nd ed. (1910), 263.)

1451

150   *Great Horwood, Bucks.*   Friday, June 18th

Pains. Item it is agreed by the whole homage that no one will be allowed to enter upon the common balks before the Feast of St Peter which is called in Chains under pain for each delinquent of 12d.

Item it is agreed that no one shall enter a separable field where grain is growing before the aforesaid Feast under pain of 6d. to the lord and 6d. to the Church as often as it shall happen.

Item it is agreed that none shall divide their meadows unless by beginning at the top of the meadow and so continuing to the bottom, under pain each one in default of 2d. as often as it happens.

151   *Elmley Castle, Worcs.*   Saturday, July 10th

It is ordered by the common consent of all the tenants there that no one of them shall pasture with his beasts in the stubble in time of autumn until forty selions in a furlong shall be fully carted and gotten in under pain for each of them in default of paying 4d.

Item it is ordered by common consent that no one of them shall pasture with his sheep in the stubble in autumn time until the whole of autumn is at an end under pain for each one of them in default of paying to the lord 4d.

Item it is ordered by common consent that none of them shall pasture with his beasts in le Brodemede except with oxen and with horses for the plough before the Feast of St James under pain for each of them in default of paying the lord 4d.

It is ordered by common consent that none of them or his servants shall gather pods in the fields there except it be in his own land and that those who have no land in the fields must have leave of their neighbours under pain for each one of them paying the lord . . .[71]

The wardens of the ordinances, well and faithfully to observe them, are John Dernell and Roger Mountford.

Item it is ordered by the steward that no man shall be wakeful or walk about [after] the hour of nine at night under pain of each of them so doing, 3s. 4d.

Item it is ordered that none of them shall have a sub-tenant unless he will undertake before the steward that he will be of good conduct and governance during the term of his residence within this demesne under pain . . .

Item it is ordered by common consent that each tenant who has a cart shall come with the said cart to fetch stone to the common street to make and mend it between the tenement of Richard Handy and the

[71] Illegible.

end ... of St James under pain for each of them not doing so of paying the lord 4d.

1453

152 *Elmley Castle, Worcs.* Wednesday, April 11th

It is ordered by the steward by the consent of the whole demesne there as well of Elmley as of Criteso that each tenant there having a cart shall cart stones for the mending of the lane called Persons Lane for two days and that every tenant having a cart shall work there in the same lane through the same time and this under pain for each defaulter of 12d.

And in like manner each one as aforesaid shall mend the lane called Wood Lane, that is for one day under the aforesaid pain.

And also they shall mend the common way from the smithy there to aldewyneshole wherever necessary under the aforesaid plan.

1454

153 *Elmley Castle, Worcs.* Friday, June 21st

It is ordered by common consent of all the tenants there that if anyone of them shall allow any beasts in the stubble of any field there after autumn to pasture before forty selions of land of the same stubble have been cleared that he shall lose to the lord as often as he is delinquent 4d.

And that if any one of them shall have any manner of beasts pasturing in the field called lordfielde, unless they be horses tethered, before the grain in the same field has been fully cleared he shall lose to the lord as often as he does it 4d.

And that if any one of the said tenants shall gather pods on the land of another unless he has obtained leave of him and the pods have been gathered along the furrows or at the end of the selions and not in the middle he shall lose to the lord as often as he does it 2d.

And that if any one of the aforesaid tenants shall take any pods or pulse for the sustenance of his beasts except from his own lands he shall lose to the lord as often as he does it 4d.

And that Thomas Hamond, Sr., Thomas Hamond, Jr., Richard Parker and Richard Daubeney are chosen wardens of this ordinance and they took oath.

1435

154 *Wistow, Hunts.* Monday, November 10th

A pain that no pigs shall be brought into the sown field from the beginning of harvest before the Feast of St Bartholomew [72] under pain of 12d. to the lord and as much to the church.

---

[72] August 24th.

And that no one shall turn his plough upon the meadows between the Feast of the Birth of the Lord and of St John the Baptist [73] under pain of 12d. to the lord and as much to the church.

And that no one shall ride over the meadows between the said feasts under the aforesaid pain.

And that no one shall sell thatch except to the lord or the lord's tenants under the aforesaid pain.

And that no animal shall be kept in the . . .[74] field from the Feast of St Martin till the Feast of the Purification of the Blessed Mary under the aforesaid pain.

And that each juror aforesaid shall keep secret the counsels of his fellows under pain of 20d. to the lord and 20d. to the church.[75]

1463

155 *Great Horwood, Bucks.* Friday, July 8th

The homage there presents that no one henceforth shall permit his foals or his calves to go openly into the grain field nor into the meadow unless tethered under pain for each one who does the contrary of 40d. as often as he does it.

And that no one henceforth shall make a common way or allow his servants there to make a common way from the stream called Dyggewellford overland to a certain place called Suddene under pain for each one who is delinquent of losing 12d. of which one-half to the use and profit of the church and the other part to the lord, etc.

1465

156 *Elmley Castle, Worcs.* Monday, November 25th

It is ordered by the consent of all the tenants there that if any of the tenants within the demesne henceforth shall sell beer in a tavern to the prejudice of any brewer he shall forfeit 20d. to the lord for what is owing.

1467

157 *Great Horwood, Bucks.* Sunday, May 31st

Ordinance for the present [*existens*]. That no one henceforth nor his wife nor his servants shall gather rushes growing on uncultivated ground or in the meadow of another tenant to offer for sale but for his own use only within this demesne, under pain for each doing the contrary of forfeiting 40d. to the lord.

[73] June 24th.
[74] MS. torn.
[75] Note that all fines are divided with the parish church.

1465

158 *Great Horwood, Bucks.* Saturday, December 17th

It is ordered by the consent of all the tenants there that no one henceforth shall wilfully allow his foals openly to go into the fields of grain after they are three weeks old unless tethered to their mothers under pain of each one doing the contrary paying 12d. namely for each foal every time.

1469

159 *Elmley Castle, Worcs.* Thursday, April 13th

The wardens of the rivulet there present that Thomas Mountford (1d.) Katerina Cole (1d.) John Martyn (1d.) Thomas Hamond (1d.) transgressed in the rivulet with their ducks. Therefore they are in mercy.

An order is made to all the tenants there that none of them shall have geese in the common rivulet in future after the third warning under pain of forfeiting their geese.

And that no one of them shall put anything filthy in the aforesaid rivulet nor shall they have their gutters running from their houses into the said rivulet, under pain for each one who is delinquent of 4d. each time.

And that everyone shall keep the rivulet opposite his tenement in its proper course under pain of each one in default forfeiting 6d. to the lord.

It is ordered by common consent of the whole homage that no one shall put any cadavers in Persons Layne under pain of 12d.

160 *Leighton Buzzard, Beds.* Monday, August 7th

It is ordained and established by the consent and assent of the steward of the Lady [76] and her tenants that every tenant and non-tenant dwelling within the demesne of Leighton shall keep his beasts and animals outside the sown fields until the Feast of St Michael the Archangel next to come unless ten acres of grain lying together have been raked and the grain thereof carted away under pain for each one doing the contrary of forfeiting 6s. 8d. to the church and 6s. 8d. to the Lady, except that each tenant may tether beasts on his own land there etc.

Item it is ordered and established by the consent and assent of the Lady's stewards and of her tenants that no one ought to rake or gather pods of beans and peas unless on his own land except by leave . . . under the pain aforesaid.

And that no one shall glean who is able-bodied (*potens est*) and can

---

[76] The Lady of Crowburg.

earn 1d. a day and 1½d. [*sic*] if any one within this demesne wishes to hire him.

And no one shall glean within the sown fields until both the grain and the land have been raked and the grain from ten acres lying together has been carted home under the aforesaid pain.

And that no one should pasture his sheep, beasts and cattle except in his own fields and in the town where he dwells under the same pain.[77]

And that everyone dwelling in the town of Exendon cum Clipson shall keep his sheep outside the meadows of the town aforesaid and his beasts outside . . . until the Feast of St Michael the Archangel next to come under the pain aforesaid etc.

161 *Elmley Castle, Worcs.* Monday, October 16th

The wardens of the rivulet there present that all is well and all pains with respect to the keeping of the rivulet that were imposed at the last court are to be continued etc.

1471

162 *Hitchin, Herts.*[78]

It is ordained by the assent of the lord's council and of his tenants that none shall enter the sown field in autumn time to gather grain or spears with rakes or by hand if they are capable of earning 2d. a day, under pain for each one doing contrary to this ordinance of 3s. 4d.

Those who are not capable of earning 2d. a day shall not enter or cross through the sown fields until the sheaves have been gathered, removed and carted from a space of four acres of land under the aforesaid pain.

And if they be boys and under age or someone's servants who are not able to satisfy the lord in respect of the aforesaid pain then their masters who have these persons in governance shall answer to the lord for the aforesaid pain.

1473

163 *Elmley Castle, Worcs.* Wednesday, May 17th

It is ordered that all who have sheep within this demesne shall remove them outside of the demesne this side the Feast of St Martin the Bishop next to come.

And they shall not keep any sheep except they be the owners of the same or their relations, under pain of forfeiting to the lord 20s.

[77] Translation somewhat conjectural.
[78] Day and month missing.

1480

164 *Great Horwood, Bucks.* Wednesday, May 17th

The township of Great Horwood is ordered to make anew part of the butts this side the Feast of the Nativity of St John the Baptist under pain for each one in default of 8d., 4d. of which, to the parish church there and 4d. [*sic*].

And if any one shoots with arrows at the metes and does not close the bars after him he shall forfeit to the lord as often as he does it 4d.

1481

165 *Elmley Castle, Worcs.* Friday, February 16th

It is ordained by common consent and assent of all the tenants that each one of them shall assist in mending a certain lane called Shortelane in the aforesaid vill this side the Feast of Pentecost next to come, under pain of each one in default paying the lord 12d.[79]

It is ordered by assent and consent of all the tenants that each tenant who brews beer to sell shall sell the beer to every neighbour as long as he has beer in his house to the amount of three gallons under pain for each one of them in default to forfeit 3s. 4d. to the lord.

1483

166 *Elmley Castle, Worcs.* Wednesday, March 26th

At this court it is ordered by the steward and by the assent and consent of all the tenants that no customary tenant within this demesne aforesaid shall sell or cut down any tree growing on the ground of any of the customary tenants except under the supervision of the parker or of the bailiff of the lord aforesaid to the end that there be no waste there and this under pain for each delinquent as often as this shall happen of 6s. 8d. to be levied to the use of the lord etc.

167 *Great Horwood, Bucks.* Wednesday, June 4th

The homage there, sworn, present that it was ordered by the common consent of all the tenants that no one henceforth shall pasture his beasts or cattle in Aldemede Shepshen and Auldonbole before the Feast of St Michael next to come under pain for each one doing the contrary of 40d.

And they choose William Slyker and Thomas Sarey overseers of the ordinance aforesaid.

And that no one henceforth shall mow in a meadow called the

---

[79] An identical by-law on Monday, April 1, 1492 was in reference to 'le laundelane' with the date Invention of the Holy Cross (May 3rd).

dolemede until all having had the same summonses shall gather under pain for each one doing the contrary of 12d.

1484

168   *Great Horwood, Bucks.*   Sunday, May 23rd

It is ordained by common consent of all the tenants that no one shall allow [his animals] henceforth to pasture by night in the common pasture called Wigwell unless they are tethered to the end that no damage come to the grain there under pain each one in default of 8d., of which 4d. to the parish church there each time and 4d. to the lord.

1486

169   *Elmley Castle, Worcs.*   Tuesday, March 28th

Ordinance by assent and consent of all the tenants that no tenant of this lord shall place hemp or flax or the offal of any animal in the common rivulet within the town aforesaid under pain of paying 12d. to the lord.

1493

170   *Dinton, Bucks.*[80]

By-law [*Bilex*]. And that at the request of the whole homage it was ordained that no tenant or inhabitant in Dinton shall tether or pasture any of their great beasts on the common of Dinton between Ieloode and Greneheved from the Feast of the Invention of the Holy Cross to the Feast of St Peter in Chains nor shall they mow grass growing on the same before the Monday next before the Feast of the Translation of St Thomas the Martyr on pain of each tenant or inhabitant to forfeit and have levied for his infraction 6s. 8d., one-half of which to the use of the lord and the other half to the use of the church of Dinton.

By-law. That no tenant or inhabitant in Doughton and Dinton shall tether and pasture his horses or other great beasts in the common of Dinton namely from Doughton Bridge to Bollestake from the Feast of Invention of the Holy Cross to the Feast of St Peter in Chains nor shall they mow grass or reeds growing in the same before the Monday next before the Feast of the Translation of St Thomas the Martyr under pain for breaking this aforesaid by-law of half a mark, one-half of which to the use of the lord and the other half to the use of the church at Dinton.

By-law. And that no tenant or inhabitant in Dinton or Doughton henceforth shall mow reeds growing on the common aforesaid before the Feast of the Epiphany of the Lord in any year under pain of half

---

[80] Day and month illegible.

a mark, one-half of which to the use of the lord and the other half to the use of the church of Dinton.[81]

1498

171 *Elmley Castle, Worcs.* Tuesday, April 10th

It is ordered by the steward and the twelve jurors with the unanimous assent and consent of the homage that if anyone shall have pigs unringed in the fields of this demesne at any time of the year . . . for each pig so found as often as he is taken, 1d.

And it is ordered that no one of the tenants shall allow his sheep to go in the fields where grain is growing until the end of autumn under pain . . . 40d.[82]

1502

172 *Elmley Castle, Worcs.* Tuesday, April 26th

And it is ordained by the steward and the homage that all tenants and inhabitants of this demesne shall mend the king's highway between . . . of this town within one month under pain for each one in default of forfeiting to the lord 11d [*sic*].

1503

173 *Great Horwood, Bucks.* Tuesday, August 1st

It is ordered by common consent and assent that all tenants having hedges on the eastern part of the town aforesaid shall cause them well and sufficiently to be repaired, namely from Colles Lane to the eastern end of the aforesaid town leading toward Little Horwood, under pain for each of them failing in default of 12d.

And under the aforesaid pair that each of them who puts his cattle on their land adjacent to their closes next to sown land shall keep them safely and securely under guard.

And that henceforth each of them who has land next to his close shall plough it and bring it into cultivation under the aforesaid pain.

1507

174 *Elmley Castle, Worcs.* Friday, October 22nd

And it is ordered that the tenants there shall ring their pigs, and this before the Feast of the Ascension of the Lord, and they shall keep them so till the end of August, under pain for each one of 6d.

---

[81] These are the first by-laws seen in these rolls, in almost unbroken continuity from 1300.

[82] MS. damaged.

1509

175 *Newton Longville, Bucks.* Tuesday, September 25th

It is ordained by consent of all the tenants that every tenant can have and keep thirty sheep for each whole virgate of land and he who holds less, less, according to the aforesaid rate. And that no one shall keep more sheep, contrary to this ordinance . . .[83]

1513

176 *Great Horwood, Bucks.* Monday, September 26th

It is ordained by assent of all the tenants that no one of them shall put their foals to pasture unherded in the fields now sown from the Feast of the Invention of the Holy Cross until autumn shall come to an end unless they are tethered, lest they do damage in the grain there sown, under pain for each one in default of 40d.

1514

177 *Great Horwood, Bucks.* Saturday, September 30th

It is ordained by assent of all the tenants that none of them shall put or keep foals in the pastures in the fields now sown called Darby felde from the Feast of the Invention of the Holy Cross until autumn is ended, unless they are tethered, to the end that they do no damage to the grain there sown under pain for each one falling in default of 3s. 4d.[84]

Item it is ordained that none of the tenants shall fork or keep their beasts in . . . called le lees in the fields there now sown after the Nativity of St John the Baptist but they shall put them in the custody of the common herd under pain for each one in default of 10s., provided however that they shall have the liberty of forking [*forcandi*] their plough horses or oxen in the aforesaid pastures after the aforesaid Feast, the aforesaid pain notwithstanding.

1515

178 *Great Horwood, Bucks.* Tuesday, October 20th

It is ordained by an agreement of the lord and the tenants that no tenant or inhabitant within this demesne shall play at dice or cards except in the time of the Lord's Nativity under pain for each one in default of 20s.

---

[83] MS. torn.

[84] Further on in the roll we find: 'Item they present that John Sharpp (2d.) Edward Tayler (2d.) John Raude (2d.) and William Bukingham (2d.) kept their foals in the sown fields untethered etc. before autumn was ended contrary to the ordinance made therein at the last court. Therefore separately in mercy as appears etc.'

And it is ordered that no one within this demesne shall take fish in Oldmedbroke nor in the other streams within the aforesaid demesne under pain of 6s. 8d.

And it is ordered that no one shall take wood by cart or on his head from the wood which is called Priorswoode without leave of the lord's officer under pain of 6s. 8d.

And it is ordered that no one shall put his pigs in the sown field called le Stoble but he shall put them with the common herd under pain of 6s. 8d.

1516

179 *Great Horwood, Bucks.* Tuesday, September 9th

It is ordained by the consent of the tenants that each tenant at will shall put and pasture his cattle on the common ways and in his own pastures from the Feast of Easter to the Feast of the Nativity of St John the Baptist and after the said Feast the said tenants shall put the aforesaid beasts with the common herd except plough oxen, and every tenant shall depasture the aforesaid oxen at will in the common ways or wherever they do not do an injury to the tenants there etc. under pain for each delinquent of 40d.

180 *Great Horwood, Bucks.* Friday, September 18th

It is ordained that all the tenants and inhabitants shall tether their foals and mares in the sown fields and not allow them to go at large in the grain of the tenants under pain for each delinquent of 40d.

And that none of the inhabitants shall cut or carry furze from the common called the Priourswode except by order of the bailiff under pain each delinquent of 20d.

And that no one shall take fish in the common fishing stream called le brok' flowing within the aforesaid town unless it be on his own ground under pain for each delinquent of 40d.

1518

181 *Newton Longville, Bucks.* Wednesday, September 23rd

It is ordained that none of the tenants shall tether horses or mares or fork his cattle in the sown fields except on his own land and this under pain each delinquent of 6d.

1519

182 *Great Horwood, Bucks.* Thursday, September 22nd

And [the jurors] say that not a few of the inhabitants there who have mares with foals allow them to go at large anywhere at all in the sown field to the detriment of their neighbours.

Wherefore it is ordered that everyone who has animals of this kind shall no longer permit nor shall any of them allow his animals aforesaid to go at large in the sown field but that mares as well as foals when they are there shall be tethered, under pain each one who is delinquent in this respect of 3s. 4d.

Every tenant there is ordered not to allow his cows to depasture henceforth on the king's way in any part of the sown field until the end of autumn under pain, each one guilty in this respect, of 3s. 4d.

1521

183 *Great Horwood, Bucks.* Tuesday, April 9th

A pain is made that no one henceforth shall allow his foals to go at large in the sown fields after they are one month old unless they be tethered with the horses under pain each delinquent of 40d.

It is ordained that no handicrafter [*laborator artifex*] or his servant shall play at tables or cards henceforth under pain each one of them in default of 12d. every time except when there is a church ale and that no one shall harbour the aforesaid players under pain of 6s. 8d. each time.

It is ordained by the assent of all the tenants there that no one henceforth shall bring in any shepherd with a flock of sheep from any outsider under pain of 40s.

184 *Elmley Castle, Worcs.* Tuesday, October 22nd

Ordinance. That everyone shall ring his pigs and sows sufficiently before the Feast of the Apostles Simon and Jude under pain of each delinquent to lose 12d.

And that no one henceforth shall break hedges or park palings under pain of each delinquent so doing to lose 12d.

1524

185 *Great Horwood, Bucks.* Monday, September 26th

It is ordained by the consent of all the tenants that each tenant within the jurisdiction of this court shall clean and mend his ditches of whatever kind sufficiently and well before the Feast of All Saints under pain for each one of them falling in default of 3s. 4d.

It is ordained by the assent of all the tenants within the jurisdiction of this court, cottagers as well as others, that each one of them for his part shall clean and repair well and sufficiently a water called the almedebroke and another water called the ffennebroke before the Feast of All Saints next to come under pain, each of them falling in default, of 12d. if he is not there at the time fixed beforehand to do this.

It is ordained that no one shall tether his mares in the field sown with wheat there unless he shall tether his foals securely with his horses aforesaid under pain for each one of them falling in default of 3s. 4d. as often as it happens.

Item it is ordained that no one shall tether nor shall he allow his horses, mares or foals to wander at large there in the meadows where their hay has been heaped up in autumn, *that is to say where any heycokke shall be made yn hayharvest* [85] under pain of 3s. 4d. every time any one of them falls in default.

Again as before it is ordained that cottagers each of them shall put his beasts with the cowherd to the end that he shall not permit his beasts aforesaid to pasture nor to go into the fields of the other tenants of the lord there, under pain for each one of them falling in default of 20d. as often as it happens.

186 *Weedon, Bucks.* Monday, October 17th

It is ordained by consent of all the tenants of this manor that no one henceforth shall make parks, that is, *pennes*, on the common green before the next court.

And if it should be found by the homage at the next court that this ordinance is for the common advantage of the tenants then a pain shall be put upon those who break the aforesaid ordinance.

1527

187 *Elton, Hunts.* Monday, October 7th

Pains and ordinances. It is ordained at this court that no cottager shall keep many cows henceforth [*plures vaccas*], each of them under pain of 3s. 4d.

And further it is ordered at this court and leet that all ditches and common passageways which are a nuisance to the people of the lord king, and similarly all hedges and fences of all the tenants here, etc., before the Feast of St Martin the Bishop in hyeme next to come under pain for each of them in default in any of the aforesaid, of 20d.

And further that no tenant of this manor shall allow or shall keep his sheep in the wheat field after Lent next to come each under pain of 40s.

And that no tenant in Overtown shall keep his sheep in the wheat field in a byherd, henceforth but in a flock with the common shepherd from the Feast of St Martin the Bishop in hyeme next to come until the end of autumn next to come, each under pain of 20s.

And that no tenant of this manor shall keep sheep or shepherds in Givenall way as far as the meadow henceforth from the Feast of the Annunciation of the Blessed Mary the Virgin next to come until the

---

[85] All the by-laws of 1550 are in English.

BY-LAWS 141

Feast of St Peter which is called in Chains next following, each under pain of 6s. 8d.

And that no tenant of this manor shall put his mares hobbled [*hoppelled*] at the fen before the end of next autumn nor shall he make there a waste [*le pennuria*], each under pain of 20s.

And it is further ordained at this court that no cowherd of this town shall keep cows or young oxen on the street henceforth from the Feast of the Apostles Philip and James next to come to the end of autumn next following, each 6s. 8d.

And that no tenant of this manor shall keep more than forty sheep for a virgate of land henceforth and if more or less according to the same rate, each under pain of 20s.

And that each customary tenant of this manor shall mend his hedges and fences between himself and his neighbour through the whole town before the Feast of St Martin the Bishop in hyeme next to come, each under pain of 3s. 4d.

And that each cottager of this town shall have in his yard before the said Feast two cartloads of wood each under pain of 6s. 8d.

Every cowherd of this town shall keep his cows with the herd in springtime and not by byherd, each of them in default under pain of 6s. 8d.

And further that in springtime each one shall tether his foals in the fields with their mothers after the Feast of the Translation of St Thomas the Martyr, each under pain of 20d.

And that no tenant henceforth shall keep his horses or mares in halters in springtime, to the damage of the lord's tenants, nor shall he keep his oxen in the fields in springtime, each under pain of 3s. 4d.

1531

188 *Great Horwood, Bucks.* Tuesday, October 3rd

It is ordered that they shall not allow their beasts to go at large before the end of autumn under pain of 40d.

It is ordered that no tenant by copy of court [roll] shall have several [*plures*] sub-tenants in one house without the lord's leave, under pain of 40s.

It is ordained that no one shall pasture any beast except oxen in the wheat field before the Feast of Pentecost under pain of 40d.

1534

189 *Great Horwood, Bucks.* Friday, October 16th

It is ordered that no one shall harbour or entertain any woman or women of ill fame more than one night under pain for each delinquent, of 6s. 8d.

It is ordained that each one shall clean his part of the rivulet from . . . bridge to the hemp pole before the Feast of the Holy Trinity under pain for each delinquent, of 3s. 4d.

It is ordained that no one shall have foals more than four weeks old untethered in the fields sown with barley and oats under pain, each delinquent, of 3s. 4d., nor foals more than eight weeks old in the fields sown with beans under the aforesaid pain.

The jurors present that William Taylor is a common trespasser in the field with his beasts, therefore etc.

It is ordained that no cottager shall have more than two cows, one horse and four pigs, under pain for each delinquent, of 12d.

It is ordained that no one shall gather beans under pain for each delinquent, of 12d.

It is ordained that no one shall put sheep in the field sown with wheat, barley and oats before the Feast of the Holy Trinity under pain, each delinquent, of 4d.

1537

190 *Elmley Castle, Worcs.* Monday, April 23rd

Item it is ordered that no tenant of Elmley shall harbour any stranger or vagabond under pain of 3s. 8d.

Item it is ordered that no tenant of Elmley shall gather any pods [belonging to] another without leave under pain of 3s. 4d.

And the tenants of Elmley are further ordered that none of them shall keep any beasts in the stubble field within a space of twenty selions of standing grain under pain for each one of them, of 3s. 4d.

1538

191 *Great Horwood, Bucks.* Thursday, October 8th

It is ordained by the assent of all the tenants that each of them shall mend his part of the road called Woluerton way before the Feast of the Purification of the Blessed Mary the Virgin next to come, under pain for each delinquent of 3s. 4d.

It is ordained that each one shall clean his part of his ditch at Hyndwell as far as the hemp pole before the Feast of Pentecost next to come under pain, each delinquent, of 3s. 4d.

It is ordained that no one shall allow foals to go at large in fields sown with wheat, barley and oats after they are of the age of one month, under pain of 3s. 4d.

It is ordained that no one shall pasture sheep in the common East field from the end of autumn to the Feast of St Edward under pain of 3s. 4d.

It is ordained that no one shall pasture his beasts in the common field before the Feast of Pentecost under pain of 3s. 4d.[86]

1542

192 *Great Horwood, Bucks.* Thursday, October 26th

It is ordained by the assent of the tenants that no one shall carry with him a hatchet or any other tool for cutting wood or underbrush in the woods of the lord nor shall he cut wood or underbrush, under pain of 3s. 4d.

Item it is ordained that no one shall pasture the common ways in the fields of Horwood with his beasts before the Feast of Pentecost, and after the Feast of Pentecost that no one shall pasture in the common ways aforesaid unless he has land there, under pain of 3s. 4d.

It is ordained that no cottager shall keep more than two beasts, one mare and one calf under pain of 3s. 4d.

Item it is ordered that no one shall allow calves to go at large in the sown field until autumn is over, under pain of 3s. 4d.

1545

193 *Newton Longville, Bucks.* Monday, April 13th

It is ordered by the assent of all the tenants that each one shall put his beasts except beasts of the plough in charge of the herdsman after the herdsman has come from the woods, under pain for each delinquent of 4d. every time.

Item it is ordained that no one shall pasture his beasts in the sown fields except on his own lands from the Feast of Pentecost next to come until the rye and wheat have been taken away under pain of 4d. each one every time.

Item it is ordained that no one shall pasture his oxen in the common ways before the Feast of the Holy Trinity next to come under pain, each delinquent, of 4d.

194 *Newton Longville, Bucks.* Thursday, September 3rd [87]

It is ordained by the consent of all the tenants that no tenant shall agist his beasts at Blechfeldey-leese by Smaldeyeey henceforth before the Feast of Pentecost under pain, each delinquent for each time, of 12d.

---

[86] On Wednesday, October 1, 1539, the last by-law was re-enacted together with the following: 'It is ordained by the assent of all the tenants that each cottager shall put his beasts in charge of the herdsman under pain each delinquent of 3s. 4d.'

[87] The second time by-laws were enacted this year.

Item it is ordained that no one shall pasture or tether horses on the common ways before the Feast of Pentecost next to come under pain, for each delinquent, of 4d. each time.

Item it is ordained that no tenant shall keep or pasture his oxen on the common ways before the Feast of the Holy Trinity next to come under pain for each delinquent for each time of 4d. unless it is on his own land.

Item it is ordained that no one shall pasture his cows or other animals in the sown fields before the Feast of St Peter in Chains next to come under pain, for each delinquent for each time, of 12d.

1546

195 *Newton Longville, Bucks.* Saturday, October 2nd

It is ordained by the assent of the tenants that no one having a plough shall take a tongue [*lingua*] from the lord's woods under pain each delinquent for each pole [*fasticule*] of 4d., *and that no man break the wood hedge* [88] under pain for each delinquent every time, of 4d.

[88] This phrase is in English.

Court Rolls

196 *Newton Longville, Bucks. Court held there on Friday next before the Feast of the Decollation of St John the Baptist in the eleventh year of King Edward.*[89]

Mercy 3d.	Henry le Dekne and Richard le Palefreman have leave to agree and the said Richard puts himself in mercy by pledge of Edmund Strettle, and the same Richard acknowledges that he is held to the said Henry in the sum of 20d. to be paid at the Feast of St Martin next to come by pledge of the aforesaid.
Mercy 3d.	Alice Wythemay and Richard le Bole for licence to agree in a plea of debt and the said Richard puts himself in mercy by pledge of Simon Bacon.
Mercy 3d.	Edmund Strettle and Ellen Thomas have leave to agree in a plea of trespass and the said Ellen puts herself in mercy by pledge of William Thomas.
Law 6 handed	Edmund Strettle plaintiff by pledge of William Hardy offers himself against Ralph Cheseman in a plea whereby he charges that the said Ralph cut down and took away thorns growing in his hedges to the value of half a mark and of this he offers suit. And the said Ralph came and said that he is in no way guilty of the aforesaid trespass and he is at his law by pledge of John Simeon.
Fine 12 cocks	It is granted by the lord to Agnes sister of Simon Bacon that she may be married, that is to say outside the fee.
	Ralph Cheseman, plaintiff, by pledge of William Haukyn versus Edmund Strettle in a plea that he ill-used him maliciously with contumelious words to the damage of the said Ralph. And the said Edmund said that he was in no way guilty of the said trespass and he asks that this be inquired and the said Ralph similarly.
Mercy 3d.	The inquest charged with this says that the aforesaid Edmund is guilty of the aforesaid trespass to [Ralph's] damage 1d. Ralph shall recover the damage aforesaid and the said Edmund is in mercy by pledge of Richard le Palfreyman.
Fine 12 cocks	It is granted by the lord to Alice Bouere that she may marry wherever she wishes in the lord's fee.
Mercy 3d.	John le Sweyn puts himself in mercy for trespass with his pigs in the lord's grain by pledge of the messor.

[89] August 27, 1283. New College Court Rolls, N.L.I. 1, 1.

Mercy 3d. Matilda Deffes puts herself in mercy for trespass with her oxen in the lord's grain.

Mercy 2d. Hugh Myntrel puts himself in mercy for trespass with his pigs in the lord's grain by pledge of John Bacoun.

Mercy 2d. The lord's swineherd puts himself in mercy for trespass with his pigs in the lord's grain by pledge of the reeve.

The lord's swineherd puts himself in mercy for trespass with his pigs in the lord's grain by pledge; condoned.

Mercy 3d. The rector of Newton puts himself in mercy for trespass with his pigs in the lord's grain by pledge of John Bacoun.

The swineherd of the town puts himself in mercy for trespass with his pigs in the lord's grain by pledge of the reeve.

Mercy 2d. John Stoke puts himself in mercy for trespass with his pigs in the lord's grain by pledge of the messor.

Mercy 2d. John Walter puts himself in mercy for trespass with his horses in the lord's meadow by pledge of the messor.

Mercy 2d. Edmund Strettle puts himself in mercy for that he made default at the tedding of the lord's meadow.

Mercy 2d. Edmund Strettle puts himself in mercy for that he made default at the cocking of the hay.

Mercy 2d. John Kempe puts himself in mercy for the same.

Mercy 2d. Walter Iuottesone puts himself in mercy for the same.

William Thomas similarly. (2d.)

Mercy 2d. John Stoke similarly.

Mercy 2d. Elinor Thomas puts herself in mercy because she defaulted in the lord's work.

Mercy 3d. Walter Bouere puts himself in mercy for the same.

The whole homage of their own free will grant the lord 40s. for his recognition that their lands and tenements be not seized into his hands.

The wardens of autumn present that Matilda Thomas (6d.), and Alice Cheseman (6d.), John Perkyn (6d.), Elinor le Souttere (6d.), Emma Cheseman (6d.), and William Bens (6d.) and William Bens the miller (6d.), John Gosse the miller (6d.), and Alice Cheseman (6d.), William Robyn (6d.), and the son of Robert Hod (6d.), and the daughter of Elinor Thomas (6d.), and John Gerrard (6d.).[90]

Sum 10s. 9d.
Afferrers John Robaud   John Simon
Sum of cocks 24

---

[90] No mention is made of the nature of their trespass, but note that in the by-laws of 1290 (Doc. 8) a fine of 6d. was fixed for breach of any one of them.

COURT ROLLS 147

197 *Newton. Court held there on Monday next after the Feast of the Translation of St Thomas in the twelfth year of King Edward.*[91]

Damages 20d Mercy 4d. Ordered	Walter Vele puts himself in mercy for default in his law versus John Haukyns in a plea of trespass. Therefore it is ordered to levy 20d. damages awarded to him by the court to the use of the same John for the debt of Walter by the pledge of Richard Zoge.
Law 6 handed	John de Campho plaintiff by pledge of Richard le Palefreman offers himself against Edmund de Streete in a plea complaining that the said John appropriated grain . . . [illegible] he has suffered damage of half a mark and the aforesaid Edmund comes and says he is in no way guilty of the aforesaid trespass and he is at his law, pledge of the law Walter Vele.
Damages 40d. Mercy 4d. Ordered	It appears by the confession of Richard le Zonge that he is guilty of the trespass imputed to him by John de Campho and damages are taxed by the court at 40d. and the aforesaid Richard is in mercy for the aforesaid trespass by pledge of Walter Vele and it is ordered to levy the aforesaid damages.
Damages 6d. Mercy 2d. Ordered	It appears by the confession of John Kempe that he is guilty of the trespass imputed to him by Walter le Vele and damages are taxed by the court at 6d. Therefore the aforesaid Walter shall recover the aforesaid damages and the aforesaid John is in mercy for the aforesaid by pledge of the messor.
Damage 1½d. Mercy 2d. Ordered	It appears by the confession of Walter le Vele that he is guilty of the trespass imputed to him by John Kempe and damages are taxed at 1½d. Therefore the aforesaid John shall recover the aforesaid damages and the aforesaid Walter is in mercy pledge Edmund Streete.
Damages 40d. Mercy 3d. Ordered	It appears by an inquisition upon which John de Campho and Julian le Man put themselves that Julian is guilty of a trespass imputed to him by the same John and damages are taxed by the court at 40d. Therefore the aforesaid John shall recover the aforesaid damages and the aforesaid Julian is in mercy for his trespass by pledge of Hugh Roberd and William Thomas.
Damages 3d. Mercy 2d. Ordered	It appears by an inquisition on which William le Vele and John . . . put themselves that the aforesaid William is guilty of the trespass imputed to him and damages are taxed by the court at 3d. Therefore the aforesaid John shall recover the aforesaid damages and the aforesaid William is in mercy pledge John Bacon.
Damages 2d.	It appears by the inquisition on which William le Vele and John Kente put themselves that the aforesaid John is guilty of the trespass imputed to him by the said William. Therefore the said

[91] July 10, 1284. *Ibid.*

Mercy 3d. Ordered	William shall recover the aforesaid damages which are taxed by the aforesaid court at 2d. and that the said John is in mercy.
Damages 6d. Mercy 4d. Ordered	It appears by the confession of Richard le Zoug that he is guilty of the trespass imputed to him by Richard le ffrense and damages are taxed by the court at 6d. Therefore the aforesaid Richard le ffrense shall recover the damages aforesaid and the said Richard le Zoug is in mercy pledge John Robaud.
Mercy 3d.	Ralph Cheseman and his pledge to prosecute are in mercy because they did not prosecute against John le Bolter de Brichull. William Vele plaintiff offers himself against John Kempe in a plea that he should render to him 4d. which he withholds unjustly to his damage etc. and the aforesaid John recognizes the unjust
Damages	detention of 2d. therefore it is considered that he shall recover the aforesaid 2d. and damages are adjudged by the court namely at 1d.
Mercy 3d. Ordered Law 6 handed	and for the unjust detention he is in mercy. And as for the other 2d. he is at his law at the next [court] pledge of the law William Haukyn.
Rendering of account	William Aleyn who has served the lord in many offices for a long time rendered his final account of all receipts, disbursements, views and expenditures relating to the grange of Wychmung, and of the collection of the rents of the lord there and elsewhere and of other business of the lord before the aforesaid lord and William de Kynepell the lord's steward. Therefore the said William in all his accounts and allowances owes the lord the sum of 13s. 4d. for the whole time until the present day.
Mercy	It appears by the whole homage except Edmund de Streete and Richard Zouge that John Bankous and his wife are in no way guilty of the trespass of which they were accused in the preceding court by Walter ... Henry le Ferour Richard Vele Simon Bacon John Walter Edmund Strettle Walter Vele William Roberd Robert Adekyns Richard le Zoug Richard Vele and Robert le Zoug. Therefore the aforesaid accusers are in mercy.
2d.	The shepherd Robert de Preston puts himself in mercy for a trespass in the meadow with his sheep.
2d.	John Gadwyne puts himself in mercy for the same.
3d.	The shepherd of the rector puts himself in mercy for the same.
1d.	Richard Bacoun puts himself in mercy for the same.
1d.	Felicia ... puts herself in mercy for trespass in the pasture.
1d.	John ... puts himself in mercy for the same.
1d.	John Haukyns puts himself in mercy for the same.
2d.	Edmund Screcale puts himself in mercy for the same.
Ordinances of autumn	It is granted by all the lord's tenants that the statutes of autumn that were ordered in preceding years be observed and enforced.

Wardens were elected namely William Robyn Walter Vele Philip Simeon John Gerrard Richard le Zoug Edmund de Strettle Henry le Ferour and Hugh Roberd and they took oath.
Sum 3s. 10d.
Names of the affeerers Henry le Ferour William Robyn

198 *Newton. Court held there Saturday next after the feast of the Apostles Peter and Paul in the eighteenth year of King Edward.*[92]

Essoins 2d.	John de Preston defendant versus Henry le fferour plaintiff in a plea of debt by John Haukyns. John Bacoun puts himself in mercy for his trespass in the lord's grain with five piglets.
3d.	Roger Adekyns puts himself in mercy for trespass in the lord's grain with three sheep and four lambs.
2d.	Richard le Zoug puts himself in mercy for trespass twice in the lord's pasture.
3d.	Richard le Zoug puts himself in mercy for trespass in gathering herbage in the lord's grain.
3d.	Agnes le Knyth puts herself in mercy for trespass in the lord's grain in the same way.
4d.	John de Preston puts himself in mercy for trespass in the lord's grain with his lambs and in the pasture with his sheep and his pigs by pledge of the messor.
2d.	Matilda Gess' puts herself in mercy for trespass in the lord's grain with her lambs.
2d.	Robert Hod puts himself in mercy for trespass in the lord's grain with one cow.
2d.	Geoffrey Seket puts himself in mercy for trespass in the lord's pasture with his sheep by pledge of John Godwyne.
2d.	William Robyns puts himself in mercy for trespass in the lord's meadow with a horse he was leading.
2d.	Ralph Cheeseman puts himself in mercy for trespass in the lord's meadow with his sheep.
2d.	Henry le fferour puts himself in mercy for trespass in the lord's meadow with his sheep.
2d.	Richard Robyns puts himself in mercy for the same.
2d.	John Bouere puts himself in mercy for trespass in the lord's meadow and grain with two calves.
2d.	Hugh Roberd puts himself in mercy for trespass in the lord's croft with his sheep.

[92] Saturday, July 1, 1290. *Ibid.*

Heriot 1 ox	The customary tenants charged with divers articles touching the manor present that Richard Matheu who held of the lord one messuage and half a virgate of land has died by whose death one ox worth 10s. accrues to the lord by way of heriot and the tenements were taken into the lord's hand. And now comes John son of the aforesaid Richard and his nearest heir and by grace of the lord he has the aforesaid tenement rendering it into the lord's hands to the use of Amice his sister whom Hugh Bacoun took in marriage. And the aforesaid Hugh makes fine with the lord by paying 40s. for having entry to the aforesaid tenements to be paid on the Feasts of St Peter in Chains and St Michael in equal shares. And he is admitted as tenant and does fealty by pledge of William Haukyns and John le Taillour and he is given livery of seisin.
Fine 40s.	
Fealty	
Heriot 1 ox	Item ordered that John Kempe native of the lord who held of the lord one messuage and half a virgate of land has died from whose death there accrues one ox worth 9s. by way of heriot and the tenements are taken into the lord's hands until etc.
	William Haukyns in a plea of trespass complains against William Hardy and he has a day at the next [court] pledge of the aforesaid William Hardy and Henry Robert.
4d.	It appears by the inquisition into a dispossession and other matters on which Matilda Geff plaintiff and Hugh Roberd defendant had put themselves that Matilda's grain was pastured by his [Hugh's] beasts and her land ploughed unlawfully and she charges the aforesaid Hugh with the aforesaid dispossession and that her land was ploughed unjustly to the width of fifteen feet at least to her damage 15d. Therefore the said Hugh is in mercy, pledge Henry Roberd, and as to Matilda's grain being depastured they are not certain therefore the said Matilda for her unjust complaint is in mercy, pledge Simon Bacoun.
2d.	Hugh Henries puts himself in mercy for trespass in the lord's grain with one horse.
2d.	Richard the lord's swineherd puts himself in mercy for trespass in the lord's grain with one pig by pledge of William Gilot.
2d.	Julian le Man puts himself in mercy for trespass in the lord's grain by gathering herbage, by pledge of William Hardi.
	John Gerard puts himself in mercy for trespass in the lord's meadow.
3d.	Walter Vele puts himself in the lord's mercy for trespass in the lord's grain with his geese.
2d.	Matilda Geff puts herself in mercy for trespass in the lord's grain with her sheep.

John Aleyn puts himself in mercy for trespass in the lord's grain with his sheep by pledge of the reeve.

Robert de Horwod puts himself in mercy for trespass in the lord's grain with one pig, by pledge of Henry le fferour.

2d. Simon Bacoun puts himself in mercy for trespass in the lord's meadow with one horse.

2d. John Walter puts himself in mercy for the same.

1d. Agnes Thomas puts herself in mercy for trespass in the lord's pasture with her geese.

2d. Henry le Sweyn puts himself in mercy for trespass in the lord's grain with his beasts of the plough.

2d. John Palfrey puts himself in mercy for trespass in the lord's meadow with one horse.

2d. Michael de Leycester puts himself in mercy for trespass in the lord's meadow by gathering herbage.

2d. William Thomas puts himself in mercy for trespass in the lord's grain with one horse.

1d. John le Taillour plaintiff and Alice Cheseman defendant are given leave to agree in a plea of debt and the said Alice puts herself in mercy by pledge of Ralph Cheseman.

Inasmuch as Alice who was the wife of William Gilot native of the lord was previously married to a certain Hugh Coyntrel native of the lord and the said Alice after the death of the said William her former husband had as a dowry the third part of one messuage and a half of one virgate of land without fine or licence of the lord on which account the lord ordered the aforesaid Hugh not to work it any longer while the said Hugh was a tenant of one messuage and one virgate of land in bondage since he is not entitled to hold so many tenements nor by the extent of the manor does he do anything therefor, which Hugh nevertheless depastures with his beasts notwithstanding the aforesaid prohibition and the said Hugh called to account on this said that he and the other tenants of the lord in such a case for all time theretofore were accustomed to hold several tenements without fine or licence or any complaint and this he is prepared to verify by the homage or other lawful means as may be necessary. And the matter is put in respite until there can be a fuller consultation etc.

Inasmuch as Alice who was the wife of John Mount native of the lord was formerly married to a certain John Stoke native of the lord, and the aforesaid Alice after the death of the aforesaid John her former husband had as a dowry a third part of one messuage and half of one virgate of land without fine or licence of the lord, it is ordered by the lord that the aforesaid John no longer work the tenements because the said John is the tenant of one messuage and one virgate of land in bondage and he does not have leave to hold so many tenements nor by the extent of the manor is mention made of the particulars. Inasmuch as the aforesaid John called to account with reference to the aforesaid matters gave the same answer in all things as the aforesaid Hugh, the matter is put in respite as above until etc.[93]

199 *Court of Newton Longville held there Thursday next after the Feast of the Translation of St Thomas the Martyr in the sixth year of the reign of Edward III after the Conquest.*[94]

Day at the next [court]	At the prayer of the parties a day was given again to Walter Vele senior and John Smith in a plea of trespass without essoin so that all matters touching the said plea shall remain in the same state as before until the next [court].
Ordered	Again as before it is ordered to distrain John Dymok to redeem his pledge taken for trespass in the lord's meadow with his sheep. As before it is ordered to distrain Roger le Mountfort to redeem his pledge taken for trespass in the lord's grain.
	Again as before it is ordered to distrain Ralph Perkin de Saldene and Roger le Mountfort for trespass in the lord's pasture.
	Reginald le Potter complains of Agnes Dauy in a plea of trespass, pledge to prosecute Robert Hood. Therefore it is ordered to attach the said Agnes to answer to the said Reginald in the said plea at the next [court].
Mercy 2d.	Hugh Quyntrel puts himself in mercy for trespass with his beasts in the lord's grain.
2d.	Robert Adekynes and Henry the Clerk by leave are agreed in a plea of trespass that the said Henry shall put himself in mercy by pledge of John Bacon. It is ordered to distrain John le Sweyn to redeem his pledge taken for trespass in the lord's meadow with his beasts.
Ordered Condoned	
2d.	Walter Vele, Jr. puts himself in mercy for the same.
1d.	John de Stoke puts himself in mercy for trespass in the [common] pasture with his sheep.

[93] There follow the by-laws as in Doc. 8. The names of the wardens elected to enforce them are only partly legible but they include Henry le fferour, John Gerard and William Haukyn. The membrane has been extensively damaged at the end where the by-laws were recorded.

[94] July 9, 1332. New College Court Rolls, N.L. I, 2, 1.

3d.	Elena Thomas is in mercy because she gathered herbage from the standing grain of the lord contrary to the prohibition. Richard Robyn is in mercy for the same.
3d.	
Ordered	It is ordered to distrain Lucy le ffrounceys to redeem her pledge [taken] because she gathered herbage in the standing grain contrary to the prohibition.
	It is ordered to distrain Richard the chaplain de Salden to redeem his pledge taken for trespass in the lord's meadow with his sheep.
3d.	Walter Gate is in mercy because he gathered herbage in the standing grain of the lord contrary to the prohibition etc.
Ordered	It is ordered to distrain John Dymok to redeem his pledge taken for trespass in the lord's grain.
1d.	Richard Bacon puts himself in mercy for trespass in the grain with a certain heifer.
2d.	Simon Bacon puts himself in mercy for trespass in the lord's meadow.
1d.	Robert Karlel for the same with his horse.
Ordered she has nothing	It is ordered to distrain Margaret daughter of Slore to redeem her pledge taken because she gathered herbage in the standing grain contrary to the prohibition etc.
Ordered	It is ordered to distrain John le Playwhritte for the same.
Ordered	It is ordered to distrain Elena le Mountfort for the same.
1d.	Simon Dymok puts himself in mercy for trespass in the lord's grain.
1d.	Walter le Vele, Jr. puts himself [in mercy] for the same.
2d.	John Simeon puts himself [in mercy] for trespass in the lord's grain with a certain horse.
2d.	Walter son of Ivette puts himself [in mercy] for trespass in the lord's meadow.
3d.	Hugh Quyntrel puts himself [in mercy] for trespass in the lord's grain with his lambs.
3d.	Walter Vele, Sr. for the same in the lord's meadow.
2d.	John de Preston for trespass in the lord's meadow with two horses by pledge of Robert Hood. Henry Robert for the same.
2d.	John Hugh puts himself in mercy for trespass in the lord's meadow.
2d.	John de Preston puts himself [in mercy] for trespass in the lord's meadow with a certain horse, pledge Robert Hood.[95]

---

[95] There are eleven other cases of trespass in the lord's meadow or grain with a horse, a cow, sheep or geese. The fine in each case is 1d. or 2d.

Inquisition	Inquisition taken by Simon Bacon, John Simeon, Hugh Quyntrel, Robert le Knyght, John Godwyne and John Walter who say on their oath that Edmund de Stretle made default therefore he is in mercy and that as to other articles there is nothing [to present].
Mercy 3d.	
Ordinances of autumn	It is granted and ordered by the homage of the lord of Newton that no one who holds land of the lord shall gather beans, peas or vetches in the field unless from land which he has sown. And if anyone shall be found acting contrary to this ordinance he shall pay the lord 12d. for each default. And that if anyone wishes to gather beans, peas and such like he shall gather them between sunrise and the hour of prime.

Item that no one shall allow his calves to pasture in the field within the standing grain without a keeper.

Item that no one shall be admitted to glean who is able to earn his food and 1d. a day if it is found that there is someone who wishes to hire him.

Item that no outsider be allowed to glean.

Item that no pauper shall gather beans within the selion but at the end or along the sides and if they shall do otherwise they shall not be allowed to glean in the fields any more and they shall lose the beans they have gathered.

Item that no one shall cart by night.

Item that no sheaves shall be paid out in the field.

Item that everyone shall cause his stiles and the lanes nearest him to be so maintained that no harm shall come to the lord or any of his tenants because of a defect.

Item that no one of them shall gather herbage from this day to the end of August in the standing grain of any one else.

Item that no one shall cause stubble to be gathered after the grain has been fully carried off until the Feast of St Martin unless on his own land. And if any one shall be delinquent in any of the aforesaid he shall pay the lord 6d. for each default except in the article concerning stubble for which each delinquent shall pay 3d. for every default. And to see to these ordinances and to present those who violate them there were chosen Simon Bacon, Walter son of Iuette, John Walton, John Robaunt, John Simeon, John Gerard and the two messors namely the messor of the lord and of the community of the town and they took oath etc.

Sum 4s. 8d.   Names of the affeerers

John Henry, John Gerrard and the lord's messor

Memorandum that John Haukyn is charged with the perquisites of the court here for the first time.

200 *Broughton [Hunts.] day of St Hugh, bishop of Lincoln, in the sixteenth year of King Edward and the third year of Abbot John.*[96]

Names of the chief pledges John Joceline John Aspelaon William son of John at the Bridge John le Bon Alexander the Woodward Ralph the Clerk John Hobbe Ralph Euerard Alexander of Bluntysham William Henry John Randolph John Gere and Henry at the Gate

Names of the jurors Elias Carpenter John Baldry Simon Crane Simon the Smith John Nunne Andrew Onty Simon Edward

6d. 8d.   Richard of Broughton John Nel William the Cooper Alan the Horseman and Alan son of John son of Hugh. They pay 6s. 8d. chevage.

From Simon le Bond because he spoke ill of the beer of Robert Curteys from whence the said Robert suffered damage in the amount of 6d. He is poor, pledge Henry son of John, and by the same pledge he shall make satisfaction to the said Robert for the damage as above and they [the pence] are granted to the clerk.

2d.   Thomas Cobbe plaintiff and John de Ely defendant are in agreement and John puts himself in mercy, 2d., pledge Richard de Balliol.

Ordered   William de Broughton, William de Lond', John Cook and Ralph Norreys are distrained to answer at the next [court] because they made default at the first boon day of autumn.

From Richard de Camera because he made default at the first boon day of autumn, a mass, remitted.

12d.   And John Nuncium le Mung' 12d. because he did not send to the first boon day of the lord as many men as he had at his own work, remitted, pledge John Wylymot.

6d.   It is found by the jury of neighbours that Walter Grave said opprobrious things to John Bennett at a work [day] for the lord in autumn therefore he shall make satisfaction to him in respect of his damages which are taxed at 1d. and for the trespass he is in mercy 6d., pledge Simon Grune.

Distraint   William de Broughton is distrained to answer at the next court for the damage done by his two horses in the lord's peas.

From Richard de Broughton because he did not come to work for the lord in ditching at Wyrlewyk, forgiven, pledge William Carpenter.

---

[96] November 17, 1288. P.R.O., S.C. 2/176, *m.* 2. Latin text printed in part in W. O. Ault, *Court Rolls of the Abbey of Ramsey* (1928), 197–201. There is an Extent of the manor of Broughton, Hunts., in *Cartularium Monasterii de Rameseia*, I, 333 ff., dated 1252, and another in the Hundred Rolls, II, 600 ff.

	From William le Cupere for damage done by his horse by night in the lord's peas, forgiven, pledge Richard de Broughton.
6d.	From Richard at the well for damage done by his beasts in the
12d.	lord's grain. From Robert the reeve for the same, pledge each other. Fine of both 6d.[97]
Distraint	Alice Robynes is distrained for her geese damaging the lord's grain.
6d.	From Richard the parson for damage done by his geese in the lord's grain. From Richard de Broughton for the same. Pledge each the other. Fine of both 6d.

From Simon Grave for his mainpast wrongfully gleaning the lord's grain in autumn 6d., pledge John Wylymot.

Henry the miller and Thomas le Hund plaintiffs offer themselves against John le Tynkere who was attached by two rings of wheat in the hands of John le boteler and John Roger who when John le Tynkere did not come [sic]. Therefore let him be better distrained.

The reeve and the beedle must be queried concerning the produce of an acre and a half which John Robert leased to John Stoke and which they should have taken to the lord's use but because the said John Stoke took away the produce against the prohibition of the said reeve and beedle by the warrant of John Roger who was not able to warrant [this he] is in mercy 6d. pledges Richard the parson and William son of Ralph and by the same pledge he shall make satisfaction to the said reeve and beadle for the aforesaid produce for which they were at first charged. The produce is estimated at 3 rings, 3 bushels and a half of rye and 2 rings, 3 bushels of peas.

John Roger acknowledges that he had warranted John Stoke the pasture of an acre and a half when he was not able to warrant this. Therefore he is in mercy, a mass, pledge John de Wistowe.

Thomas Prat acknowledges that he is in debt to Agnes Gylot for goods to the value of 6d. Therefore he shall make satisfaction to her for the aforesaid 6d. and for the detention he is in mercy, a mass, pledge Edward Edeline. Day of payment on the Purification of the Blessed Mary.

Andrew Onty was attached to answer for that he carried away the produce of half an acre of land which John Gere rented from the said Andrew but because it was witnessed by William Nuncium that he had leave he is quit thereof.

The tasters namely Alexander the Woodward and Richard de Hyrst say that the wife of Elias Carpenter broke the assize of beer.

---

[97] Three others are fined for the same trespass.

COURT ROLLS 157

	Therefore she is in mercy 2s., pledge Geoffrey the Marshal.[98]
Ordered	The chief pledges say that the bailiff of the lord abbot made two pits in the town, to its nuisance. Therefore the bailiff and the reeve are ordered to put them right.
	And they say that William Russel harboured a certain Nicholas de Eton' who is outside the assize. Therefore he is in mercy, a mass, pledge John the Beedle.
6d.	And they say that Hugh Knyt harboured a strange woman who is not profitable to the town, 6d., pledge John Gore.
	And they say that John son of Agnes Matheu is not at all faithful and he withdrew himself. Therefore let him be taken if he shall come within this liberty.
	And they say that John the Tynekere made an assault in the home of Thomas le Hund and wounded him. Therefore let him be attached by his body. And let it be remembered that 2 rings of wheat are in the lord's possession, wherefore let them be kept.
6d.	And they say that John Robert is a tanner of leather but he gives
1 capon	6d. per annum. From Robert Curteys for the same, one capon.
1 capon	From Thomas Colbe for the same, one capon. And they say that
4d.	John Robert is a tanner of leather but he gives the lord 4d. per annum.
6d.	And they say that Henry the Miller took false tolls in the mill. Therefore he is in mercy 6d. pledge Walter the Miller.
12d.	And they say that Robert Strypling pastured the grain of the neighbours by night. Therefore he is in mercy, a mass, pledge John Ballard. From Henry son of John for the same with his beasts 6d., pledge John le Bon.
12d.	And they say that the wife of Thomas le Hund was a gleaner against the common statute of the town. Therefore she is in mercy pledge the reeve. From Mariota Gylbert for the same, pledge the beadle. From Alice daughter of Robert Matheu for the same, pledge the same John. From Johanna, daughter of Ralph Eureard for the same, pledge the reeve. From Robert Strypling because he took sheaves out of the field, pledge the reeve. From Felicia daughter of John le Straker because she gleaned contrary to the statute, pledge Hugh the Stalkere. Fine of all of them 12d. The jurors say that Richard le Camera made a pit in the royal way across from Simon Crane which is a nuisance. Therefore let it be amended. And they say that Reginald Gylbert surcharged the pasture with twenty sheep. Therefore he is in mercy 6d.,

---

[98] Twelve others were fined for the same offence. The fines are, respectively 12d., 6d., 30d., 30d., 12d., 12d., 18d., a mass, 18d., 4s., a mass, and 12d.

pledge William Kepline. And they say that William Kepline paid with sheaves in the field in autumn contrary to the common statute of the township. Therefore he is in mercy 12d., pledge the reeve.

Emma, daughter of Robert le Clerk, complains of William Gylbert for that while she was harrowing in the field of Broughton on the land of Agnes Gylbert on Wednesday next before the Purification of the Blessed Mary in the sixteenth year of the reign of King Edward [99] the said William came and threw her to the ground and by force and violence raped her and drew blood against the peace of the lord king, etc. And the said William being present denied force, violence and the shedding of blood and said that he did not rape the said Emma but that for the past three years he had known the same Emma by her own free will whenever he wished and he asked, and the said Emma likewise, that this be enquired by the thirteen chief pledges and the twelve jurors whose names are at the top of this view. Who came and say that the said William did not rape the said Emma on the day specified nor did he know her against her will as she charged but in the way he was used to knowing her nor did he shed her blood. Therefore the said William is quit and the said Emma for her false claim is in mercy. She is poor.

Richard de Broughton, clerk, complains of Alexander Bluntysham, William Ketline and John of Broughton for that they pastured their lambs on half an acre of growing wheat at Haycroft to his damage 2s. etc. And the aforesaid Alexander, William and John came and acknowledged it all and asked an assessment of the damage, and they were taxed at one ring of wheat with which

18d. they should recompense the said Richard and for their trespass they are in mercy 18d., pledge each other.

Ordered From John de Boteler for unlawful detention of 6d. from Johanna Euererad, a mass, pledge his father. And by the same pledge he shall pay the said Joanna the said money.

From Alexander frere for green [wood] 6d. From William Gernoun for the same 6d. From William son of John Long for the same 6d. Pledge each other.

6d. John Hume was attached to answer for green [wood] by pledge of
Ordered William Byssop but the same John did not come. Therefore the said William is in mercy 6d., and the said John shall be put in better pledge.

John Cateline was the pledge at the last view of William de Weston and Bartholomew le Wells for 12d. to be paid to John

[99] February 3, 1288.

Ordered	Euerard of which nothing has been paid. Therefore the said John is in mercy, forgiven. And it is ordered etc.
	From the reeve and the beadle because they did not have the book for charging the jury as is proper, forgiven.
6d.	From Geoffrey Smith of Ripton for his son taken with green [wood] 6d., pledge Thomas at the bridge. From Walter Geroun for the same, above; pledge Robert Rychard. From William Margery for the same 6d., pledge Robert Richard.
Ordered	Andrew, son of Walter of Prestel', is distrained to answer at the next court because he was attached with green [wood].
6d.	From Absalom the reeve because he did not have the roll of the halmote of the last court so that it could be looked through and the pleas carried forward, 6d.
10s.	From the chief pledges because they did not present Richard de Camera who made a pit in the royal road nor Roger Gilbert who surcharged the pasture with his sheep, and from the jury who concealed John son of Agnes Matheu who has withdrawn himself for the time being and from the whole township for not keeping watch in due form, 10s.
12d.	From Alexander Woodward and Richard de Hyrst tasters for many concealments of the trespasses of the brewsters and because they did not do their office in due form in tasting the beer of the brewsters and for other trespasses, fine of both 12d.
51s. 6d.	Sum 51s. 6d.

201 *Court of Horwood [Great Horwood, Bucks.] held on Saturday next after the Ascension of our Lord in the thirty-third year of King Edward* [100]

Essoin	Richard, parson of Horwood, versus Edmund son of Ralph in a plea of debt, by Thomas son of John.
	Ralph son of Ralph plaintiff offers himself against Richard the parson of Horwood defendant in a plea of debt. The said Richard essoins himself the second time and he has a day at the next [court] and the said Richard has a day to remedy his many defaults as above.
	The lord grants to John son of John le Mester one half virgate of land which was John's his father, the said half virgate to have and to hold in villeinage and to do for it all the customs and services which his father was accustomed to do for it. The said John gave the lord 20s. for this grant, half to be paid at the Feast of the

[100] May 29, 1305. New College Court Rolls, G.H.I., 2, 1̂.

Nativity of St John the Baptist and the other half at the Feast of St Michael, and he did fealty.

Item he granted to Sir Richard the chaplain to hold the aforesaid half virgate from the Feast of St Michael in the thirty-third year of the reign of King Edward son of King Henry to the end of a term of fourteen years, doing the customs and services in all things as the father of the said John was accustomed to do, and he shall repair and maintain the houses and buildings and he shall sustain the said John in all necessities and he shall pasture two ... [illegible] of the said John during all the said term and both for the repairs and maintenance of houses and buildings and for the aforesaid pence. He shall pay at the terms written above. And the aforesaid Richard finds pledges for keeping the aforesaid agreement, namely Robert Sanders and Thomas Berner.

Fine 20s.

At this court the lord prior granted to John Hayron one half virgate of land which was Walter Hayron's his father, to have and to hold the said half virgate of land in villeinage according to the custom of the manor, doing for it all the customs and services in everything just as his father was accustomed to do. For having this grant, moreover, the aforesaid John gave the lord prior 26s. 8d., half to be paid at the Feast of St Michael next after the making of this enrollment and the other half at the Feast of the Nativity of Our Lord next following, and he shall maintain the houses and buildings in as good a state as he received them or better and for the aforesaid pence as well as for the maintenance of the houses and buildings the aforesaid John has pledges, that is, Robert Sanders, Walter Baynard, Richard at the Brook and Ralph son of Ralph, and he is given livery of seisin and does fealty.

Court of Horwood held on Tuesday next after the Feast of St James in the thirty-third year of the reign of King Edward.[101]

Essoin   Richard, rector of the church of Horwood, essoins himself against Ralph son of Ralph in a plea of debt by Richard son of Richard de Ierdelee, second time.

Day   Ralph son of Ralph plaintiff offers himself against Richard rector of the church of Horwood in a plea of debt. Essoined, and they have a day until the next [court].

Richard rector of the church of Horwood who has a day came to

---

[101] Wednesday, July 28, 1305. See Doc. 22. This is the session next following the court held on May 29th.

COURT ROLLS 161

Mercy
12d.

this court to remedy his many defaults by pledge of Richard le Kyng, 6d., and John Godwyne 6d., and because the said rector did not come it is adjudged that Richard le Kyng and John Godwyne are in mercy, pledge each the other. And the said rector of the church of Horwood shall be put under better pledges.

The lord, of his grace, has granted to Geoffrey son of Hamon the Smith one virgate of land with appurtenances which Hamon his father [held] to have and to hold in villeinage according to the custom of the manor doing all the customs and services that his father was wont to do. And for this grant the aforesaid Geoffrey paid the lord a fine of 4 marks by pledge of Hamon Makyn, Walter Noreman, John the Smith and Richard the Smith. And he has a day to pay two marks at the Feast of St Michael next to come and two marks at the Feast of Easter.[102]

202 *View with court of Great Horwood held there on the Monday next after the Feast of the Ascension of the Lord in the thirteenth year of the reign of King Edward son of King Edward.*[103]

Essoins

Richard Steuens of the common by John ——. First time.
John of London of the same by Henry son of Nicholas.
William le Newelond of the same by Richard Newelond. First time.
The tithingmen namely John ffraunk John Asculf William Baynard Jeffrey le fferour Thomas Roger and John Payn present that Master Roger of Bauere, 12d., made default of the common [suit] and that Walter de Ryngested, 3d., made default of the common and that John de London, 2d., who should have made an essoin made default.

Distraint

Item they present that Richard son of Hamo le Brut entered upon the lord's field without leave. Therefore let him be distrained to show at the next court why he entered etc. Afterwards he made fine with the lord for the said entrance with 6d. by the pledge of Hamo le Brut.

Distraint

Item they present that John le Gard took Johanna daughter of Stephen le Gard in marriage without the lord's leave. Therefore it is ordered that the said Stephen be distrained to answer at the next court why he married his daughter Johanna without leave.
Item they present that Henry Campion raised the hue justly

---

[102] There follow the by-laws as in Doc. 22. There the record ends.
[103] May 12, 1320. New College Court Rolls, G.H.I, 2-2.

against Thomas Degneis, 3d. forgiven. Therefore the said Thomas is in mercy by pledge of John ffraunk, and John Gerard etc. And because the said John and John became the pledges of the said Thomas and did not have him at this court therefore they are in mercy 2d.

Mercy 6d. And they present that William le Sommomer raised the hue justly against Ralph Baldewyne, 6d., and drew blood from him therefore the said Ralph is in mercy by pledge of John Maykyn and Robert Saunders.

And they present that Alice Gilote raised the hue justly upon Robert Blakenan and he is dead at his own hands.

Mercy 2d. And they present that Alice Durant raised the hue justly upon Margery [last name illegibile]. Therefore the said Margery, 2d., is in mercy by pledge of Walter Steuenes.

Mercy 2s. And because the tithingmen, 2s., did not present the trespass made between Walter le Sommener and Ralph Margery in due form they are in mercy by pledge of each other.

Mercy 6d. And they present that Ralph Baldewyne drew blood from Richard le Lockyere. Therefore the said Ralph, 6d., is in mercy by pledge of John Simond and John le Smyth.

Mercy 12d. And because the tithingmen, 12d., did not attach the said Richard the Lokiere therefore they are all in mercy by pledge each of the others.

William Jeanekins is placed in the tithing of William Baynard and it is sworn etc. Ralph son of William Jenekyns is placed in the tithing of Thomas Roger and is sworn etc.

Aletasters Walter Steuenes and Richard Margary ale-tasters present that Richard Haroun (2d.) Ralph son of Richard (6d.) Stephen the Carter (6d.) Thomas Roger (6d.) Henry Bycoun (3d.) Walter Norman (6d.) Hammond Ashby (3d.) Matilda Boyercotes (3d.) John le Coupere (3d.) Alice Hayroun (3d). William Baynard (3d.) John Ffrank (3d.) William son of John (3d.) Matilda Bycoun (2d.) John Harcoun (2d.) Richard Fforge (3d.) Jeffrey Faber (3d.) John Gerard (2d.) (forgiven) Idonna Ffrankelyn (2d.) John Ffaber (2d.) brewed and sold contrary to the assize. Therefore they are all in mercy.

Memorandum concerning four skins delivered to the reeve of Newington.

Matilda wife of Robert ffrankelyn of Little Horwood plaintiff offered herself against Thomas le Sweyn in a plea of debt and John son of John Gerard and Henry Bycoun are pledges to prosecute. Therefore it is ordered that the aforesaid Thomas be summoned to answer to the said Matilda at the next court etc. (Matilda also has a plea of debt against Stephen le Carter, Agnes

COURT ROLLS 163

daughter of Stephen le Carter, and William Campion, John son of John Gerard and Henry Bycoun are pledges to prosecute).

Ralph Margery and Richard Haroun have come to an agreement by leave of the lord about a certain trespass against the said Ralph by the said Richard. Therefore the said Richard (2d.) puts himself in mercy by pledge of John Maykyn.

Richard Haroun pays the lord 12d. for leave to remain in the lord's fee coming and going at will by pledge of Ralph Margery who is also pledge of the aforesaid Richard that he will be of good conduct while he is in the lord's fee and that there shall be no claim against the tithing while he is in the fee aforesaid.[104]

Stephen le Carter gave the lord one-quarter of oats for leave to marry Johanna his daughter to John of Westbury paying at the Feast of St Michael next to come by pledge of Ralph Margery and John le Bolt.

Mercy 2s. 11d. John le Newman had two calves, Robert Pech one calf, Henry Campion (2d.) two calves, Agnes who is the wife of Richarde Kyng (2d.) two calves, Richard [last name illegible] two calves, Alice Haroun (1d.) one calf, Henry Bycoun (2d.) two calves, Robert Saunders (1d.) one calf, Richard Margery (2d.) two calves, Alan le Rype (12d.) two calves and he broke the pound, John Gerard, Sr. (forgiven) three calves, Hamo le Brut (1d.) one calf, Henry le Shepherd (1d.) for his one calf, and Alice (2d.) who is the wife of Richard Payn two calves, and Margery Mayn (2d.) two calves, and William Euerard (2d.) two calves, and John ffrank (forgiven) one calf and he broke the pound, and Richard Haroun (2d.) two calves, and Richard Baynard (2d.) two calves, and William Janekynes (1d.) one calf, entering and damaging the grain of the town of Horwood contrary to the common ordinance of the same town. Therefore they are in mercy, each of them pledge of the others.

Inquest Walter Steuenes complained of Ralph son of Richard Baynard, William Janekynes and John ffrank, William Baynard, Robert Saunders, Alice le Rous, William Saunders, Richard Blakeman, Thomas Benet, John Payn, John Gerard, Richard Margery, John Isonde, John Maykyn, Ralph son of Richard, Richard Baynard, Robert Saunders that they had depastured his grass with their beasts.[105] And the aforesaid Ralph and the others came and were not able to deny it and thereupon the aforesaid Walter asked that it be inquired on the oath of good men of the neighbourhood

[104] Walter le Taylour paid the lord 6d. for the same privilege pledge William Steuenes.

[105] This item can be seen word for word in the record of a court held on Monday, August 13, 1319.

what damaged he incurred. They say on their oath that he suffered damage to the extent of 19½d. Therefore it was adjudged that the aforesaid Walter should recover his damages against them and they are all in mercy, each of them pledge of the others.

Sum: 17s. 11d.

203 *Court of Horwood held there on Wednesday the Feast of St Margaret the Virgin in the sixteenth year of the reign of King Edward son of King Edward.*[106]

Again as often before it is ordered to distrain Hayman Kane to answer to the lord for many defaults and Geoffrey Smith in plea of debt.

Richard Cross and William Stott by leave of the lord are agreed in a plea of trespass so that the said William puts himself in mercy (6d.) by pledge of Robert Sanders.

Alice of the graveyard puts herself in mercy (8d.) for a rescue made by her mainpast from the messor of the town, by pledge of Ralph Margery.

John Gerrard and John Hildich are agreed by leave of the lord in a plea of trespass so that the said John Hildich puts himself in mercy (3d.) by pledge of Ralph Margery.

Ordered John le Newebond was distrained by six sheep to answer to Ralph Margery in a plea of debt and Henry the Shepherd rescued the aforesaid sheep from Nicholas le Honte. Therefore it is ordered

Ordered that the said Henry be distrained, to answer to the lord for the rescue at the next [court] and the aforesaid John le Newebonde to answer as before to Ralph Margery in a plea of debt.

Mercy Alan le Roper puts himself in mercy (2d.) for a rescue made and a pound broken against [the will of] the messor of the town, by pledge of Robert Sandres.

William Beynard undertook to have Matilda Wutenhan and Scholastica daughter of the said Matilda here to answer to John Makyn in a plea of trespass. The aforesaid Matilda and Sco-

Mercy lastica did not come therefore the said William is in mercy (2d.). And nonetheless it is ordered to distrain the said Matilda and

Ordered Scolastica to answer to the aforesaid John Makyn in a plea of trespass at the next [court].

Ordinances It is agreed and ordered in full court by the whole homage of the
of autumn town of Great Horwood that no one among them shall be allowed to glean who is able to earn his food and a penny a day for his

---

[106] July 20, 1323. New College Court Rolls, G.H.I, 2, 1.

COURT ROLLS 165

labour and further that no one of them shall harbour an outsider gleaning among them. And that no one of them shall cause his grain to be taken from the field by night. Nor shall anyone of them pay anyone with grain in the field. Nor shall anyone of them allow his workers to carry grain from the field to the use of any one except it be one of his own family and because his lord has need of it. Nor shall they do anything else contrary to the ordinances made in the preceding year, under pain of paying 6d. to the lord for each default. And to keep the foregoing [ordinances] and to present those who do the contrary as often as they do it William Baynard, Hugh the reeve, Geoffrey the smith and Robert Sandres were elected by the community of the town and sworn.

Mercy — It is presented that Stephan le Carter made default. Therefore he is in mercy (2d.).

Fine
one capon
one cock — Lucas de Bauecote shall give the lord one cock and one capon annually as long as he shall remain in the lord's fee, paying the cock at Christmas and the capon at the Feast of Ss John and James, by pledge of John Hildich who is also pledge of the said Lucas that he will comport himself well and faithfully so long as he remains in the fee etc.

Day at the next [court] — John Maykyn and Scolastica daughter of Matilda Wyttenham put themselves on inquest in regard to a certain trespass and a day is given them at the next [court] and the said Scolastica found a pledge to hear the said inquest at the next [court] namely William Baynard.

Ordered — All the lord's customary tenants are ordered to remove all outsiders dwelling in the fee who do not have leave before the Feast of St Peter in Chains under pain of paying the lord 40d.

    Sum 3s. 11d.   affeerers
    John ffraunk   Walter Steuenes

204 [*Great Horwood*] *Extent of the manor of the lord prior of Longville Gyfford made there on Saturday the Feast of the Invention of the Holy Cross in the thirteenth year of the reign of King Edward son of King Edward* [107]

On the oath of John Gerard Henry Marger Walter the Yronmonger William Baynard Ralph son of Ralph Geoffrey Smith William son of John John the Smith Hugh le Cere John Mayklyn John Somer and

[107] May 3, 1320. New College, Liber Niger, f. 36a–40d.

Walter Newman [108] who say on their oath that there is in the demesne a chief messuage containing two acres of which John Baynard formerly Roger Bedford holds one half rendering for it 2s. 6d. a year and John Carlyl and Alice his wife hold the other half of the said messuage rendering per annum 3s., and one capon for a certain place between their messuage and the cemetery of the church.

Item they say that in the eastern field there are 107 acres of arable land of which each acre is worth 2d. a year. Item in the southern field there are 21 acres of arable of which 14 are above Lynlond the price of each acre 2½d. In the same field there are 7 acres above the . . . ditch, each acre is worth 1½d.

Item they say that in the western field above Laydenhull in the northern part there are 10 acres each worth 2½d. and 16 acres worth 1½d.

Item they say that each acre will be sown with two bushels of wheat or three bushels of peas or three bushels of rye or four bushels of drage or four bushels of oats most years.

Sum total of arable land seven score and eighteen acres. Sum total of rent 25s. 8½d.

Meadow

Item they say that in the meadow of Longehamme there are 2½ acres of meadow price of each acre per annum 4s. and in the meadow of Shepesham there are 3½ acres of meadow price of each acre 2s. 6d. and that in ryageweynsende there is one acre of meadow and it is worth per annum 18d. and in the assart there are five acres of meadow worth per acre per annum 12d. Sum of acres of meadow 12. Sum of pence 22s. 6d.

Pasture

Item they say that in the cowmede there are 2½ acres of pasture price of each acre per annum 12d. Sum of pence 2s. 6d.

Item there is a water mill and it is worth above maintenance 6s. 8d. per annum.

Free Tenants

William Adam formerly Henry Bykon holds one messuage and one virgate of land with its appurtenances rendering therefor 8d. per annum and he owes suit of court from three weeks to three weeks and he owes wardship, marriage and relief.

Robert William formerly Hammund Bret owes one messuage and one virgate for the same rent and service.

Robert William formerly Alice Rous holds one messuage and three furlongs for three shillings and she owes suit like the above Henry and she holds by charter.

[108] These men were all unfree; see Index of Liber Niger.

John Hykedon formerly Richard Steuenes one messuage and one furlong for 8d. rent and service like the aforesaid Henry.
The tenement formerly held by Richard Exir, one messuage and a furlong for 11d. rent of which Robert William formerly Hammund Bret owes 4½d. and Richard son of Agnes Steuenes 1d., Alice le Rus and William the Newman 4d. and Richard son of John Steuenes 2d. and the said tenement owes suit etc. like the aforesaid Henry Bykon.
Richard Frankelyn formerly John Frankelyn one messuage and one virgate for 19½d. per annum and he owes suit etc. like the aforesaid Henry.
Richard Bayld' formerly Richard Margery, one messuage and one virgate, 8d. per annum and suit like the aforesaid Henry.
John Clerk formerly John ffrank', one messuage, one virgate 15d. rent. The same John pays a penny and a half per annum for a certain fish pond and suit of court like Henry.
Sum of all the rents 5s. 1½d.

Customary tenants of one virgate of land

John Smyth holds of the lord one messuage and one virgate of land and one butt containing one rood of land, rendering therefor 4s. 4d. per annum at the aforesaid terms and at the death of the aforesaid John he shall give a heriot namely his best beast and if the said John does not have a beast he shall give the lord as a heriot the produce of the best half acre of land under crop on the said land and for the said heriot the wife of the said John shall remain on the said land for one whole year after the decease of the said John doing the services and customs due and accustomed from it without making fine and after the expiry of the said year the tenement shall remain in the lord's hands until fine is made for it according to ancient custom.
Item the aforesaid John ought to plough with the lord at the winter sowing for one day with what beasts he has in the plough by reasonable summons three days in advance for the reason that his plough-beasts often depasture in the woods where they cannot be found at the will of the said John, and if he does not have plough-beasts then he shall plough with the lord with his plough and this work is worth a penny and a half.
And he ought to harrow with the lord for one day with one man and one horse at the winter sowing and he shall have his food or a ha'penny and this work is worth besides the food 1d.
Item he ought to plough at the Lenten sowing in the aforesaid manner and this work is worth a penny and a half and he ought to harrow at the same season with one man and one horse and he shall have from the lord a measure of oats worth a farthing and in addition to the oats this work is worth 1d. And he ought to plough the fallow in the aforesaid manner,

when his plough-beasts pasture the herbage, and this work is worth 1d., and he shall find one man to weed with the lord for one day and this work is worth a ha'penny.

And he owes one man to mow in the lord's meadow for one day and he shall have of the lord one loaf of wheat bread price a ha'penny for this work and he shall have one bundle of hay as much as he can lift with his handfork price a farthing and this work is worth beside the hay 2d.

And the same John together with all the customers when they ought to mow shall have one live sheep to the value of 18d. and they shall have in common one shovel full of salt valued at a penny and the said John also should turn and make the lord's hay with one man for one day and this work is worth 1d.

And he ought also to carry the lord's hay to the court of the lord of the manor for one day with one cart and he with the other customers shall have his food namely a loaf of wheat bread, beer and cheese as food for the said John and his boy, 2d., and if he does not have his food he shall cart no more and this work is worth besides the food 1d.

And he ought also to reap the lord's grain for one day in autumn with two men without food and this work is worth 4d., and again he ought to reap with the lord with all his family except his wife at the great boon day and the same John shall go to see that his family does their work well and he ought to gather the sheaves together [in shocks] and at noon they shall come for their food to the lord's court at the lord's expense with his whole family carrying napkin, cup and dishes and they shall carry away with them all the scraps left over in a napkin and a cup full of beer.

Item and he ought to mow the demesne with two men for one day if need be without food and this work is worth 4d.

And he ought also to work at enclosing the lord's assart with one man for one day and in the evening he shall have a bundle of brushwood to take with him to his home and this work is worth, besides, a ha'penny.

And he owes one man for one day to gather nuts for the lord if there shall be nuts in the lord's wood and after that day the said John together with the other customers shall have the nuts that remain in the said wood; and he owes suit of court.

Sum of rents 2s. 2d. Sum of works $19\frac{1}{2}$d.[109]

[109] The other virgaters are John Warner, formerly Hugh Nell', William Adam formerly Alice Bouton, Richard Baynard formerly John Gerard, John William formerly John Makyn, William Hogges formerly Robert Saunders, Robert Coupere formerly Walter Yermonger, Stephen Smith formerly Robert Saunders, Walter Hawkyn formerly Ralph son of Ralph, John Hawkyn formerly William Baynard, William Frankelyn formerly Ralph Wyttyngham, John Clerk formerly Johanna daughter of Johanna, John Wilkyn formerly Hugh the Reeve, John Smith formerly Walter Smith, John Clerk formerly Walter Norman.

Customary tenants of one half virgate

Robert Rede formerly William Saunders holds one half virgate of land rendering therefor per annum 2s. namely at the Feast of St Martin 12d. and at the Feast of St James 12d. and after his death he owes a heriot namely his best beast and if he shall not have a beast the lord shall have as a heriot the produce of the best half acre of land under crop in his tenement and for the aforesaid heriot his wife shall remain in the said tenement for one whole year after the decease of the said William for the services due and accustomed without making a fine and after one year has elapsed the aforesaid tenement shall remain in the lord's hands until a fine has been made to the lord according to ancient custom.

Item the said William ought to plough with the lord at the winter sowing with as many plough-beasts as he has in the plough with three days' notice in which to take the animals depasturing in the woods where he may not be able to find them when he wants to and if he shall not have animals then he shall plough with the lord with the quarter part of one plough and this work is worth a ha'penny and a farthing and he ought also to harrow for one day with one man and one horse at the winter sowing and he shall have his food or a ha'penny and this work is worth besides the food 1d. and he ought to plough at the Lenten sowing in the manner aforesaid and this work is worth a ha'penny and a farthing and he ought to harrow at the same season one man and one horse for one day and he shall have one measure of oats to the price of a farthing and this work is worth besides the oats 1d. and he ought to plough at fallow time in the manner aforesaid when his plough-beasts can feed on the herbage and this ploughing is worth a ha'penny and a farthing.

And he owes one man at the weeding for one day and this is worth a ha'penny and he owes one man at the mowing in the lord's meadow for one day and he shall have from the lord one loaf of wheat bread price a ha'penny and he shall have one bunch of grass as much as he is able to lift with his handfork price a ha'penny.

And the same William together with all the customers who mow shall have one live sheep price 16d. and they shall have together in common one shovel of salt price 1d. and this is worth besides the provisions 2d.

And the said William shall also turn and carry the lord's hay with one man for one day and this is worth 1d. and he ought to carry the lord's hay to the court of the said lord of the manor for one day with the said [sic] cart and he along with the other customers shall have his food namely a loaf of wheat bread, beer and cheese, the value of the food 1d., and if he does not have his food he shall not cart any more and this work is worth aside from his food a ha'penny.

And he ought to reap the lord's grain for one day with one man without food and this work is worth 2d. And he ought to reap with the lord at the great boon of autumn with all his family except his wife and the same William shall go to see to it that his family do their work well and he ought to shock the sheaves and at noon he shall come to the lord's manse for his food at the lord's expense, husband and wife with his whole family bringing napkin, cup and dishes and they shall carry away all the scraps in their napkins and a cup full of beer.

The same William ought to reap with one man for one day the lord's grain if it is necessary and this work is worth 2d.

The same William ought to make an enclosure with one man for one day around the lord's assart and he shall have one bundle of brush wood to take to his house and this work is worth in addition to the brush wood a ha'penny.

Item he owes one man to gather nuts for the use of the lord for one day if there are nuts in the lord's wood and after that the said William together with all the other customers shall have the nuts that remain in said woods.

Sum of rents 12d. Sum of works $19\frac{1}{2}$d.[110]

Cottagers

Roger Milleward formerly Geoffrey Smyth holds one cottage rendering per annum 2s. and he owes one man to weed for one day and this is worth a ha'penny and he owes one man for a day to toss the grass after mowing and he shall have from the lord for his labour one loaf of wheat bread worth a ha'penny and he owes one man to turn and lift the hay for one day and this work is worth 1d. and he owes one man for one day to make a cock of the hay and this is worth 1d. and he owes one man for two days to bind the grain in autumn after the reaping and he shall have each day at evening one sheaf of the kind of grain he has bound to take with him to his home, worth 2d. and this work is worth 2d. besides the sheaf. And he ought to come to the great boon day with all his family and he shall bind after the reapers and he shall come for his food with all his family just as the aforesaid customers and he owes one man for one

[110] The following are the names of the customary tenants of one half virgate who owe rents and services like those of William Saunders: Richard Bedforde formerly Thomas Heriot, Walter Hawkyns formerly Alice Serat, Richard Taylor formerly Walter Best, Walter Smyth formerly Ralph le Meister, Robert Tomlyne formerly Robert son of Tomlyne, Richard Hund formerly Johanna Est, Robert Bedeford formerly Alice Durant, Adam Richard formerly Margery Mayn, Richard Twychyn formerly Johanna Yorardvtz, Johanna Warner, Matilda de Boycote, Nicholas Gylmot formerly Edith Couper, Robert Bayly formerly Johanna Payntz, Robert Taylor formerly Johanna Hyldyd, Emma Chyrchey formerly Johanna Okteley, William Maygee formerly Stephen le Carter, Johanna Baynard formerly Richard Baynard, William Wilkyn formerly Thomas son of Roger, Johanna Frankelyn formerly Henry Campyon, Robert Bykon formerly Johanna Hayron, Johanna Page formerly William Kyng, Johanna Baynard formerly Johanna Godwyne, Johanna Hykalon formerly Johanna Ysonde, Richard Chyrchey formerly Julian son of Walter Yremongere.

day to gather nuts like the aforesaid customers do and he owes suit at the two great courts.

Sum of rents 12d.   Sum of works 4½d.[111]

The rector of the church of Horwood holds a certain place enclosed in his court which was of the land of Peter Godewyn returning 6d. per annum and two suits of court at the two great courts.

William Gobyon formerly John Isonde holds one cottage next to Sladedych and a certain plot of meadow called hyllymede returning 15d. rent per annum.

Richard Chyrchey formerly Alice Chyrchey holds one messuage and one virgate of land paying 5s. 2d. rent per annum and he owes a heriot and suit of court every three weeks.

Memorandum: that the whole township as well free as customers give the lord 60 cocks per annum the value of each 1½d.

205   *Court of Halton [Oxon.] held there on Thursday next after the Feast of St Peter in Chains in the third year of the reign of King Edward third after the Conquest.*[112]

	Hugh de Oxident by leave of the lord demised to John Symond 4½ acres of his arable land lying in the fields of Halton of which 1½ acres lie in Meredenesdene next to the land of Thomas Gudrych and one half acre lies in the Outelong next to the land of Richard Reynald and one half acre lies in Shortelebrunde next to the land of Richard Dourten and one half acre lies above le Stone next to the land of the said Richard and one half acre lies at the Wertlonge next to the forge of William Coupere and one acre lies divided in le dych furlong—to hold for the term of the life of the said John Symond and pay a rent to the said Hugh annually at the usual terms of 18d. for all services and the said Hugh shall do the lord all other services pertaining to the said
Fine 5s.	land for the said 18d. And the said John gave the lord 5s. for the said land, pledge the said Hugh.
Mercy 6d.	Thomas Godrych pleads guilty to a false complaint against Juliana Wodeme in a plea of trespass, pledge himself.
Mercy 6d.	The said Thomas pleads guilty to the same against the same Juliana in a plea of debt by the same pledge.

---

[111] The following cottagers owe the same services as Roger with their rents varying from 3d. to 6d.: Richard Milleward formerly Richard Claydon, Walter Haukyn formerly Thomas le Sweyn, John Pecur formerly Hugh Neel, Walter Smyth formerly John Pykard, Robert Benet, John Page formerly Johanna Isonde, Hammond Gerard formerly Johanna Gerard, William Mayge formerly William Steuykle, Alice Haukyn formerly Ralph Wyttynham, William Cebyson formerly Richard Disicus, Thomas Taylor formerly Johanna Faber.

[112] Thursday August 3, 1329. Halton Rolls, *loc. cit.*, 1–16–45.

Inquest	It says that Robert le ffynch is in default, therefore let him be
Distraint	distrained. Item John le Carpenter (12d.) John le . . . [illegible] (3d.) John le Lynch (3d.) Robert Silberman (2d.) Roger Tristram (6d.) Dionisius le Hanch' (2d.) Hugh atte Style (6d.) and Hugh
Mercy 3s. 4d.	Huercke (6d.), natives are in default therefore [they are] in mercy.
Heriot 10d.	William Cugelman came in full court and rendered into the lord's hand one messuage next to the lord's mill for which the lord has for a heriot one customary [pig?] worth by estimate 10d. And Richard son of William West, a native of the lord, came and is siesed of the said messuage holding [it] in villeinage according
Fine 10s.	to custom and he gives 10s. for entry and pays annually at the usual terms 3s. 6d. for all services and he does fealty as a native, pledge William West.
Ordinance of autumn	It is ordered by the lord's bailiffs and by the consent of the whole homage both free and customary that no one shall glean who is able to earn a penny a day and food. Item that gleaners young and old shall glean faithfully and well. Item that no one shall harbour any, whether denizens or outsiders, who trespass in gleaning or in other ways. Item that no one shall have egress from his close over the land of another and if he has an exit over his own land he shall save his neighbour harmless. Item that no one shall enter a field with a cart after sunset to cart grain. Item that no one shall enter the stubble with his sheep and other beasts before it has been depastured by the beasts of the plough. Item that no one shall tether a mare in the fields of grain, reaped or standing, where she can do damage. Item that no one shall make a footpath, driveway, or track for his grain cart over the grain of another to the damage of the neighbours, by night or at any other hour of the day. Item that henceforth no one shall look for green beans or peas in the field except between mid-prime and prime. And these ordinances are to be kept under pain of 6s. 8d. And to keep watch over these ordinances and attach those who break them and present at the next court all those who break them as often as they do so there were elected and sworn Philip atte Lynch Thomas le Cook Thomas at the Pit William West Thomas Hemmyng and Richard de Mordene.
	Again as before it is ordered to distrain all outsiders who have not given security.
Distraint	Again as before it is ordered that John atte Street be distrained to show in what manner he has entered the lord's fee.
Take over	Again as before it is ordered that the land which Nicholaus Whyt held of the lord in villeinage be taken into the lord's hands.

Sum 20s. including heriot.

206 *Halton [Oxon.]. View with Court, Wednesday next before the Feast of St Martin in the third year of Richard II after the Conquest.*[113]

Cert money one-half mark	Robert Smyth William West William Waryner Thomas Bendekyn Thomas Trystram and John Poygnauit, tithingmen and ale-tasters present that they give cert money on this day of half a mark.
Mercy 19d.	And the Lady Isabella, Thomas Wendemere, John Strete Thomas Marewelle (2d.) John Martyn (2d.) made default. Therefore they are in mercy. And that the tithingmen do not have the whole tithing, in mercy (6d.), and that Thomas Royuald (2d.) makes default, therefore he is in mercy and the tithing for concealment is in mercy (2d.).
Mercy 4d.	And that William Cooper unjustly took toll therefore he is in mercy.
To be enquired	And that Walter Spenser and Thomas Deram caught a duck with a net in the lord's woods, and later it was acknowledged by the bailiff that they had a licence from the warden, therefore etc.
Mercy 10d.	The ale-tasters present that Richard Martyn, once (1d.), Richard Reynold, once (2d.), Robert Smyth, once (2d.), John Poynauyt, once (2d.), Walter West, once (2d.), brewed and broke the assize therefore, in mercy.
Twelve jurors	John Sandewell, Richard Baron, Thomas Reygnald, John Pegge, John Sandewell, William Martyn, Richard Martyn, Philip Smyth, Thomas at the Pit, Richard Compayn, Edward Sawyer, Walter West, Thomas Wodeward, Richard Knight sworn present that . . . [this sentence is left unfinished].

There follows the little court.

Attachments of the messor Mercy 13d.	Richard Chaundler (2d.) Mathew Donne (1d.) John Sprynger (2d.) John Crosse (2d.) William Sheperde (2d.) Robert Smyth (2d.) John Skryngyn (2d.) Robert Smyth (1d.) put themselves in mercy for trespasses in the grain and wood of the lord.
Native	The homage presents that Thomas Merewell living at Rykmersworth is a native of the lord and has withdrawn himself from the lord's demesne, therefore etc.
Mercy 2d. Ordered	Item they present that Walter West has a house that is in poor condition therefore he is in mercy and it is ordered that he repair it before the next court under pain of 2s.
Wardens of the by-laws	John Pougnauit Thomas Wodeward and Thomas at the Pit wardens of the by-laws [*belawes*] present that Roger Marewell (2d.) John Short (2d.) William Martyn (2d.) William Merdene

[113] November 16, 1379. Halton Rolls, *loc. cit.*, 1–16–47.

Mercy 8d.	(1d.) had their sheep in the stubble in autumn time before the cattle [*animalia*] had depastured it, which is contrary to the ordinance of autumn, therefore they are in mercy.
And that Alice Deram gave Margery Haket a sheaf contrary to the said ordinance, therefore she is in mercy.
And that Matilda Trystram (3d.) stole four sheaves in autumn therefore she is in mercy.
Ordered to levy	They [the jurors] present that John Martyn who holds one messuage and one virgate of land of the lord according to the custom of the manor for the term of his life is in arrears with his rent, namely, 6d. for the two preceding years, for which the bailiff is charged in his account, and his customary labour to the value of 6d. and he has put his land at farm without leave of the lord, that is, to Richard Martyn, William Martyn, William Heyward, John Martyn, Jr., John Marewell, Thomas Trystram, Thomas Sandewell. Therefore these who occupy the land without leave are in mercy and it is ordered that the said rent and the value of the works be levied from the said tenants of the land to the use of the said bailiff because his account is charged with the said rent and services.
Ordered to seize	Item they present that the said John Martyn relinquished his said tenement and virgate of land and withdrew himself from the demesne with his chattels by night but where he dwells they do not know because of his divers debts to the lord and others. Therefore it is ordered that the bailiff seize the said tenement of land to the lord's hands and render to the lord the profits thence ensuing etc.
Fealty	And that Richard Haket who held half an acre of the lord has died and he has no animal which the lord can have for heriot and Margery his widow claims to hold the said half acre of land of the lord while she is sole by custom of the manor and she does fealty.

Sum, 11s. 4d., and 12d. of rent withheld.

The expenses of the steward holding the court there and overseeing the manor for one night 2s. 2d., one bushel of oats, one duck, and one capon.

INDEX

INDEX

INDEX TO INTRODUCTION

Access, right of, 55
Acre, size of the medieval, 22; of the Statute, 22

Balks, 22–3
Beane, 38–40
Blackstone, on gleaning, 31
Boon-works, 29
Boundaries, 52–4
Boundary marks, 54; in New England, 54
By-herds, 48
By-laws, earliest, 19; enforcement and penalties, 60, 61

Carting by night, 36–7
Churchwardens, 64
Coaration, 20; in New England, 78
Common consent, 58–9; lord of the manor and, 59
Commonage, right of, in New England, 78

Extent, manorial, 18

Fallow, cultivation of, 44–6; pasture of, 42
Fences, 51–2; of crofts, 51; of fields, 52
Fines, 63; shared with the village church, 63–4
Freeholders, 58
Furrows, length of, 22; stealing of, 23

Gleaners, 28
Gleaning, by-laws of, 29–31
Gore, 23

Harlestone, Northants., agreement of the inhabitants, 75
Harvest, 27–34
Harvesting, early machine for, 38; McCormack reaper, 38
Hay, scarcity of, 25
Haying, 25–7
Hayward, *see* Messor

Hemingford, Hunts., lease of to the men of the town, 68–72
Highway Act of 1555, 57
Highways, overseers of, 57
Horses, 43; mares with foals, 44

Ine, Laws of, 16

Kingsthorp, Northants., lease of to its tenants, 72–5

Labourers, Statute of, 32, 33
Lanes, 54
Leasing of manors, 68
Legumes, 38–40

Manor, court of, 65; extent of, 18; lord of, 59
Manure, 17
Meadows, 25; lotting of, 26
Messor, 63
Mowing, by-laws of, 26

New England towns, 17, 77–8; by-laws of, 78
Nitrogen fixation, 17

Open-fields, origin of, 15–16

Parish churches, embellished and enlarged, 64
Parishioners, responsibilities of, 63–4
Parson, economic importance of, 58–9
Pasture, 40–6; of meadow, 41; of stubble 17, 42
Paths, 55
Peas and beans, 38–40; by-laws of, 39–40
Pigs, 48–9; feeding of, 49; herding of, 49; ringing of, 50
Plebiscite, 66
Plough twist, 22
Ploughing, 20–3; by-laws of, 23
Ploughs, 20
Poor, the, 31

Reapers, wages of, 32–3
Reeve's account, 18
Right of way, 55–6
Roads, 54–7; maintenance of, 56–7

Selion, 21–2
Sheaf stealing, 34–8
Sheaves, by-laws concerning, 35–8
Sheep, 46–8; by-laws concerning, 47
Shepherds, 48
Shrewton, Wilts., manor of dismembered, 67
Sowing, 23–5; by-laws of, 24
Straw, 41–2
Stubble, 17, 42

Tethering, 43–4
Tithe sheaves, 36

Vill, 64–5; of divided lordship, 75–7
Village assembly, 67

Walsoken, Norfolk, community of the vill of, 76–7
Wardens of the by-laws, 60–3; number, 60; presentments of, 62–3
Wimeswold, Leics., by-laws of, 75–6
Woodwards, duties of, 65; election of, 65

INDEX OF MANORS

The by-laws and court rolls are listed under the names of the manors from whose rolls they were taken. References are to the numbered documents followed in each case by the date in parentheses.

Brightwaltham, Berks., 16 (1293), 61 (1340)
Broughton, Hunts., 7 (1288), 200 (1288), 98 (1391), 109 (1405), 137 (1430)
Burwell, Cambs., 122 (1411)

Castleacre, Norf., 27 (1309)
Chatteris, Cambs., 2 (1273)
Cheddington, Bucks., 3 (1275)
Cuxham, Oxon., 21 (1296), 32 (1315), 58 (1338)

Dinton, Bucks., 170 (1493)

Elmley Castle, Worcs., 83 (1373), 85 (1376), 97 (1390), 101 (1391), 105 (1398), 121 (1411), 123 (1412), 126 (1412), 129 (1416), 131 (1416), 141 (1432), 145 (1439), 147 (1446), 149 (1449), 151 (1451), 152 (1453), 153 (1454), 156 (1465), 159 (1469), 161 (1469), 163 (1473), 165 (1481), 166 (1483), 169 (1486), 171 (1498), 172 (1502), 174 (1507), 184 (1521), 190 (1537)
Elton, Hunts., 187 (1527)
Eynsham, Oxon., 19 (1296)

Great Horwood, Bucks., 9 (1290), 22 (1305), 201 (1305), 24 (1306), 29 (1310), 31 (1314), 33 (1316), 36 (1319), 202 (1320), 204 (1320), 203 (1322), 38 (1322), 41 (1327), 46 (1330), 50 (1331), 51 (1332), 55 (1335), 57 (1337), 60 (1339), 63 (1341), 65 (1343), 66 (1343), 70 (1346), 72 (1349), 73 (1351), 74 (1353), 75 (1354), 76 (1356), 77 (1357), 78 (1362), 80 (1364), 81 (1368), 84 (1374), 88 (1385), 91 (1388), 93 (1389), 94 (1389), 102 (1391), 104 (1397), 112 (1405), 113 (1406), 115 (1407), 116 (1408), 127 (1415), 132 (1417), 136 (1429), 142 (1433), 144 (1436), 150 (1451), 155 (1463), 157 (1461), 158 (1463), 164 (1480), 167 (1483), 168 (1484), 173 (1503), 176 (1513), 177 (1514), 178 (1515), 179 (1516), 180 (1516), 182 (1519), 183 (1521), 185 (1524), 188 (1531), 189 (1534), 191 (1538), 192 (1542)

Halton, Bucks., 17 (1295), 44 (1329), 205 (1329), 87 (1379), 206 (1379), 108 (1403), 128 (1415), 196 (1546)
Hemingford, Hunts., 20 (1296), 117 (1409)
Hitchin, Herts., 162 (1471)
Houghton, Hunts., 13 (1291), 28 (1310), 110 (1405)

INDEX 179

Launton, Oxon., 89 (1385), 95 (1389), 107 (1401), 148 (1446)
Leighton Buzzard, Beds., 160 (1460)

Newington, Oxon., 1 (1270), 5 (1286), 10 (1290), 35 (1318), 40 (1326), 45 (1330), 48 (1331), 67 (1345), 69 (1348), 119 (1410), 130 (1416)
Newton Longville, Bucks., 196 (1283), 197 (1284), 198 (1290), 8 (1290), 11 (1291), 14 (1293), 18 (1295), 37 (1322), 42 (1329), 43 (1329), 47 (1330), 49 (1331), 52 (1332), 199 (1332), 53 (1333), 54 (1335), 56 (1335), 59 (1339), 62 (1341), 64 (1342), 68 (1346), 71 (1348), 90 (1387), 92 (1388), 106 (1401), 114 (1406), 133 (1422), 134 (1426), 143 (1436), 175 (1509), 181 (1518), 193 (1545), 194 (1545), 195 (1546)

Podington, Beds., 103 (1395)

Ripton Regis, Hunts., 12 (1291), 34 (1317)
Roxhill, Beds., 25 (1307), 26 (1308), 39 (1322)

Staines, Middlesex, 4 (1276)
Stukeley, Hunts., 23 (1305)

Therfield, Herts., 15 (1293)

Upwood, Hunts., 30 (1311), 82 (1369), 111 (1405), 124 (1412), 135 (1428), 140 (1430)

Warboys, Hunts., 86 (1378), 96 (1390), 100 (1391), 120 (1411), 125 (1412), 138 (1430), 146 (1440)
Weedon, Bucks., 186 (1524)
Welwyn Rectory Manor, Herts., 6 (1287)
Wistow, Hunts., 79 (1363), 99 (1390), 118 (1410), 139 (1430), 154 (1455)

INDEX OF BY-LAWS

The principal subjects with which the by-laws deal are listed alphabetically. References are to the numbered Documents.

Axe, carrying in lord's wood, prohibited, 192

Balks, must not be pastured till 1 August, 150
Beans, gathering of prohibited, 189; landholders may gather on own land, only, 31, 199; poor may gather, but only at end or sides of selions, 8, 199
Beer, must be sold for a half-penny, 20
Brewers, must brew through whole of autumn, 140; must not brew during Church Ale, 112; must sell 3 gallons to each neighbour, 165; must not sell beer more than 4 days old, 164
Butts, villagers must repair, 164; those who shoot arrows, must replace the bars, 164
Byherds, prohibited, 75; of cows, in summer, prohibited, 187; of sheep, in grain fields, prohibited 11 November to end of autumn, 187
By-laws, repealed, 37; re-enacted, 9, 11, 18, 37, 41, 49, 50, 53, 54, 57, 60, 62, 63, 68, 70, 71, 128, 161; enacted for a trial period, 186

Cadavers, must not be put in the lane, 97, 159
Calves, must not pasture before other animals, 8; excluded from fields of grain, 24, 31, unless herded, 47, 52, 93, 199, unless tethered, 155; must not go at large in sown fields till end of autumn, 192; excluded from the meadow, 31, 65; must not pasture anywhere unless tethered, 106
Carting of grain by night prohibited, 8, 24, 36, 38, 42, 46, 47, 51, 52, 59, 67, 76, 77, 109, 122, 199, 203, 205; prohibited unless cart was in the field by day, 48; of marl and manure, must be in the accustomed way, 65
Carts, must not enter a field of grain after dark, 44
Common or waste, pasturing and tethering prohibited, 3 May to August, 170; mowing in, prohibited before 7 July, 170

180   OPEN-FIELD FARMING IN MEDIEVAL ENAGLND

Common ways, horses may not pasture or be tethered in before Pentecost, 194; oxen may not pasture, before Trinity Sunday, 193, except on own land, 194; each tenant must mend his own part, 191

Common ways in the fields, pasturing before Pentecost except by landholders, prohibited, 192

Cottagers, may not have byherds of sheep, 24; may not have cattle in the fields of other tenants, 185; their cattle must be in the common herd, 185; stints of, 192

Cows, must not pasture the King's way through the sown field till end of autumn, 182

Crofts, common of, reserved to tenants, 125; fences of, *see* Fences

Ditches, must be cleaned, before the next court, 138; by 11 November, 139, 187; each tenant must clean his own, 191

Ducks, not allowed in the brook, 101; must not enter the fields of grain before end of autumn, 145

Enclosures, trespassing in, prohibited, 44

Feast days, work on, prohibited, 89, 99, 107, 140, 148; all autumn work on, prohibited, 124

Fences, all breaks and gaps must be repaired, 36, 46, 187; breaks and gaps next to open fields must be repaired by every tenant, 3, 74, 96; fences between neighbour and neighbour must be repaired, 187; croft fences must be kept tight, 41, 42, 47, 51, 69

Fines, for breach of by-laws, doubled if by night, 8; of boys under age and of servants unable to pay, must be paid by their masters, 162; shared with the church, *see* Parish Church

Fishing, prohibited, 178; except on tenant's own ground, 180

Foals, excluded from common fields of grain, 24, 86, 122; excluded till all grain has been cleared, 79; excluded from the fields 1 August to 29 September, 139; excluded till 8 September, 118; excluded, unless tied, 100, 140; must not follow the carts in autumn, 135, 138, 146; must be tied to dams after 7 July, 187; must be herded or tied, 3 May to end of autumn, 176, 177; less than one month old, must not go at large in the grain fields, 158, 191; one month or over, must not go at large in grain fields, 183; 189, more than eight weeks old, must not go at large in bean fields, 189; under one year, may not enter a sown field untied or untended, 76, 78, 135, 180; one year old and over, may be pastured in field and meadow only if herded, 93

Folds and pens, none may be placed on the common, 186

Fuel, each cottager must have two loads of wood in his yard, 187

Furze, must not be taken from the common without leave, 180

Geese, none allowed in the brook, 150; not till Michaelmas, 129

Glean, none may who are able of body to reap, usually, for a specified wage, 5, 8, 22, 38, 42, 44, 48, 51, 55, 59, 67, 72, 76, 77, 90, 92, 94, 103, 110, 111, 113, 114, 115, 118, 119, 120, 122, 123, 124, 130, 135, 138, 139, 140, 145, 160, 162, 199, 203, 205; only those may who are too young or too old to reap, 44, 61; no outsiders may, 36, 46, 51, 52, 69, 77, 199, 203, 205; no outsiders, unless vouched for, 8, 42, 47

Gleaners, must enter field by one of the four lanes, 77; must return with gleanings by King's way, 81; by royal way, not through gaps, 115

Gleaning, not till all the grain has been gathered into sheaves, 121; not till all sheaves have been carried away, 123; 131; not till a space of 4 a. has been cleared of sheaves, 162; not till 10 a. have been raked and the sheaves taken away, 160; not till 40 selions have been cleared, 45; between sunrise and sunset, only, 115

Green beans, must be gathered

INDEX

between middle of prime and prime, 33, 44
Green crops, may not be gathered in another's land after 1 August, 42, 47, 52

Harbouring prohibited, of those who play illicit games, 183; of strangers and vagabonds, 33, 190; of women of ill fame, 189; of those who glean wrongfully, 3, 4, 26, 27, 39, 44; of outsiders, in autumn, 5; of outsiders, in the town pasture, 21; of those who carry grain unlawfully, 22
Headlands, may be pastured only after meadow has been mown, 93
Hedges, must be repaired by all tenants, 173; must be mended by 11 November, 187; customary tenants must repair, between neighbour and neighbour, 187; must not be cut or carried, 202; must not be broken, 184
Herdsman, all animals must be in his keeping, 73, 193; each tenant must contribute to his wages, 133
Horses, excluded from meadow till Michaelmas, 79; may not enter fields night or day unless tethered, 105

Illicit games, labourers, artisans and servants forbidden to play; 183; forbidden, except at Christmas time, 178

Labourers, wages specified, 146; must work in their own village, 116
Lambs, may not pasture on another's land, 56
Lanes, all tenants must repair, 165; must be mended with stone carted by those with carts, 152

Manure, must not be taken from the meadow, 66
Mares, must not be tethered with horses, 146; mares only, allowed in the stubble, 120; may not be put in the fen, hobbled, till end of August, 187
Mares with foals, must not go at large in sown fields, 182, 185; must not be tethered in grain fields or meadows, 75; must not be tethered next to the grain day or night, 123; must be tethered at end, not side, of a land, 78, 92
Meadows, must not be mowed till all assemble, 167; none may ride over between Christmas and 24 June, 154
Meadows, pasturing of, not before 22 February, 81; not before Michaelmas, 167; not till end of August, 145; not till hay has been carried away, 65, 80, 131; not till all tenants agree, 141; not by any animals before Pentecost unless tethered, 65; no foals or calves unless tethered, 155; no pigs, 101
Meadows, separable, must be divided beginning at the top, 150
Messor, elected a warden of the by-laws, 53, 80
Metes and bounds, must be set and encroachments presented, 23; all tenants and residents 12 years and over must survey, 149

Night walkers, none after 9 o'clock, 151

Oxen, must not pasture common ways before Trinity Sunday except on owner's land, 194; must not pasture common ways after Trinity Sunday, 193

Parish church, one-half the fine allotted to, 106, 112, 117, 137, 138, 139, 140, 146, 150, 154, 155, 160, 168, 170; stolen sheaves given to, 63; tenants and residents assemble in, 149
Pasture, separable, must be in common after 24 June, 133, 179; after 1 August, 127, 132, 143, 150; if adjacent to sown fields, animals must be herded, 173
Pasturing, general rules: no animals may go at large till end of autumn, 80; no animals may pasture fallow, meadow, sown fields or common ways, 31 May to June, 104; no animals except oxen may pasture common fields before Pentecost,

188; for as long as a night and a day, without right, penalized, 91; beasts on the common must always be herded, 144; at night, prohibited, 113, 115, 144

Pasturing the roads, ways and paths: between Easter and Trinity prohibited, 96; Easter to 24 June, permitted, 179; 29 October to Pentecost, prohibited, 133; limited to 2 oxen or 2 cows, 200; no sheep 25 March to 1 August, 187; no cows in the royal way to end of autumn, 182

Pasturing the stubble: not till 3 weeks after harvest, except cart horses, 82, 205; not till 10 acres have been cleared, 51, 80, 90, 114, 160; 14 acres, 92; 15 acres, 101; one land, 8; one stadium, 98, 102, 109, 110; one furlong, 146

Peas and beans, landholders may gather on their own land, only, 8, 46, 52, 55, 81; must be gathered between sunrise and prime, 8, 17, 47, 52, 81, 205; landless must have consent of neighbours, 151, 190; must be gathered from the furrows and at ends of the selions, not the middle, 153

Pigs, may not pasture stubble with larger animals, 90; excluded from the meadow till end of autumn, 102; excluded from Lenten field, 35; must not pasture grass in fields of grain, 122; excluded from stubble till 40 selions have been cleared, 123; may pasture common field by leave of the reeves of autumn, 135; must be herded by day, 64, 119, 130, 178

Pigs must be ringed: at all times, 171; with iron rings, 19; from Ascension Day till end of autumn, 174; before 28 October (by-law of 22 October), 154

Pits, must be filled up, 118

Plebiscite, by-law so called, 128, 142

Plough, beasts of the, allowed to pasture first, 44; need not be herded, 193; may pasture meadow if herded, 78; not subject to usual rules of pasture, 179

Plough, wood for, not to be taken from royal wood, 195

Ploughs, those having two must cart 20 loads of stone, 197

Polluting a stream prohibited, 139, 159; with hemp, flax or garbage, prohibited, 169

Poor, may gather beans, 8; but only at end and sides of selions, 47, 52, 199; fines must be paid by those who vouch for them, 63

Pound, location and dimensions specified, 136

Quisquilias, may be gathered on landholder's own land, only, 110

Reap, all able of body, men and women, must, and not glean. *See* Glean and Gleaners

Reapers, wages specified, generally with and without food, 8, 12, 22, 24, 26, 38, 39, 42, 44, 46, 47, 51, 52, 55, 59, 67, 69, 72, 76, 77, 90, 92, 94, 103, 110, 111, 113, 114, 115, 118, 119, 120, 122, 123, 124, 130, 135, 138, 139, 140, 145, 160, 162; forbidden to leave town for higher wages, 113, 122, 125, 130; forbidden to work outside the town till end of autumn, 120. *And see* Glean

Reaping, by night, prohibited, 24, 109; before 15 August, prohibited, 94

Reeds, mowing before Epiphany prohibited, 170; between 11 November and 3 May, prohibited, 125; before March, prohibited, 124; must not be sold to outsiders if any tenants wish to buy, 146

Roads, all customary tenants must mend, 95; all tenants and inhabitants, 172; all who have carts must haul stone to mend, 151; each tenant must mend the road along his land, 118

Rushes, must be gathered for own use only and not to sell, 157

Sheaves, must not be handed out in the field, 4, 7, 16, 24, 36, 38, 39, 42, 47, 51, 52, 55, 59, 67, 145, 199, 203; must not be handed out in the field as gifts or as wages, 69; may

INDEX

be handed out in the field only to those who reap for sheaves, 48; must be handed out at farmstead and not elsewhere, 108

Sheaves taken from the field, if by workers, for the use of their masters, only, 36, 38, 42, 46, 51, 55; workers may not carry them on their heads, 81; must be carted, 15; but not at night, 122, 124, 145; nor after carrying time, 103

Sheep, must not pasture before larger animals, 48, 87, 90, 119, 205; must not be pastured without leave of reeves of autumn, 135; must not be pastured in the common way 25 March to 1 August, 187; must not pasture grass plots in common fields at any time, 122

Sheep must not pasture the meadow till 8 September, 118; till end of autumn, 102

Sheep must not pasture sown land, 117; before harvest, 63

Sheep must not pasture the stubble, till the end of autumn, 145, 151, 171; till all the grain has been taken away, 32, 100; until a space of 10 a. has been cleared, 106; 20 a., 92; 40 selions, 123

Sheep must be folded, on the common or in the fields 3 May to 13 October, 214; but no folds on sown lands, 114

Sheep of outsiders, none may be kept, 163, 189

Shepherds of foreign sheep, may not be received, 184

Stiles, must be kept in good repair, 8; must be kept in repair by the tenant nearest, 35, 52, 199

Stints specified, of calves, 192; of cows, 187, 189; of pigs, 189; of sheep, 134, 175, 187

Stubble, must be gathered on own land, only, 24; unless it has been bought, 66; must not be gathered on another's land till 11 November, 46, 51, 52, 53, 55, 199

Stubble, pasturing. *See* Pasture and Pasturing

Tavern, taking neighbours to one out of town, prohibited, 71

Tethered, all animals pasturing in the fields must be, or herded, 90, 205; cattle, horses and mares must be, except on your own ground, 181; calves and foals in the field must be, 75; cows may not be before end of autumn, 146; horses may be, in fields and meadow, from the beginning of mowing till end of August, 58; horses must not be, in the fields of growing grain, 44; horses and mares must not be, in the fields, till Michaelmas, 138, 146; horses and mares must not be tethered at night, 123; mares with foal may be, at sides of a land, only, 90, 93, 114, 115, 116, 127; mare and foal must be tied together, 185

Tethering, on your own ground, only, till Michaelmas, 110; among the sheaves in a space of 3 a., only 115; after removing another's grain, prohibited, 51

Trees, none may be cut down or sold without licence, 166

Trespass, in another's grain, with cart or cattle, forbidden, 44, 205; with four or five horses together, forbidden, 44

Undertenants, copy-holders may not have without licence, 188; must be vouched for, 151

Vagabonds. *See* Harbouring

Wardens of the by-laws, election of, 2, 9, 18, 22, 24, 38, 40, 41, 42, 43, 44, 45, 46, 47, 48, 49, 51, 52, 53, 55, 59, 60, 62, 63, 67, 68, 69, 70, 71, 77, 80, 81, 82, 85, 86, 90, 91, 92, 93, 98, 100, 101, 104, 106, 108, 109, 110, 111, 113, 114, 115, 116, 118, 119, 121, 123, 127, 128, 129, 130, 131, 132, 142, 144, 145, 151, 153, 167; re-elected, 50, 54, 57; awarded one-third of the fines, 107, 148; presentments of, 48, 66, 67, 73, 87, 89, 96, 97, 125, 130, 145, 148, 159, 161, 177

Water course, must be cleaned by joint labour of all the tenants, 142; each tenant must keep his own part in good order, 159, 185, 189

Women of ill fame. *See* Harbouring

6

For Product Safety Concerns and Information please contact our EU representative GPSR@taylorandfrancis.com
Taylor & Francis Verlag GmbH, Kaufingerstraße 24, 80331 München, Germany

www.ingramcontent.com/pod-product-compliance
Lightning Source LLC
Chambersburg PA
CBHW061835300426
44115CB00013B/2390